Helping Your
ADD Child

Helping Your ADD Child

Revised 3rd Edition

*Hundreds of Practical Solutions
for Parents and Teachers
of ADD Children and Teens
(With or Without Hyperactivity)*

John F. Taylor, Ph.D.

PRIMA PUBLISHING
3000 Lava Ridge Court • Roseville, California 95661
(800) 632-8676 • www.primalifestyles.com

WARNING—DISCLAIMER
Prima Publishing has designed this book to provide information in regard to the subject matter covered. It is sold with the understanding that the publisher and the author are not liable for the misconception or misuse of information provided. Every effort has been made to make this book as complete and as accurate as possible. The purpose of this book is to educate. The author and Prima Publishing shall have neither liability nor responsibility to any person or entity with respect to any loss, damage, or injury caused or alleged to be caused directly or indirectly by the information contained in this book. The information presented herein is in no way intended as a substitute for medical counseling.

All products mentioned in this book are trademarks of their respective companies.

Pseudonyms have been used throughout to protect the privacy of the individuals involved.

Library of Congress Cataloging-in-Publication Data
Taylor, John F.
   Helping your ADD child : hundreds of practical solutions for parents and teachers of ADD children (with or without hyperactivity) / John F. Taylor—3rd ed.
      p.   cm.
   Includes bibliographical references and index.
   ISBN 0-7615-2756-7
   1. Attention-deficit-disordered children. 2. Attention-deficit disorder in adolescence. 3. Problem children—Behavior modification. I. Title.
RJ506.H9 T383 2001
618.92'8589-dc21   2001021083

01 02 03 04 DD 10 9 8 7 6 5 4 3 2 1
Printed in the United States of America

How to Order
Single copies may be ordered from Prima Publishing, 3000 Lava Ridge Court, Roseville, CA 95661; telephone (800) 632-8676 ext. 4444. Quantity discounts are also available. On your letterhead, include information concerning the intended use of the books and the number of books you wish to purchase.

Visit us online at www.primalifestyles.com

To Tammie, Dana, Beth, Amy, Michael, and the thousands of precious and wonderful children whose lives have been affected by the conditions and factors portrayed in this book.

Contents

Introduction

IN THE PAGES of this book, it is my great privilege to be able to present you with the most comprehensive guide ever published to practical solutions for attention deficit hyperactivity disorder (ADHD). It provides a panoramic catalog of the stresses faced by the family and hundreds of suggestions for relieving those stresses. Although addressed primarily to parents, it is also intended for members and students in all of the relevant helping professions.

No successful carpenter, with a complicated task at hand, would attempt to build with only three or four tools in the tool kit. This tool kit has hundreds of tools, from cover to cover. These tools provide new hope for solving the puzzle of ADHD and its closely related conditions of oppositional defiance, conduct disorder, depression, learning disabilities, Tourette's syndrome, Asperger's syndrome, pervasive developmental delays, and autism.

No successful carpenter, on the other hand, would attempt to use a hammer when a screw driver is called for. Every technique isn't suitable for every child. Please feel free to select whichever approaches seem to hold the most promise. Don't hesitate to use the index to locate the specific topics you're interested in.

The attention deficit hyperactivity syndrome colors an individual's experiences in every arena of life. It has had many names, the most current reflecting the key symptoms of hyperactivity and attention disorder—attention deficit hyperactivity disorder, abbreviated in this book as ADHD. Those who have only inattention symptoms and those who have only hyperactivity symptoms are included under this same label, as are those who have both symptom clusters. ADHD is the most common child psychiatric disorder and accounts for at least half of all referrals to child guidance clinics. From 5 to 10 percent of the children in the United States are afflicted with this syndrome. Its causes and outcomes are incompletely understood and its level of impact on the child ranges from very mild to very severe. Early indications are often not recognizable, and controversy surrounds almost every aspect of the topic.

As its apparent incidence has increased over the past few decades, a giant gap has developed between scientific knowledge and what has been conveyed to parents, teachers, and counselors. Inconsistent and inaccurate professional training continues to spawn disagreement and confusion about this disorder, from initial diagnosis to the difficulties that can be expected. ADHD is still grossly misdiagnosed and incorrectly managed. It is both overdiagnosed and underdiagnosed.

Many books in this field written for the general public are superficial, incomplete regarding treatment practices and controversies, and silent on key issues of family life such as the marital relationship, parents' feelings, supervising play activities, getting cooperation on chores, and sibling rivalry.

During three decades of raising children with ADHD and working professionally with hundreds of children, adults, and adolescents who have ADHD, I have learned to respect the potency of the biochemistry of the nervous system. In general, I find it best to use physiological treatment combined with psychosocial, sensorimotor, and academic efforts. A simplistic treatment approach will not bring the benefits you and your child need and deserve.

During the 1950s, 1960s, and early 1970s, only one physiological treatment was used for ADHD with any degree of success—prescribed stimulant and antidepressant medication. Some professionals and researchers in this field prefer to cling to a narrow viewpoint that proclaims prescribed medication as the only effective form of direct physiological treatment. I have discovered that there are six organ systems involved in ADHD and closely related conditions: the brain, the skin, the immune system, the digestive system, the body fuel system, and the blood. As I travel throughout North America presenting training seminars, I teach that you must address all six organ systems if you want maximum success at knocking out ADHD symptoms. Prescribed medication addresses only one of the six.

In the early 1970s the startling discovery was made that limiting exposure to certain chemicals capable of interfering with normal brain chemistry greatly reduces ADHD symptoms. My extensive experience and familiarity with controlling chemical exposure has provided me with a broader view of how to facilitate normal biochemical processes in the nervous system to alleviate ADHD symptoms. Because it doesn't involve a diet, but instead focuses exclusively on avoiding exposure to toxic irritants, I call this avenue of helping a child with ADHD "toxinsulation."

In the 1980s and 1990s prolific additional research pinpointed two additional clusters of practical, effective techniques for assisting brain and body chemical processes and reducing ADHD symptoms. One is the dietary and nutritional avenue for helping these children. It includes providing key nutrients as well as avoiding foods to which the child's body reacts with a sensitivity or immune response. The other is the sensori-motor avenue of providing special procedures using skin, muscles and sense organs.

There are actually four major avenues for intervening on behalf of your child: physiological (which includes medication, diet, and toxinsulation), academic, sensorimotor, and psychosocial. Research now indicates that the more, the merrier. Use as many as seem relevant. Don't stop at one or even two.

Because medication is the most common method of treatment, I have included guidelines and forms for using medication. I have included instructions for adjusting dosage level and controlling for toxic side effects.

During this discussion I assume that you prefer medication as the treatment method. I don't append each sentence with "or, if that doesn't work, consider using the chemical exposure control method or altering nutrition." Please feel free, however, to consider the other two approaches in the physiological tool kit.

Although the backbone of the ADHD syndrome comprises abnormalities in the other five organ systems, the flesh of the disorder consists of psychological factors caused by underlying abnormalities in the brain. Children with ADHD have good days and bad days, just as everyone else does. They grow angry and rebellious if mistreated, they become criminal if neglected or abused, they are excited and pleased when they receive sincere appreciation and acknowledgment of their efforts, and they become discouraged and want to quit if faced with continued frustration and failure. I urge you to remain open-minded about the possibility that several factors may combine to influence behavior and mental efficiency.

I have included guidelines for preventing and overcoming the most common and troublesome disciplinary situations that occur with these children, including away-from-home times. The emphasis must be on orderly routines, clear communication of feelings and needs, and close family relationships based on mutual respect.

Research clearly shows that orderly family processes and firmness help a child with ADHD adjust successfully. The relationship between you and your child is far more critical and powerful than any relationship your child could ever establish with a teacher, physician, psychologist, counselor, or other helping professional. Therefore, I have included elaborate discussion of how to relieve marital stresses, sibling rivalry, and the emotional roller-coaster that parents experience in coping with a child who has ADHD. In addition, I have provided an entire chapter on how to join or organize a support group. Appendix A, "For More Help," provides information on additional resources and organizations for further help. This is broken down by chapter.

ADHD in general, and hyperactivity in particular, poses severe stresses on a marriage; I have witnessed divorces stemming from arguments about how to deal with a child with ADHD. The misbehavior, chaos, and stress can be relentless and overwhelming. Intense sibling rivalry is the norm. Your family will become more united or more divided in response to ADHD; its effect will not be neutral. The focus throughout this book is on strengthening the self-esteem of parents and children along with rebuilding harmony among family members. Everyone can share a sense of mission and purpose, a common goal of working to counter a shared stress.

Most public school teachers face children with ADHD every school year, and a significant proportion of those children are taking prescribed medication or attempting to control chemical exposure. Teachers, however, are probably the most overlooked and underused professionals with the potential to help the child with ADHD. I have included three chapters on school adjustment along with checklists and numerous suggestions for how teachers can be more successful with these challenging students.

Management of your child, with or without the use of prescribed medication, should involve an individualized, comprehensive, and cooperative effort among helping professionals and your family. Because there are few comprehensive references for parents, teachers, and healthcare providers about medication, dietary control of ADHD, and controlling for chemical exposure to reduce symptoms, this book devotes considerable attention to these three forms of physiological treatment. Teachers can be much more helpful to physicians by using the checklists in this book for giving feedback about response to treatment and diagnostic information about ADHD.

You have a choice of several levels of awareness and intervention. After reading chapter 1, for example, you might decide your child displays several traits cataloged there, yet still not conclude that ADHD is an accurate label. You might also agree those traits are causing many difficulties for your child and other family members, yet believe those difficulties can be overcome without physiological intervention. If you choose to forgo using diet, toxinsulation, or medication, and put all your effort into training your child to adapt, you can still use this book as your guide. It shows you how to help your child develop better self-control, temptation resistance, social skills, study habits, decision making, friendship building, relaxation techniques, anger control, assertiveness, problem solving, and various other skills for day-to-day functioning.

This book can become a powerful resource to share with friends, relatives, caregivers, child-care providers, and others who want to help. It can also become source material for a discussion group or college course on this disorder. A group of parents meeting weekly, for example, can share their experiences and approaches, discussing two chapters each week with the aid of the study and discussion questions in appendix B. Such a discussion group does not require a professional leader.

A recent trend in this field is to diagnose overlapping (called co-morbid) conditions along with ADHD. The child with "pure" ADHD is a rarity; the vast majority have other difficulties that merit additional psychiatric diagnoses. I believe that Asperger's syndrome, autism, depression, and pervasive developmental delays can be placed on a continuum with ADHD. Their physiological mechanisms are similar to those involved with ADHD, and the treatment interventions seem to work about the same. I have included discussion of these comorbidities in chapter 2.

My goal is that this book will provide practical assistance for parents and others who want to understand and help an individual with ADHD in a powerful, balanced, sensible manner. You are always welcome to visit my Web site, www.ADD-plus.com, for constantly updated helpful links to additional resources. For this book's limitations, I give you my humble apology and will gratefully accept your feedback with an eye to upgrading for the next revised edition. As for its strengths, I ask simply that you use them to make life work better, then let me know what worked for you.

CHAPTER 1

Understand Hyperactivity and Attention Deficits

ATTENTION DEFICIT HYPERACTIVITY disorder (ADHD) is the most common psychiatric disorder among children. Usually up to five other organ systems besides the brain are involved in this disorder—they are the digestive system, the immune system, the skin, the body's fuel system (blood sugar), and the blood itself. Yet seldom are all six organ systems taken into account in treating this disorder, and it is mishandled in every conceivable way, with thousands of children, adolescents, and adults incorrectly diagnosed. Its symptoms are not necessarily obvious and start at various stages of infancy, toddlerhood, and childhood. Some people show signs of the disorder even before they are born; others are not suspected of having it until their preteen years.

The disorder overlaps with several other conditions (called co-morbidities). The number, severity, and types of symptoms differ from one child to the next, and each child shows a unique pattern of behavior and personality. There are, however, certain similarities among children with ADHD.

A COMMON SYNDROME WITH MANY NAMES

ADHD was described as early as 1845 by the German physician Heinrich Hoffmann in his classic *Der Struwelpeter* (*Slovenly Peter*), a collection of humorous moral tales for children. The heroes were drawn from his observations of children, including "Fidgety Philip."

Recent popular names for the syndrome, or for closely overlapping syndromes, include attention deficit disorder (ADD), ADD with hyperactivity (ADD-H), ADD without hyperactivity (ADD-noH), brain damage syndrome, dyslexia, functional behavioral problem, hyperactive child syndrome, Irlen syndrome, hyperkinesis, hyperkinetic impulsive disorder, learning disabilities, minimal brain damage syndrome, minimal brain dysfunction syndrome, sensory integration disorder, minimal cerebral dysfunction syndrome, minor cerebral dysfunction syndrome, postencephalitic disorder, and specific learning disabilities.

> *The term attention deficit disorder, or ADD, is a lay term and not the correct professional label for this condition. Throughout this book I will use the correct label of "ADHD."*

The term attention deficit disorder, or ADD, is a lay term and not the correct professional label for this condition. Imagine a house with three rooms in it. One room has hyperactive children without attention focusing problems. They are referred to as having ADHD hyperactive-impulsive type. The second room has children in it who have attention focusing problems. Those children are referred to as having ADHD inattentive type. The third room has children in it who have both hyperactivity and attention focusing problems. Those children are referred to as having ADHD combined type. Throughout this book I will use the correct label of "ADHD" for all three subtypes.

Research studies consistently point to a 5 to 10 percent proportion of children who have the ADHD syndrome. Some experts believe the true number is closer to 20 percent of the general population. Differing prevalence rates from nation to nation have resulted from differing methods of defining and cataloging ADHD symptoms. When these differences are taken into account, the prevalence rates for most European countries, China, and Australia coincide reasonably with those in North America.

CHARACTERISTICS OF CHILDREN WITH ADHD

Many features of children with ADHD are socially appropriate and desirable. Their spontaneity, zest, tirelessness, enthusiasm, intensity, curiosity, stimulating brashness, and life-of-the-party energy have useful moments and serve as social catalysts.

There is probably a link between ADHD and giftedness. These children have rich imaginations and are aware of nuances and sensations others miss. They can combine unrelated ideas in novel ways so their art productions and written compositions show a special measure of creativity. When these individuals are successfully treated, their personal expressions display even greater variety, depth, and attention to detail. Some of the most creative persons in history, including Thomas Edison and Albert Einstein, apparently had this disorder.

> *Many features of children with ADHD are socially appropriate and desirable, including their spontaneity, zest, enthusiasm, curiosity, and life-of-the-party energy.*

No child with ADHD will have all the traits discussed in this chapter. The following general trends are more consistently shown by children with ADHD than by children without ADHD.

ADHD is difficult to diagnose because, like all behavior disorders, it tends to appear gradually. Neurological and physiological studies indicate that individuals with ADHD have a wide range of biochemical imbalances and uniqueness. Symptoms phase in and out in various settings and change somewhat from moment to moment. For some, the symptoms tend to fluctuate in several overlapping cycles.

Some children with ADHD who live in colder climates, for example, seem to become worse in most symptoms every spring. They are allergic to blossom pollens. Those who become worse in the summer are allergic to grass pollens, and those who become worse in the autumn are allergic to weed pollens. There is also a four-hour protein cycle, in which the child becomes noticeably more symptomatic during the third and fourth hours after the last meal, then becomes better shortly after consuming a protein-rich snack or meal.

Often there has been no previously normal behavior pattern for parents or professionals to use as a basis of comparison in deciding which of the actions are symptoms of ADHD. The hyperactive child, for example, often seems mentally alert, smiling, energetic, and interested in contact with others. One of the most difficult aspects of this disorder is deciding how much of the unusual behavior is "normal."

There is no simple test for ADHD. The apparatus and procedures for measuring such key traits as attention span and reaction time are elaborate and expensive, and are currently confined to experimental use. Physicians cannot measure blood or urine to assess biochemical imbalances in the nervous system of these children. The most accurate diagnostic method is a review of the child's history and behavior at home and at school.

> *The most accurate diagnostic method is a review of the child's history and behavior at home and at school.*

Imagine giant decks of 200 cards each for all children. On each card is a trait of the ADHD syndrome and its overlapping conditions: difficulty following teachers' instructions, bed-wetting, entering a sibling's room without permission, excessive flatulence, liking to take long showers and baths, craving cheese and sugar, grinding teeth, talking too loudly for the situation, sweating while asleep, and so forth. Each child receives some cards from the deck that represent particular behaviors. Some children receive only a few cards. Others might receive over 100 cards.

Those who receive many cards have enough traits to become noticeably different from most other children. Even though two ADHD-identified children might have the same number of cards—say, 103—the collection of traits that one child has is different from the array occurring in the next child. And each of those 103 traits is constantly fluctuating in severity, acted upon by various idiosyncratic factors such as the amount of sleep obtained the night before and even what was eaten for breakfast.

GENDER DIFFERENCES

Among children with ADHD, 60 to 80 percent are boys. Compared to girls who have ADHD, boys with ADHD are more likely to be overactive, aggressive, disruptive, and referred for child guidance services. Both girls and boys are physically active and rowdy, with the girls being tomboyish. School behavior commonly reported about girls with ADHD includes doodling, excess giggling, excess talking with classmates, great interest in sports and dancing, and excess daydreaming.[1]

One study found that boys with ADHD display more attention problems than girls with ADHD, regardless of grade level.[2]

The traits associated with the inattentive type of ADHD are generally correlated with gender—there tend to be more girls in that subtype than in the hyperactive-impulsive subtype. Therefore, girls with ADHD, on average, are more likely than boys to become depressed, suffer from anxiety, be overlooked by their teachers, be self-critical and self-blaming, and so forth. They are at risk for teen pregnancy compared with non-ADHD peers, in part because of their low self-esteem and in part because of their impaired decision-making skills. I suspect that they are also at risk for the eating disorders anorexia and bulimia.

> Compared to girls who have ADHD, boys with ADHD are more likely to be overactive, aggressive, disruptive, and referred for child guidance services.

Underneath it all, however, girls with ADHD are cut from the same piece of genetic and physiological cloth as their male counterparts. They have the full range of ADHD symptoms and respond just as well to the various academic, psychosocial, sensorimotor, and physiological approaches given in this book.

Diagnosing ADHD Subtypes

Doctors currently divide people with this condition into three sub-types: those with hyperactivity, those with attention deficits, and those with both. Here is a simplified summary of the criteria in the *Diagnostic and Statistical Manual of Mental Disorders* (fourth edition), published by the American Psychiatric Association. To be diagnosed as a true case of ADHD, (A), (B), or (C) must apply.

(A) Six or more of these *inattention* symptoms have occurred for at least six months. For each item, the child must *often:*

- ❑ Not give close attention to details or make careless mistakes in schoolwork or other activities

- ❑ Not sustain attention in tasks or play

- ❑ Not seem to listen when spoken to directly

- ❑ Not follow through on instructions or finish schoolwork

- ❑ Have difficulty organizing tasks or activities

- ❑ Avoid, dislike, or be reluctant to engage in tasks requiring sustained mental effort (schoolwork or homework)

- ❑ Lose things needed for tasks (toys, assignments, pencils, books)

- ❑ Become distracted easily by extraneous stimuli

- ❑ Appear forgetful in daily activities

(B) Six or more of these *hyperactivity-impulsivity* symptoms have occurred for at least six months. For each criterion, the child must *often:*

❑ Fidget with hands or feet, or squirm in seat

❑ Leave seat in class or other situations where remaining seated is expected

❑ Run about or climb excessively when inappropriate (in teens, simply feeling restless qualifies)

❑ Not play or engage in leisure activities quietly

❑ Be "on the go," acting as if "driven by a motor"

❑ Talk excessively

❑ Blurt out answers before questions are completed

❑ Have difficulty waiting his or her turn

❑ Interrupt or intrude on others, butting into conversations or games

(C) To be diagnosed with ADHD combined type, a child would have at least six symptoms in the hyperactivity category *and* at least six symptoms in the inattentive category.

In addition, some symptoms have to occur before age 7, impairment must occur in at least two settings (home plus school, for example), there must be clear evidence of clinically significant impairment of functioning (below the level expected from the child's age), and the impairments must not stem from other causes (such as psychotic conditions).

THE KEY TRAITS

Here are the clusters of mental, physical, and emotional traits that comprise the ADHD syndrome. All ADHD traits come from the universe of normal experience. Not all individuals with ADHD have all of these symptoms, but most have a majority of them. They indicate the ADHD syndrome when they appear consistently, when the child is unable to change them, and when they don't stem from psychological causes or from ADHD-imitator conditions.

Mental Difficulties

Distractibility.   Children with ADHD have a faulty mental gatekeeper. They have little ability to block out noises in order to concentrate. A noise outside the window, a cough, or a dropped pencil is equally as important as what the teacher is saying. Stimulation from experiencing the feel of cloth rubbing against their skin, created by wiggling in the chair, is as important as eating.

> *These children typically have a short attention span and a tendency to be distracted by whatever is unimportant and irrelevant.*

These children typically have a short attention span and a tendency to be distracted by whatever is unimportant and irrelevant. They flit from activity to activity, discontinuing efforts before each task comes to a proper completion.

Motivation plays a large role in determining attention to a task. Parents and teachers consistently have trouble differentiating between the circumstances in which children with ADHD can't focus and those in which they aren't interested in focusing. These children are especially distracted when mental discipline or self-restraint is needed, as when functioning in a group or performing a difficult or uninteresting task.

Confusion.   Children with ADHD have trouble recognizing an object that stands out from the background. This trait also applies to handling ideas. They are poor at prioritizing, recognizing what is important, and making decisions based on the relevant factors. These children have trouble organizing and arranging schoolwork; for example, they may be tempted to go skateboarding on the night before an important exam. They might appear scatterbrained, absentminded, and forgetful. Performance varies, so that they seem to learn something one day but completely forget it the next.

These children have trouble understanding ordinary conversations or lectures, especially sorting out details, listening for key information, and sifting through what the other person is saying for points of agreement. They are confused by instructions, especially those involving three or four steps.

They have difficulty computing logically. They can become sidetracked by an unimportant detail. Faulty reasoning ability leads to poor impulse control, decreased ability to plan and predict consequences of their own actions, weak social judgment, and impaired academic skills.

Their perception is selective. They tend to notice and remember only the specific parts of personal experiences that fulfill hopes, wishes, or prior beliefs. They might make contradictory statements without being aware of the inconsistencies. When asked how well school is going, they might recall high grades on one or two homework assignments while forgetting the many failed tests and homework assignments not turned in or graded low.

Faulty abstract thinking.   Concept formation, or abstract thinking ability, is poorly developed in children with ADHD. Recent research has uncovered considerable evidence of nutritional deficiencies, dehydration, and the probability of heavy metal toxic deposits in ADHD brain tissue that inhibit the ability to conduct abstract thought. Since these children have difficulty restating a sentence or paragraph in different words, their note taking is often inept. They have difficulty understanding what they read. Abstract subjects like

The Inattentive Type of ADHD

Children who have many ADHD symptoms but few or none that directly reflect fidgetiness or impulsivity have a more restrained personality. They tend to have few conduct problems and rarely become involved in delinquent behavior or drug abuse in adolescence. They are socially withdrawn, shy, and unpopular with peers.

They often have learning disabilities, and they are at high risk for academic difficulties and retention. Their problems tend to cluster around mental confusion factors, such as difficulty concentrating and finishing a task, poor organization of schoolwork, daydreaming, inattention, problems following instructions, absentmindedness and forgetfulness, drowsiness (not because of medication overdosage), and being slow moving.

Their low overall satisfaction and low happiness level are distinctive characteristics, and they are more likely to become depressed

mathematics and topics involving long sequences, like spelling, are especially difficult for them.

These children have trouble thinking hypothetically in "what if" fashion or understanding cause and effect in "if-then" reasoning. Rather than using an example as a general guideline, they personalize or misinterpret it. Because these children are especially weak in social situations involving abstract concepts, they interpret the teacher's reminder to sit still as "the teacher is picking on me."

Fragmenting of their experiences is another symptom. They have trouble applying information from previous experiences to current ones and often appear lost and confused when asked to apply a learned tactic to a new situation. They might claim not to know a geography fact because they haven't been there, for example.

They have trouble with situations that require using information from a past experience to handle a new one. In emergencies or crises,

than other children with ADHD. Lacking in confidence, they tend to appear anxious and worried. Since their self-doubts include their appearance and strength, they are less likely than their classmates to participate in sports. In contrast to hyperactive children, these children are more likely to:

- Lie rather than fight
- Be diagnosed as having a phobia, depression, or anxiety
- Be tense and nervous
- Plod through work and be generally slow acting
- Be self-doubting and critical of their appearance
- Avoid fights and be nonaggressive
- Show inhibited, but not bizarre, behavior
- Feel guilty and remorseful

children with ADHD are especially at a loss. They generally need a routine and close supervision to cope with new or ambiguous situations.

Inflexibility.   Children with ADHD are often too rigid in their approach to situations. They have trouble switching from one activity to another and tend to adjust poorly to changes in their surroundings. Rearranged furniture or a new day-care environment can bring on tantrums. These children persist in their approach and point of view despite new information, and they reject better solutions even after several unsuccessful attempts with their current approach.

Poor verbal skills.   Finding the words with which to express their thoughts and feelings is often difficult. Stuttering and stammering are common parts of the syndrome. These children can do poorly on tests because of difficulty remembering the correct words to use in an exact required sequence to express the complete idea. Girls with ADHD often have more problems with these skills than boys with ADHD.

Aimlessness.   One of the most common reports from parents is never knowing what to expect. These children lead disjointed, chaotic lives. They seem to profit little from past errors, so they continue to make academic and social blunders. The combination of impulsiveness and failure to appreciate danger results in accidents and mishaps among those with hyperactivity. Although they know the rules, they seem to lack the self-control to follow those rules. There seems to be a general weakness in the ability to self-regulate and to resist temptations for acting improperly.

> *In emergencies or crises, children with ADHD are especially at a loss.*

Spontaneous to a fault, they seem never to plan ahead and have little concern or preparation for the future. Those who have the inattentive type of ADHD will ponder, fret, take in a great deal of data, and remain indecisive for extended periods of time.

Perceptual difficulties.   These children can become confused about common opposites. Differentiating "upside down" and "inside out" may be difficult. For example, they might put clothing on inside out without realizing it.

They may use letters like *w* and *m*, *d* and *b*, and *p* and *q* interchangeably. Sometimes the reversals occur within words, as when *dog* is seen as *god*, or *was* as *saw*. They might put their shoes on the wrong feet or simply have trouble remembering which hand is left and which is right. Understanding position, such as vertical and horizontal or backward and forward, and recognizing relationships like over, under, beside, and between cause confusion. Skills such as telling time, reading maps, and doing math problems require spatial awareness and are especially difficult for some children with ADHD. About a fourth can be diagnosed with dyslexia. They may try to read from right to left and from the bottom to the top of the page.

Accurate visual perception requires seeing things as a whole. Instead, these children break down a picture or design into parts and do not perceive the parts as connected to each other. Their reading is disjointed, only one word at a time with no flow between words and incorrect pauses for punctuation. They might not be able to fill in missing parts of what they see or hear. Handwriting is notoriously poor for about one-third of children with ADHD. They may perceive corners of objects as protruding farther than they do or not as far. This poor depth perception results in clumsiness, awkwardness, and occasional stumbling and running into things.

> *Poor depth perception results in clumsiness, awkwardness, and occasional stumbling and running into things.*

Perceptual problems can also affect their sense of hearing. Many of the reading problems these children have stem from difficulties hearing and remembering the separate sounds made by letters and letter combinations. They omit words and letters when reading and have weak rhyme perception. Analyzing words into sound units may be troublesome: *ing* may be pronounced as *in* plus *g*. Their ability to hear harmony, melody, and rhythm in music is also often impaired, and they may have trouble singing on key. In contrast, a small group of children with ADHD have rich musical and rhythmic talents.

Inattention to body states.   Many children with ADHD have an incorrect perception of their internal and external body states. They seem to be somewhat insensitive to pain; they might injure themselves severely, then fail to report the injury until much later. They might not feel hunger even though they haven't eaten for an entire day. They have a poor sense of the passage of time. These problems reflect a high-overlap condition for ADHD, sensory integration disorder.

From 40 to 50 percent of children with ADHD have problems with bowel and bladder control. Daytime wetting and soiling occur because they are underresponsive to their internal body signals, thinking their bladders are empty when they are not.

Physical Difficulties

Constant movement.   Those children who are hyperactive act as if driven by a giant mainspring wound too tightly. There is poor channeling of energy, with irrelevant and useless movements of various body parts. They jump, fidget, squirm, rock, wiggle, and run. They often run ahead, flit around, and need to be called back by supervising adults when in public.

Children with ADHD are often underresponsive to their internal body signals.

They need to be constantly busy and are unable to sit quietly and restfully. Even when focusing on a television program or computer screen, they change body position, rhythmically move their feet, or make tapping noises. They poke, touch, feel, and grab, especially in stores and in school hallways. Repetitive behaviors such as thumb sucking, nail biting, scratching and picking at sores and fingernails, teeth grinding, and pulling out hair one strand at a time are common.

These children also seem to be constantly moving their mouths. They are consistently noisy and loud at play, making clicks, whistles, and other sounds and producing an endless stream of chatter. One mother summarized her 10-year-old's constant movement of the mouth: "He goes from loud to louder. He said his first word at 8 months and hasn't stopped talking since."

Variable rates of development.   During infancy and toddlerhood, some children with ADHD develop faster than their peers—for example, learning to walk and talk earlier than other infants. Occasionally, they skip a stage, the most common being learning to walk without first learning to crawl.

Does Your Child Have Mouth-Based Indications of Hyperactivity?

Here are tip-offs to true hyperactivity pertaining to the mouth. These indicators apply from toddler age through adult:

- Talking too loud for the situation
- Making many clicks, whistles, and other sounds
- "Tongue tour" around the outside of the mouth when concentrating
- Teeth grinding (often a sign of the magnesium deficiency common among individuals with ADHD)
- Tics, twitching, and grimacing around the lips and mouth
- Chewing on things (hair, cloth, fingernails, pencils, gum)
- Being a chatterbox

More often, however, these children are slow in passing the developmental milestones. They might not start crawling until after 10 months or walking until after 18 months. Some show delayed development of speech skills and a small vocabulary. Carried to extreme, this delay in development is grounds for applying an additional diagnosis of developmental delay, which is associated with Asperger's syndrome and autism.

Food cravings. The three most commonly craved food categories for children with ADHD are salty and highly seasoned food (craving minerals, which most children with ADHD appear to be deficient in), cheese (craving amino acids, which most children with ADHD appear to need an unusually high amount of), and sugar (desperate for more fuel, the brain of the child with ADHD probably is attracted to sources of immediate energy).

Allergies and sensitivities.   Children with ADHD often show signs of allergy to offending substances such as animal bites and stings, chemicals, medicines, pet dander and feathers, dust, mold, and cosmetics. The most common food allergies among children with ADHD are to chocolate, corn and corn products, eggs, milk (especially skim milk), nuts, pork, sugar, soy, and wheat products. These children also have allergies to pollens, resulting in an increased risk of hay fever and asthma. Eczema and other skin rashes also occur often in individuals with ADHD.

Sensitivities, on the other hand, don't involve the immune system but reflect the body's mistaken attempt to incorporate foreign substances into normal biochemical processes. Individuals with ADHD tend to be sensitive to just about any chemical refined from petroleum and chemical relatives of petrochemicals. Most of these irritants are phenol-based. The molecules appear to be picked up and misused by the nervous system, sabotaging the manufacture of its normal products. The resulting imbalance within the brain creates ADHD symptoms. Phenol-based unstable compounds are found in virtually all petrochemicals and most highly aromatic substances such as gasoline, paint, smoke, and perfume, as well as in coal-tar products such as dyes.

> *Eczema and other skin rashes occur often in individuals with ADHD.*

Fair-featured children (blue or green eyes and blond or red hair) account for 40 to 50 percent of all children with ADHD in the Caucasian category. These same features characterize the majority of patients of allergists, as there seems to be a genetic connection between being fair-featured and having a biochemically sensitive body.

Sleep problems.   These children may not want to sleep and might oppose going to bed, even though they have been active throughout the day. It may be hard for them to get to sleep after going to bed. Some children with ADHD have very shallow, short periods of sleep rather than an ordinary eight hours. The sleeping patterns

Is Your Child Allergic?

Revealing the entanglement of allergies with the behavioral components of ADHD is one of the most exciting developments in this field. Especially with young children, the subtle, almost hidden role of these underlying bodily imbalances is sometimes hard to ferret out. One parent summarized such an experience:

> When my son was a "terrible 2"-year-old, my husband and I tried to get help for his behavior problems. He was driving us crazy! We were in and out of doctors' offices for his ear infections and frequent bouts with croup. At every opportunity, we asked the doctors what we could do about his tantrums, destructiveness, nightmares, and aggression.
>
> "Perfectly normal" is what we heard over and over. "He'll grow out of it." We dealt with the problem as best we could, using loving discipline (and at times, not-so-loving discipline). We tried eliminating petrochemicals from his food. What a surprise to see our dream of a "normal" child after just one week! His ear problems and respiratory infections cleared up as well.

of many of these children are quite irregular and subject to various disturbances.

Coordination problems.   Children with ADHD may have a poor sense of balance and problems with large muscle coordination. Riding a bicycle, a two-wheeled scooter, or a skateboard can be a challenge. Hopping on one foot, jumping rope, balancing on a trampoline, and skipping backward can also be especially difficult tasks.

Small muscle coordination problems appear when these children try to draw, write, or color. About one-third of children with ADHD have distinctively sloppy handwriting. If there is a coordination problem,

Does Your Child Have Sleep Disturbances?

Here are the most common sleep disturbances associated with ADHD. Count each as occurring if it happens more than once every six months.

❑ Sleep talking, including muttering and murmuring

❑ Sleep walking (appears half asleep, half awake)

❑ Nightmares or night terrors

❑ Teeth grinding (a sign of magnesium deficiency, one of the most common mineral deficiencies in children with ADHD)

❑ Bedwetting (if after seventh birthday)

❑ Sweating excessively (a sign of the faulty lipid metabolism that occurs in the majority of children with ADHD; the body is trying to correct its salt-to-water balance)

❑ Excessive movement

❑ Fitful, disturbed sleep pattern resulting in less than eight hours of sleep

children with ADHD are usually not impaired in both the large and small muscle groups simultaneously.

Skin problems.   One of the most common medical complaints for which children with ADHD are taken to their pediatricians is skin rash. The skin problems of children with ADHD reflect their difficulty with lipid metabolism. Basically their bodies have lost some natural moisturizers in the form of essential fatty acid derivatives and are suffering from a form of dehydration. The skin then becomes itchy and develops rashes. Sometimes you notice tiny red dots underneath the upper arms of infants and children with ADHD. Sometimes their hair or nails will be dry and brittle.

Emotional Difficulties

Self-centeredness.   Children with ADHD sometimes lack awareness of their impact on others, seeming not to pay sufficient attention to social signals and cues. They often seem surprised, alarmed, and confused about why others are so upset with them. They may do harmful acts without meaning to hurt others, then be surprised when others show anger. Because they don't feel personally connected to the situation, they are quick to resent others for being angry at them and consequently for treating them unfairly.

They tend to blame others and external circumstances for their difficulties rather than accepting responsibility. Everything is someone else's fault. These children have difficulty identifying needed self-improvements, and they seldom admit to being wrong.

Especially for the hyperactives, their own wants, needs, and whims often appear to be their dominant concern. When denied what they want, they pester and harp until adults give in. They have an "I don't care" attitude if threatened or punished. They want the rules changed to their own advantage.

Children with ADHD tend to relate poorly to other children, especially in group settings. Though at first they may attract friends, hyperactives are not able to keep them. They are incredibly bossy, dominate play situations and intimidate their playmates, are bullheaded and stubborn about getting their own way, and remain inflexible to the appeals of another child. They sabotage cooperative endeavors because of their weak sensitivity to others' feelings and their intrusions on others' boundaries.

The inattentive-type children, on the other hand, seem better able to connect with friends, but they are less likely to attract new friendships. The hyperactives attract but don't bond; the inattentives bond but don't attract.

Impatience.   Hyperactive children are typically negative, contrary, oppositional, and hard to please. Parents report that these children always seem to find something to complain about and manage to tamper with every situation.

The impatience of hyperactive children is reflected in impulsiveness and acting without first asking permission. They respond too quickly before understanding the entire instructions for a task, becoming impatient to get started and just as impatient to stop. While standing in line, these children poke, push, and shove to get ahead. Hyperactive children seem unable to wait for anything!

> *The impatience of hyperactive children is reflected in impulsiveness and acting without first asking permission.*

Recklessness.   Hyperactive children tend not to be diligent. They make many careless errors and take a slipshod approach to tasks, as though they take nothing seriously. Their thoughts tend to be of the reflex variety, with little apparent mental effort. In their "I don't know and I don't care" attitude, they disregard safety and health, with little concern for obvious dangers. The devil-may-care child may have no fear of heights, strangers, animals, traffic, traveling alone, or wandering away from home.

These children tend to be too rough at play, wearing out clothes and toys long before other children do. They are destructive, not only from recklessness but also from anger and inquisitiveness. Social inhibitions may be rare. Hyperactives tend to be assertive, intrusive, and without shyness. Curiosity may seem unbridled, and they may seem to pry and be nosy.

Their recklessness shows in their susceptibility to peer influence and temptations. They gravitate toward peers who are uncritical and undemanding and who have their own difficulties getting along with authority figures. Children with ADHD seem to find and attract each other.

Extreme emotionalism.   Hyperactive children often lack restraint or cushioning of their emotions. They show rapid mood changes and extreme excitability. Low frustration tolerance is a hallmark trait. They are irritable, are easily upset, and react angrily to being teased; vicious and extreme acts of violence are not uncommon. Emotional highs and lows illustrate the compartmentalized and fragmented view of life of many hyperactive children. They are moody and unpredictable, quick to forgive and forget, angry one moment and happy the next. Anger control training is often helpful for these children.

Weak conscience.   Many children with ADHD have poor respect for invisible boundaries such as the following:

- *Property.* Borrowing without permission, stealing trinkets and candy from stores and money from family members, invading purses and drawers of parents and siblings, and failing to return items they have borrowed.
- *Living space.* Entering without knocking, sneaking into siblings' bedrooms, and interrupting others in the bathroom.
- *Privacy.* Intruding on private conversations, listening on extension telephones, reading others' e-mail, being too curious and probing with offensive questions.
- *Limits.* Pounding on the door and repeatedly ringing the doorbell while waiting to enter, badgering and demanding explanations when given an undesired answer, unwilling to accept no, and defiantly refusing to do things when asked.
- *Body space.* Speaking too loudly, standing too close, poking and grabbing, tickling, or hitting.

INDICATORS OF THE ADHD SYNDROME

These factors, which seem to be associated with ADHD, can be interpreted somewhat like pieces of evidence—the more there are, the firmer the diagnosis. Most are associated with a greater-than-chance likelihood of the syndrome.

Prenatal Indicators

About 40 percent of preborn children who are later diagnosed as having ADHD tend to show symptoms of hyperactivity in the womb. Recent research has shown that many characteristics and problems, including most learning disabilities, have their beginnings in abnormal branching and placement of the brain nerves during the fetal stage. Such aspects as intelligence and overall temperament seem now to be highly influenced by very early developmental phenomena.

The human brain is most vulnerable to toxic attack by irritant chemicals during the fetal stage, when its cells are most rapidly dividing. Several of the key protective enzyme systems that would otherwise protect a human brain from toxic chemicals in the bloodstream are not developed until long after birth.

Anything that interferes with correct growth and development of brain nerve cells will be a risk factor for causing ADHD, autism, or related conditions. The most toxic substances are petrochemicals (anything refined from petroleum, such as insecticides), phenols (such as perfumes and dyes), carcinogens (anything that causes cancer), mutagens (anything that disrupts DNA functions), and neurotoxins (anything that damages or kills research animal brain nerves). In addition, there is danger from five heavy metals: copper, lead, aluminum, mercury, and cadmium. According to recent research, fetuses can become milk allergic, and this phenomenon also seems to occur at greater-than-chance frequency among babies who are later diagnosed as having ADHD.

We must await definitive research before "food additives" can legitimately be added to the list of very dangerous substances for the expectant mother to consume. However, there are logical reasons for such a precaution. Because of their chemical properties and their apparent pharmacologic effects, it is highly probable that most petrochemical food contaminants (such as pesticide residue) and dyes get through the placenta. A mother's exposure to airborne phenols such as paint or gasoline fumes is also potentially toxic for the unborn child.

These are common prenatal indicators of ADHD syndrome:

- Apparent hyperactivity in the womb, especially when the mother is sitting still: From the sixth to the ninth month of gestation, a glass of water placed on the expectant mother's abdomen would spill immediately.

- Poor maternal health.

- Mother under 20 years of age.

- First pregnancy.

- Elevated blood pressure during pregnancy (preeclampsia).

ADHD is the core symptom cluster in fetal alcohol syndrome.

- Convulsions in the mother (eclampsia) during the latter stages of pregnancy or during childbirth.

- Maternal alcohol abuse: Alcoholic beverage use during pregnancy is perhaps the best known of the toxic causes of later ADHD in a fetus. Dozens of studies have shown that nearly all babies of alcoholic mothers who continue to consume large quantities of alcoholic beverages during their pregnancies are born with ADHD. In fact, ADHD is the core symptom cluster in fetal alcohol syndrome. The most damaging period is the first trimester, when many of these mothers don't even realize they are pregnant.

- Heavy maternal smoking: Smoking during the pregnancy— and even simply being exposed to secondhand cigarette smoke during the pregnancy—can send all three dozen of the neurotoxins in cigarette smoke into the preborn child's bloodstream and fragile developing brain. The results, of course, are disastrous. Stacks of scientific studies have elaborated on what can go wrong for the preborn child exposed to so many toxins over a period of several months. Asthma, SIDS, miscarriage, leukemia, and dozens of other misfortunes all have a greater chance of occurring.

As for increased ADHD risk, one researcher found in a mammoth study of 30,000 children that pregnant women who smoked more than two packs daily had a 13 percent rate of producing hyperactive children. A matched group of nonsmoking mothers had the national average rate of 7 percent. In other words, the risk for producing a hyperactive child doubles if the expectant mother smokes heavily.

- Drug abuse: Marijuana, the most commonly used illicit substance among pregnant women, also seems to be toxic to a developing human brain. Some interesting studies assessing large numbers of babies and following them up to 10 years later found that maternal marijuana use during pregnancy was correlated with producing children who by age 10 showed distinctive patterns of "hyperactivity, impulsivity, and inattention symptoms . . . increased delinquency . . . and externalizing problems." The abuse of drugs such as cocaine by the expectant mother is also associated with ADHD in the developing child.[3,4]

- Extreme psychological stress: Women who are under severe stress during their pregnancies experience an abnormally high level of adrenalin, which gets into the fetal bloodstream. The result is a risk for long-term behavioral problems in the child. Monkeys exposed to loud noise during their pregnancies, for example, tend to have offspring that are inclined to behave like the simian equivalents of hyperactive children.

Birth Indicators

Many of these indicators are somewhat controversial because of insufficient controlled scientific studies, but most textbooks on ADHD cite them as worthy of concern:

- Extreme prolonged lack of oxygen at birth.

- Extended labor lasting longer than 18 hours.

- Birth injuries.

- Congenital problems or physical malformations.

- Fetal alcohol syndrome: This syndrome includes low birth weight, small head size, birth defects, withdrawal symptoms, and mental retardation.

> *The risk for producing a hyperactive child doubles if the expectant mother smokes heavily.*

- Prematurity: Studies of low birth weight babies suggest a relationship between prematurity factors and the syndrome. In one study, prematurity was found to be associated with hyperactivity at age 7. In another study, the ADHD rate was 18 percent in low birth weight children.

- Low placental weight.

- Breech presentation.

- Chorionitis: Inflammation of the outermost of the two membranes enveloping the fetus can sometimes create more problems.

Early Infancy Indicators (Birth to 6 Months)

While useful for diagnosis, many of the following indicators also occur widely among babies who *don't* develop ADHD:

- Inadequate sleep
- Irritability and seeming hard to soothe
- Excessive crying and colic
- Feeding problems: difficulty nursing, difficulty accepting a formula, or differing appetite levels
- Health problems such as allergies, colds, asthma, upper respiratory infections, and fluid in the ears

- Poor bonding: isn't cuddly and responsive, is restless, or is difficult to manage during such routine activities as bathing, diaper changing, or feeding

Late Infancy Indicators (6 to 18 Months)

As I travel throughout the United States and Canada giving seminars on ADHD and oppositional defiant disorder, many parents and professionals have asked me at what age ADHD can be first diagnosed. They are usually quite surprised at my answer: infancy. These late infancy indicators reflect unstable physiology, particularly in the digestive and immune systems, as well as impairments in brain function as reflected in bizarre movements or abnormal passing of developmental milestones:

- Unusual crib behavior such as foot thumping, excessive rocking, head banging, climbing out of the crib, and taking the crib apart
- Rapid or delayed development of muscle (motor) skills such as crawling, sitting, standing, walking, and running
- Rapid or delayed development of verbal skills such as saying the first word prior to 9 months or after 15 months of age
- Low adaptability to change
- Difficulties getting to sleep, staying asleep, or obtaining restful sleep

Toddlerhood Indicators (18 to 36 Months)

The first letters of the five key toddlerhood indicators spell *radio:*

- **Reckless.** Accident prone, careless with common dangers such as traffic, and susceptible to accidental poisoning.
- **Aggressive.** Pushes, shoves, pinches, kicks, bites, grabs toys, and can't play cooperatively for a sustained period.

Does Your Baby Have Colic?

The earliest indication of ADHD after birth is trouble with feeding, crying, or sleeping during the first six months. Commonly called colic, this condition reflects the numerous digestive problems that children with ADHD are at risk for having.

One father described his experience with a daughter whose colic and other ADHD symptoms were rapidly solved in infancy:

> Terri would not sleep and in fact slept less than my wife and me. We would take turns being up with her til two or three in the morning. She would wake up at seven and be up all day!
>
> Month by month, the problems just got worse. She would cry all day, and when I got home from work, Martha would be at her wit's end, exhausted from a tiring day with Terri. There was not a part of the day, from morning to night, that Terri did not disrupt. I can remember rocking her in the rocking chair trying to put her to sleep, and she would just lie in my arms, eyes wide open, hands outstretched, tense. The evenings were filled with Terri just literally bouncing off the walls and furniture.
>
> We started on the Feingold program, and without exaggeration, I can say that we saw a change in her personality within four days.

- **Destructive.** Breaks, throws, and tears apart things, toys, and clothing because of anger, curiosity, or general high activity level.

- **Incorrigible.** Underresponsive to parental correction, unconcerned when threatened with punishments, and requiring constant attention, reminding, and restraining.

- **Overactive.** Acts as if driven by a mainspring that is wound too tightly, resulting in nonstop movement and an inability to sit quietly for more than a few minutes.

Preschool Indicators (3 to 5 years)

The preschool years can be very stressful for parents. Many symptoms start simultaneously, and answers seem few and far between. These are some of the prominent preschool symptoms:

- **Stomach problems.** The digestive system is one of the organ systems most often impaired among children with ADHD. Troubles with digestion can lead to many behavioral complications. According to research, by the time they are 5 years old, children with ADHD on the average have had more serious gastrointestinal complaints resulting in contact with physicians than their peers.

- **Lack of coordination in large or small muscle group activities.** The child tends to produce sloppy and messy seat work at preschool or kindergarten, or may be especially clumsy.

- **Off-task behavior.** These children wander away from their tables at school and may seem to require an excessive amount of attention and supervision.

- **Overactivity.** Hyperactive children won't sit still and pay attention, fidget during story time, are out of their seats too often, talk out of turn, and make inappropriate comments to classmates and the teacher.

- **Intrusiveness.** Hyperactive children are almost universally unpopular throughout their childhood and adolescence. They bother other children by talking to them, touching them, or intruding on their projects and play, as well as by inappropriately seeking attention, such as by clowning.

- **Aggressiveness.** These children are aggressive toward class-mates and can't play cooperatively. They take their classmates' toys and hit them, kick them, and make them cry.

- **Distractibility.** These children appear to have too short an attention span when compared with other children of the same age.

- **Parent-child conflict.** Patterns of family disruption, such as ignore-nag-yell-spank cycles, become established. The parents perceive the child as a negative influence on the family.

PREDICTOR FACTORS

Psychological studies of families of children with ADHD have uncov-ered a number of factors that indicate a higher-than-chance likeli-hood of ADHD. The more of these factors that occur, the greater the chance of the child's having ADHD.

Familial Factors

These "tip-off" conditions occur consistently among near relatives, providing additional support for the mounting evidence that ADHD is primarily genetically determined:

- **ADHD in near relatives.** The occurrence of the disorder in blood relatives such as parents, grandparents, aunts, uncles, and siblings is a predictor. An increased prevalence of ADHD of about 25 percent is found in non-twin siblings, and a much higher percentage is found in identical twins.

- **Alcoholism in near relatives.** Alcoholism is one of the most common major conditions associated with ADHD, with about one-third of male alcoholics having it.

- **Sociopathy in near relatives.** Criminal tendencies in parents, grandparents, aunts, and uncles are associated with ADHD in the children.

- **Depression in near relatives.** Along with alcoholism and sociopathy, depression in parents, grandparents, aunts, and uncles is also a predictor, especially among female relatives.

- **Allergies and sensitivities in near relatives.** Having close relatives who suffer from hay fever, asthma, sensitive skin, or allergies increases the likelihood of the presence of ADHD.

- **Adoption.** About 2 percent of U.S. children receive foster or adoptive care. These children, however, are at extreme risk for behavioral and emotional problems. They appear at counseling services at about five times the incidence of nonadopted children. Often the services they require have to do with ADHD and related conditions like oppositional defiant disorder. About one out of every four adopted children has ADHD.

  These children are at risk for low self-esteem, as they sometimes feel rejected by birth parents. They often view their foster and adoptive parents' expectations as being too high for them to reach. The parent-child communication difficulties typical of ADHD families may be worsened because adoptive parents tend to be somewhat older than birth parents, creating a larger generation gap.[5]

Physiological Factors

Two of the best known comorbid conditions to ADHD seem to be caused by disrupted body chemistry. These are:

- **Phenylketonuria (PKU).** This inherited disease results in a biochemical imbalance in the brain. Some studies suggest over one-half of children with PKU have ADHD. Children who have PKU are invariably fair-featured also.

- **Tourette's syndrome (TS).** This condition represents a worst-case scenario of obsessive-compulsive tendencies. It usually involves tics, which are jerking muscle movements starting in the face and spreading to the neck and shoulders, then finally to the trunk and limbs. Several dozen other symptoms are also possible, including uttering of odd sounds, making irrelevant comments, and experiencing a host of ADHD and autism symptoms such as distractibility and restlessness.

  The symptoms seem to phase in and out with fluctuations in brain chemistry. Nearly one-fourth of individuals with TS experience total disappearance of symptoms for extended periods. Significant ADHD symptoms occur in over one-half of those with TS, and about 6 percent of children with ADHD have TS.

ADHD DURING ADOLESCENCE

Severely symptomatic youngsters are more likely than borderline and mildly symptomatic children to retain their symptoms during adolescence. Problems with aggression, poor self-concept, impaired peer relationships, and poor school performance become prominent. The typical adolescent with ADHD has at least one extended period of depression.

Those children with ADHD whose observable symptoms continue into adolescence are at greater risk when their parents have severe psychiatric disorders or substance abuse. Such children have higher rates of delinquency, depression, and conduct disorders as well as lower IQs and academic achievement scores than those whose symptoms seem to decline rapidly during early adolescence.

> *The typical adolescent with ADHD has at least one extended period of depression.*

Conduct Disorder

Children with a conduct disorder (ADHD-cd) show repetitive, persistent actions that violate the rights and property of others and major societal norms and rules. They rarely acknowledge

Does Your Child Have a Weak Conscience?

The two most common overlapping conditions to the hyperactive-impulsive and the combined types of ADHD reflect inadequate conscience. Oppositional defiant disorder (ODD) is the most frequent one for hyperactive children and teens. The indicators must have occurred for at least six months and include:

- Negativism
- Hostility
- Defiant behavior involving frequent loss of temper
- Arguing with adults
- Refusal to comply with rules and requests
- Deliberate attempts to annoy others
- Blaming others rather than accepting responsibility
- Frequent display of resentment and anger
- Being "thin-skinned," easily offended, or easily annoyed
- Displaying spiteful or openly vindictive actions

Conduct disorder (CD) is roughly equated with juvenile delinquency. Children and teens typically start with ODD, then deterio-

their antisocial behavior; they admit to problems of overactivity and attention deficits much more readily than to conduct disorder behaviors.

They are more likely to display these behaviors if they are raised in poverty, if they are abused, if the parents have psychiatric disorders, or if they belong to a conduct disorder friendship group.

A significant proportion of adolescents in the juvenile justice system and adults in the penal system have a history of ADHD. As many as 30 to 40 percent of teens from the ADHD-cd subgroup eventually get into trouble with authorities as adults. Of all children with

rate further into CD. Indicators include violation of the basic rights of others and of standard social and ethical norms and rules. The violations must have occurred over at least a 12-month period and include:

- Bullying
- Initiating fist fights
- Using a weapon while confronting or assaulting others
- Being physically cruel to people or animals
- Stealing while confronting a victim (robbery, purse snatching)
- "Conning" people
- Sexually abusing someone (of any age)
- Setting fire to cause damage
- Destroying property
- "Breaking and entering" crimes
- Stealing and shoplifting
- Violating curfew
- Running away
- Being truant

ADHD, this group is at greatest risk for adult antisocial and criminal behavior. In one survey, nearly 50 percent of adults with ADHD-cd had arrest records for a felony. Most researchers find an overlap of hyperactivity and conduct disorder in from 30 to 65 percent of the cases they investigate. These traits tend to be relatively stable. Children with ADHD-cd who show aggressive tendencies, lie, or steal often continue to show antisocial tendencies in adolescence.

A high incidence of alcoholism and character disorders is evident among fathers of children with ADHD-cd, and these children have siblings who also have a high likelihood of conduct disorders. Anti-social parents are more likely than psychiatrically healthier parents to have a child with ADHD-cd.

Aggression

There are four types of aggression:

1. **Person-oriented.** Fighting, bullying, using weapons.

2. **Object-oriented.** Breaking, kicking, tearing, slamming doors, and throwing toys, other objects, and furniture.

3. **Verbal.** Cursing, name-calling, teasing, criticizing, bossing, and harassing.

4. **Symbolic.** Making threatening, aggressive, obscene, or otherwise offensive gestures.

A significant proportion of adolescents in the juvenile justice system and adults in the penal system have a history of ADHD.

Aggressiveness toward others is one of the key factors determining whether a child or teen with ADHD will be accepted by peers. Less aggressive children are better accepted. Because aggressiveness is one of the most stable and least changeable of the ADHD personality traits, it is vitally important to provide anger control and social skills training and to focus on developing conscience.

Drug Abuse

Having a romance with or being a close friend of a drug user greatly increases the chance that a teen with ADHD-cd will abuse substances also. The usual lag between the time the teen starts abusing drugs and the time parents realize it is approximately six months. If you suspect drug abuse, get help immediately. Confronting your teen might not result in much immediate improvement. Almost every drug-abusing teen denies the problem when confronted. Even with a confession

Is Your Teen Abusing Drugs?

Here are telltale signs of drug abuse by your child or teen. The greater the number, the more serious the problem. Many of these indicators, such as food cravings and irritability, reflect classic ADHD traits, so hunt for sudden changes.

- **Energy changes.** Fatigue, sleepiness, changes in hours of sleep, difficulty waking, too much or too little sleep, staying up all night, periods of unusual excitement and drivenness.

- **Physical changes.** Reddened or watery eyes, drooping eyelids, colds, runny nose, infections, hacking cough, shortness of breath, peculiar breath odors, pale cheeks, sweating or chills, stomach or intestinal problems, clumsiness, coordination problems, sudden food cravings, appetite change.

- **Mental changes.** Slurred speech, lack of emotion, forgetfulness and absentmindedness, talking in incomplete sentences, losing train of thought, nervousness, irritability, distorted sense of time, paranoia, depression, suicidal threats, strange and bizarre thoughts, hallucinations.

- **Social changes.** Withdrawal from normal contacts, dropping friends, seeking out less desirable acquaintances, idolizing questionable adults, attraction to drug-lyric music and performers.

- **Attitude changes.** "I don't care" attitude about school; avoiding homework; resentment of teachers, police, and other authorities; flagrant disregard for rules.

- **Emotional changes.** Rapid mood swings, extreme irritability, angry outbursts, unexplained crying, intense worry, oversensitivity to criticism.

- **Nighttime activity changes.** Frequent short visits from strangers, secretive phone calls, refusal to tell names of new acquaintances, traffic violations, possession of drug equipment and smoking devices, strange odor on clothing.

and a promise to discontinue, the possibility of repeated drug use is quite high.

ADULTS WITH ADHD

More than one-half of adults with ADHD never come in contact with mental health or correctional systems; they lead normal, well-adjusted lives.

One mother of a young adult with ADHD summarized the gradual blossoming of adjustment during late adolescence and early adulthood:

> The very traits that used to work against him now work for him. He's so aware of how others are doing and how they are feeling. He strikes up conversations and has an easy time making good friends.

Many teens with ADHD adjust better after high school, when their academic problems are finally over. As a group, their work status and employer ratings tend to be somewhat lower than the non-ADHD adults. One predictor of more positive adult adjustment that consistently appears in the research is a supportive authority figure, most often the mother, who expressed confidence and positive expectations about the young person's ability to be successful in life.

AN ACCURATE, EASY-TO-USE SCREENING CHECKLIST

No single checklist is final proof of the existence of ADHD. The one that follows makes a crude division between hyperactivity and other behavior problems. It is not a comprehensive list of all symptoms but lists the most differentiating symptoms—those likely to occur in hyperactive individuals and unlikely to occur in nonhyperactive individuals. Experience with this scale over the years has indicated that it is accurate from age 2 through adulthood. The items lean rather significantly in the direction of the fidgetiness and hyperactivity components

THE TAYLOR HYPERACTIVITY SCREENING CHECKLIST

For each of the 21 behaviors, put an X in one of the three boxes to show the typical behavior. Rate the behavior when the child or teen is not being supervised, helped, or reminded; not watching television or a computer screen; and not receiving any kind of treatment to control behavior.

Indicate the trend. Try to avoid column B ratings; a 51 percent trend in either direction should merit an A or C rating. Compared with others of approximately the same age, this child typically shows behavior:

A. Somewhat more like this	B. Absolutely no trend	C. Somewhat more like this
1. Quiet person		Noisy and talkative person
2. Voice volume is soft or average		Voice is generally too loud for the situation
3. Few mouth or body noises		Noisy, makes clicks, whistles, hums, cracks knuckles
4. Walks at appropriate times		Flits around, runs ahead, needs to be called back, is jumpy
5. Keeps hands to self		Pokes, touches, feels, grabs
6. Appears calm, can be still		Always has a body part moving, fidgets with hands or feet, is squirmy
7. Can just sit		Has to be doing something to occupy self when sitting, is quickly bored
8. Contemplative, deliberate, not impulsive		Too quick to react, impulsive, engages mouth and muscles before brain
9. Understands why parents/teacher/others are displeased after misbehavior		Feels picked on, is surprised and confused about why others are displeased, doesn't connect own actions to others' reactions
10. Plans ahead; thinks about what the results will be before taking action		Careless, doesn't plan ahead; doesn't consider consequences before taking action
11. Cautious about mischief, avoids it		Attracted to or involved in mischief, doesn't distance self from it

A. Somewhat more like this	B. Absolutely no trend	C. Somewhat more like this
12. Obeys authority, concerned about consequences		Defies authority, has "I don't care" attitude about consequences
13. Trustable, follows through, obeys directions		Disobedient, forgetful, needs reminding to ensure compliance
14. Calm, emotionally stable, has mild or slow mood changes		Moody, unpredictable, quick to anger or tears
15. Easygoing, handles frustration without much anger, is patient, can be teased		Inflexible, irritable, impatient, easily frustrated
16. Intensity of displayed emotion is mild or moderate		Emotions are extreme and poorly controlled; no "damper pedal" on emotion; explosive, has tantrums
17. Cooperative, obeys and enforces rules of work and play		Oppositional; complains about rules, routines, or chores; wants to be the exception
18. Gives up when denied a requested privilege, item, or activity		Argues, badgers, won't take no for an answer
19. Stays on-task despite distractions, focuses, concentrates		Gets off-task, too distracted by noises and people nearby, short attention span
20. Follows through, has an organized approach to activities, finishes projects		Flits from activity to activity, starts things without finishing them, gets sidetracked
21. Doesn't try to bother or hurt others with words		Needles, teases, is mouthy, has to have the last word

The score is the total number of items in column B plus twice the number of items in column C. The range of possible scores is 0 to 42. An individual (age 2 through adult) scoring 24 or less is probably not hyperactive; 25 to 27: borderline hyperactive; 28 to 32: mildly hyperactive; 33 to 37: moderately hyperactive; 38 to 42: severely hyperactive.

Development and validity data for the original form, which had slightly different wording on some of the items but assessed the same traits on all items, are available from A.D.D. Plus, P.O. Box 4326, Salem, OR 97302.

of the ADHD syndrome. For persons with attention deficits but without a hyperactivity component, use items 8 through 20 and hunt for at least half to be rated in column B or column C.

SEVERITY OF HYPERACTIVITY

Borderline and mildly hyperactive children, typically scoring 25 to 32 on the Taylor Hyperactivity Screening Checklist, tend as a group to show somewhat different behavior from moderately and severely symptomatic children, who score 33 to 42. In general, the *more severe* the hyperactivity and the *higher* the score on the checklist, the more likely the child is to:

- Consistently show symptoms of ADHD from setting to setting
- Require high dosage levels of prescribed medication
- Show sensitivities to many environmental irritants and chemicals
- Be allergic to foods, pollens, animal dander, mold, dust, or medicines
- Have noticeable symptoms before age 2
- Experience little or no decrease in symptoms during adolescence
- Have many symptoms as an adult
- Have many cognitive impairments
- Show severe behavior disturbance
- Benefit little from counseling
- Be aggressive toward others
- Be enrolled in special-education programs

The *less severe* the hyperactivity and the *lower* the score, the more likely the child is to:

- Show variation in displayed ADHD symptoms from setting to setting

- Respond to lower dosage levels of medication
- Tolerate exposure to some environmental irritants and chemicals without showing ADHD symptoms
- Have fewer allergies
- Appear symptom free until after age 2
- Experience decrease in many symptoms during adolescence
- Have few or no symptoms as an adult
- Have few cognitive impairments
- Show little behavior disturbance
- Benefit from counseling
- Get along well with other children
- Remain in regular classrooms without special academic help

Once you understand that your child has ADHD, possibly with one or more overlapping conditions, you are ready to proceed with significant steps to improve your child's adjustment. Usually, professional help is needed, partly to continue the diagnostic process and rule out ADHD imitator disorders and partly to proceed with the various psychological, academic, sensorimotor, and physiological measures available to assist your child. Chapter 3 explains how to find the best professional help and obtain an accurate diagnosis.

THE BRAIN TOXICITY CONTINUUM

ADHD is among several disorders on a scale from minimal to maximal disruption of brain chemistry by toxic substances. Each condition involves symptoms that are shared somewhat by the adjacent conditions. When children with "ADHD inattentive type" have an S-R (symptom-reactive) state, for example, they don't suddenly become hyperactive. Instead, they become whiny, fussy, irritable, indecisive, sullen, or depressed. When children with "ADHD combined type" have an S-R state, they start showing the kinds of bizarre behavior expected from children with the more severe diagnosis of Asperger's syndrome. The most severe of all is autism, which usually reflects abnormalities in several different simultaneous chemical chain reactions affecting the functioning of the brain.

The following continuum of behavioral disorders reflects the approximate overall level of toxic processes (from lowest to highest) occurring in brain tissue:

- Depression
- ADHD inattentive type
- ADHD hyperactive-impulsive type
- ADHD combined type
- Asperger's syndrome
- Pervasive developmental delays (PDD)
- Autism

Recent research indicates that many of the same physiological approaches useful with ADHD can also help the other conditions on this continuum. The next chapter provides information on the last three conditions on this list.

CHAPTER 2

Meet ADHD's Big Brothers— Asperger's Syndrome, PDD, and Autism

O N T H E C O N T I N U U M from minimal to maximal toxicity in brain chemistry, depression represents the least deviation from normal and autism the greatest. ADHD is on this continuum, and the other disorders have similarities to ADHD. The continuum was introduced in chapter 1.

ASPERGER'S SYNDROME

Children with this syndrome have lost much of the highest order of mental functioning in terms of abstract thinking ability. They are very concrete, literal, and too specific in their thought patterns. Mostly boys, they have profound obsessive tendencies. They can become preoccupied with a favorite subject and talk about it in a monotone for hours.

Children with Asperger's syndrome can memorize facts and numbers in "little professor" style. They seem intelligent, and their language is superficially normal, but they seem to lack common sense and seldom have ordinary conversations. Abstract mental abilities like problem solving, understanding humor, having eye contact, showing empathy, and having true social relatedness are hard for them. Not usually mentally retarded, these children often have profound difficulties with internal body signals, with associated muscle coordination problems, touch defensiveness, and visual perceptual difficulties, along with ADHD symptoms.

> *Children with Asperger's syndrome can memorize facts and numbers in "little professor" style, but they seem to lack common sense and seldom have ordinary conversations.*

Here is one father's description:

Todd was a fussy baby who didn't sleep well. During his first year, he was on a regimen of antibiotics for his chronic ear infections. But his most dramatic problems were bouts of extreme behavior that began in the second year, after we introduced milk products and table food. Todd was happy much of the time but would lapse into severe sadness and anger, crying uncontrollably and sometimes screaming so hard that he actually broke blood capillaries in his face.

He was a bright, loving child, with a large vocabulary, but his motor skills were only average. A professional we consulted told us Todd had Asperger's. We later found intolerance to both gluten and caseine.

PERVASIVE DEVELOPMENTAL DELAYS (PDD)

PDD syndrome is a loosely defined collection of traits characterized by failure to achieve expected milestones of development at critical ages during early childhood. Mental retardation is often part of the picture. There are numerous causes of PDD syndrome, and it is often confused with Asperger's syndrome and autism. Use the charts in appendix C, "Emerging Patterns of Behavior," to assess whether your child is significantly behind in development of key skills.

AUTISM

Autism is a genetically based lifelong developmental disability with onset usually in the first three years of life and a constantly fluctuating continuum of severity, from mild to severe. It is a behaviorally defined syndrome characterized by uneven rates of development and profound disturbances in social interaction, communication, and perceptual skills. It often is associated with other conditions reflective of brain structural or chemical abnormalities, such as fragile X syndrome, mental retardation, ADHD, and Irlen syndrome.

Common observations about children with autism by their parents include difficulty in mixing with other children, acting as if deafness is occurring, resisting learning, absence of normal caution around danger, excess reliance on gesturing instead of normal language use, inappropriate giggling and laughter, touch defensiveness, refusal to be cuddled, obsession with and possessiveness toward specific objects, sustained periods of bizarre play, and a standoffish manner that prevents normal emotional connectedness with others.

PDD syndrome is characterized by failure to achieve expected development milestones at critical ages. Mental retardation is often part of the picture.

The incidence of autism seems to be rising rapidly. A survey in California, for example, showed a 273 percent increase over a recent 11-year period. Florida reports a 571 percent increase and Maryland a 513 percent increase in a recent 5-year period. As usual with anything controversial, some authorities in the ADHD field question the notion of an increase in the incidence of autism, dismissing it as the result of better diagnostic procedures or changing definitions of autism.

Genetic Factors in Autism

Some evidence of genetic factors in autism comes from studies of the parents of children with autism. Often, these parents have symptoms of inadequate supplies of protective sulfates in their digestive tracts

What's It Like When Autism Symptoms Begin?

Here is how one father summarized the sudden, tragic deterioration that often marks the beginning of Asperger's syndrome or autism in an infant or toddler:

My son, Jason, was born healthy. As a toddler, he was beautiful and tall. He was outgoing and talkative. He enjoyed company and going places. Then his mother took him for his routine immunizations, and all of that changed. That night, Jason had a slight fever, and he slept for a long period of time.

When he was awake, he would scream a horrible high-pitched scream. He would scream for hours. He began dragging his head on the furniture and banging it repeatedly. Over the week and a half after the vaccinations, Jason would stare into space and act like he was deaf. He would hit himself and others, which was something he had never done. He would shake his head from side to side as fast as he could. He lost all language.

and of problems with toxic exposure, immune function, and lipid (fat) metabolism. These evidences include migraine headaches, assorted allergies, autoimmune conditions like arthritis and hypothyroidism, excessive thirst, hay fever, and skin rashes.

In one study, the parents of children with autism were compared with parents of matched groups of mentally retarded and normal control children with regard to a history of having been exposed to toxic chemicals prior to conceiving their children. Parents who had been exposed to toxins accounted for 21 percent of the children with autism, compared with 3 percent and 10 percent figures for parents of the normal and mentally retarded children. In fact, 25 percent of the parents of the autistic children turned out to be chemists![1]

According to some of the latest reliable research, the ultimate cause of autism often involves some sort of toxic buildup in the brain, combined with deficiencies in needed brain nutrients. There are numerous chemical pathways by which such a buildup can occur:

- Through the collection of deposits of heavy metals—the same heavy metals that can trigger ADHD symptoms

- By the buildup of toxic waste products from body-unfriendly yeast, mold, and fungi allowed to proliferate within the digestive tract because of excess antibiotic use

- By the buildup of toxic by-products of incorrect handling by the digestive tract of certain hard-to-digest proteins commonly found in wheat and milk

- By the buildup of sulfur in the body

> *According to research, the ultimate cause of autism often is a toxic buildup in the brain, combined with deficiencies in needed brain nutrients.*

Phenol-Sulfotransferase and Autism

Normally, a human body adds oxygen to sulfur, creating sulfates that perform the protective function of preventing large food particles from escaping through the intestinal wall and triggering food-allergic reactions. Sulfates also protect the lining of the intestines and prepare waste products for discharge.

Research indicates that the necessary enzymes for transforming sulfur into sulfates are low or missing in some children with autism. Needed nutrients don't get through to the bloodstream, while allergenic particles trigger hormonal disturbances through a food allergy mechanism. These same enzymes are probably low in some individuals with corn allergies. Sulfur is found as a residue in corn products and corn syrups and is one of the reasons for the widespread incidence of corn allergy and the co-occurrence of corn allergy and autism.

In autism, there seem to be more genetic "hits"—more faulty gene processes that result in greatly diminished or missing enzymes—than in ADHD. Phenol-sulfotransferase deficiency and pepsidase deficiency are examples of such genetic anomalies that are responsible for some cases of autism.[2,3,4]

Allergy-induced autism, caused by an abnormal shortage of the detoxifying enzyme phenol-sulfotransferase-P, results in the usual cluster of food allergy and lipid-deficiency symptoms that also occur among children with ADHD—excessive thirst, nighttime sweating, low blood sugar, diarrhea, bloating, runny nose, bright rosy cheeks or ears, and dark circles under the eyes.

The "Yeast Connection" to Autism

Recent research has uncovered that many children with autism have fungal metabolites (furan compounds, tartaric and citric acid analogs) that seem to interfere with the brain's normal energy supply mechanism. Many of these compounds indicate an abnormally high amount of yeast in the intestinal tract.

Here is one mother's description of what is a typical case of digestive tract–related autism:

> My 5-year-old son had chronic ear infections from birth that were treated with antibiotics for his first two years. When he was about 1 year old, he developed chronic diarrhea and lost weight. Around this time, he was starting to babble and point, but he regressed, and the language and social skills he had been developing were gone. At 2 1/2, he was diagnosed with autism. He still had the diarrhea, but doctors could find no reason for it. He then had tubes put in his ears and the antibiotics were discontinued.
>
> We were sent to an allergist, who started my son on an anti-yeast medication. Shortly after this, the diarrhea stopped. Within three months of the diarrhea stopping and the yeast level coming down, my

son began talking and hasn't stopped. Signs of autism are now mild, though the ADHD gives him trouble.

Another mother reported a similar experience with her son:

In my search for help for our autistic son, I came upon a document by a physician who said his research showed that a common oral antifungal drug helped alleviate some outward symptoms of autism. After reading and rereading the material, I eagerly shared it with our family physician. Our doctor didn't share my enthusiasm.

He prescribed the medicine for Matthew anyway, at my insistence. After one week of medicine, people who regularly worked with Matthew wanted to know what I was doing differently; we all saw incredible improvements.

Wheat Allergy and Autism

Gluten intolerance (also known as celiac disease or celiac sprue) is a condition involving the gliadin fraction of gluten, a protein found in wheat, rye, and related grains. The gliadin fraction should be further broken down by enzymes, but if they are missing, the gliadin causes damage to the internal lining of the intestinal wall. The result is a denuding of the lining of the upper small intestine. Fewer nutrients get absorbed into the body, and full-blown malabsorption conditions often occur, with symptoms like diarrhea, weight loss, abdominal distention, anemia, and (in infants) the failure-to-thrive syndrome.

Some of the gluteomorphins—opiod breakdown products from digesting gluten—get through the denuded intestinal wall and into the bloodstream, a place where they don't belong. When they arrive at the brain, they probably lodge into opiate receptors and disrupt neurotransmitter production, triggering ADHD and/or autism symptoms.[5,6]

A salivary test for antigliadin antibody is a convenient, noninvasive, and highly reliable (though not infallible) indicator of the presence of celiac disease. The same test can be used to assess a child's compliance with a wheat- and gluten-free diet.[7,8]

Milk Allergy and Autism

A similar chemical chain of events occurs when milk protein breaks down to form casomorphine. Note that both gluten and caseine intolerances stem from faulty digestive processes, not tainted wheat or milk.[9–15]

Faulty Immune System Functioning and Autism

One mother's experience illustrates the close connection between immune system malfunction and autism:

> For two months, we reveled in the changes we had seen in our autistic son, Kirk, as his asthma seemed to have disappeared. Then, following a series of bouts of pneumonia and ear infections, his behavior deteriorated. He began biting up and down his arms, banging his head, staring vacantly into the flickering television screen. The fragile hold we had gained in Kirk's world slipped away. Our little boy sat for hours staring dreamily into space at nothing, or he rampaged through the room, ripping apart everything in his path. Sadly, after all we had been through, the new Kirk was gone.

Some research has discovered elevated interleukin-2 in children with autism, which indicates an abnormally high level of immune system activity. In other words, the body thinks it is under attack, probably because of toxic by-products from the faulty digestive tract.[16]

Another study showed children with autism to be abnormally low in IgA, the main antibody lining the interior walls of the digestive tract. This finding indicates that digestive problems are involved and that the immune system is not functioning properly. Protein and calorie depletion and/or malnutrition cause global suppression of almost all aspects of immune function.[17]

At this time, about a dozen scientific studies in professional journals claim to measure immune functions of children with autism, with inconsistent findings. Some show an overactive immune system, others show an underactive immune system, and still others show both over- and underactivity of various components of immune function. Certainly, immune functions are disrupted in children with autism, but the pattern of disruption is not a simple or unilateral one. Any nutrient that strengthens and stabilizes immune function will likely be helpful (or at least not harmful) to a child with autism, and any potentially toxic substance will probably bring about further symptoms or at least create further disruption in an already chaotic internal chemistry.

> *The safety of immunizations for infants and toddlers has recently come into serious question.*

Metal Toxicity and Autism

Scientific evidence of the safety of immunizations for infants and toddlers has recently come into serious question. Safety studies have generally measured only short time periods—often just a few weeks. There is now an increasing appeal for long-term safety studies assessing potential negative effects one or two years after an immunization. Such an effect is now suspected as a culprit in some cases of autism and Asperger's syndrome.

Can Mercury Poisoning Cause Autism and ADHD?

Mercury contained in thimerosal, a preservative, is a potential hidden villain in many vaccines, including the MMR vaccine commonly administered to babies. In 2000, the U.S. Food and Drug Administration called on vaccine makers to phase out vaccines containing thimerosal. Shortly before, the U.S. Public Health Service issued a statement admitting that infants in the United States are at risk for mercury-based toxicity from the high number of thimerosal-containing vaccines they receive.

Mercury is suspect because:

How to Have Your Child Shot

- Insist that your child be immunized only with the new mercury-free vaccines, never with a mercury-preserved vaccine.

- Refuse to allow vaccinations at any time your child appears at less than full health and vigor.

- The older, the better, so wait as long as you can for your child's natural protections to develop against the toxic aluminum and formaldehyde that will be introduced by the vaccine.

- Insist that the vaccine for each disease be given separately and that several days elapse between vaccinations.

- Autism (and sometimes ADHD) symptoms appear suddenly with no other apparent cause after, not before, the vaccination is given.

- The symptoms displayed in infants and toddlers are identical to the known symptoms of mercury poisoning.

- Autism usually hits before the age when the human body's tox-insulation systems are operative.

In a recent large study involving 503 children with Asperger's syndrome, autism, and PDD, over 99 percent were missing metallothionein, the chief toxinsulating protein the human body uses to discharge disruptive metals like mercury and prevent them from settling into brain tissue.

A large majority of children with autism who received the MMR vaccination have antibodies to brain tissue in the form of antibodies to myelin basic protein, the protein that helps form the sheath around

- Have your child consume cold-processed freshwater blue-green algae daily for three weeks prior to receiving the vaccination and for a week after. (The only algae harvesting organization that uses cold processing at this time is Cell Tech. I don't recommend the algae sold in stores.)

- Avoid unnecessary booster shots. Ask for a lab test of the child's blood for the presence of antibodies to the disease. If the antibodies are present in sufficient number, there is no need for a booster.

- Keep abreast of the latest information relevant to your child's vaccination needs. For useful Web site links, log on to www.ADD-Plus.com.

the axons of brain cells. There is a strong correlation between antibodies to myelin basic protein and antibodies to measles.[18,19]

Irlen Syndrome and Autism

Irlen syndrome can imitate autism or, in some cases, occur with it as a comorbid (associated) condition. Here are some autistic-like symptoms of Irlen syndrome that can cloud the diagnostic picture. A child who shows a number of these indicators could have one or both of these conditions.

- Rubbing of surfaces
- Sensitivity to bright lights
- Squinting or closing of one eye in bright light
- Obsession with TV set color and brightness controls
- Bizarre behavior changes under fluorescent lights

- Several blinks at a time
- Looking at an object in a series of short glances
- Rubbing or pushing of eyes
- Sideways glances
- Appearing startled when approached[20,21]

One adult who had severe symptoms of Irlen syndrome and autism as an adolescent described the experience:

> I had always known that the world was fragmented. My mother was a smell and a texture, my father a tone, and my older brother was something that moved about. Nothing was whole except the colors and sparkles in the air. The lack of integration of my senses became the lack of integration of my emotions with my body and my mind.

Pharmaceutical Treatment

Treatment of autism with pharmaceuticals often entails several simultaneous psychoactive medications. A typical combination would be something to control nervousness (buspirone), something for ADHD symptoms (methylphenidate), something to control obsessive-compulsive symptoms (anaphranil), and something to control explosive acting-out (clonidine).

Toxinsulation Treatment

Autism, Asperger's syndrome, ADHD, sensory integration disorder, and Irlen syndrome are conditions that reflect brain toxicity. All five often worsen when children are exposed to toxins and improve with the toxinsulation method outlined in chapter 7. Here is one mother's experience:

> Derrick at 2 1/2 was diagnosed with autism. He made very little eye contact and spent hours in self-stimulatory behaviors: spinning around, sliding a toy back and forth over and over again, focusing on objects rather than people, and spending hours lining toys up.

Derrick had severe temper tantrums, sensory integration problems, and very little social interaction. His temper tantrums would become especially severe when he was given antibiotics for his frequent ear infections.

When Derrick became 3, he showed a keen interest in potty training but was having trouble with diarrhea. When he drank grape juice, the diarrhea stopped, but the temper tantrums increased to horrific levels.

He had a big problem with touch defensiveness. He would wear only swimsuits. To force him to change into other clothes would mean a temper tantrum that could last hours.

Then came the "cupcake" revelation. Derrick ate that famous cupcake with the white surprise inside and had a temper tantrum that lasted four hours. My husband and I could do nothing but hold him down as he kicked and screamed! The rest of the day, he lay on the floor, in a stupor, and rolled a toy truck back and forth until it made a crease in the carpet.

On another day, we saw a dramatic reaction after Derrick ate four jelly beans. It was like watching fireworks! At first, we thought sugar was to blame, but then we realized he never acted that way when he ate my homemade treats.

TREATMENT OF AUTISM AND ASPERGER'S SYNDROME

> *Two-thirds of children with Asperger's syndrome or autism have a wheat or milk allergy.*

Always hunt for toxic buildup. Two-thirds of children with Asperger's syndrome or autism will have either a gluten (wheat) or caseine (milk) allergy. Follow the food allergy recommendations in chapter 6.

A promising new treatment method for autism is the use of secretin, a naturally occurring hormone that improves digestion. It has been available as a medicine for many years and has an excellent history of safe use for pancreatic disorders. The method has had approximately a 50 percent success rate decreasing autism symptoms and often diminishes food-allergic reactions as well. This method is brand new and must await careful scientific trials before it can be generally recommended.

For that matter, anything that improves digestion, strengthens immune function, nourishes brain tissue, or improves visual organization will probably help. Visual training can also be helpful for children with autism and Asperger's syndrome. Avoidance of all six categories of irritants described in chapter 7 will also probably help.

I've included this chapter because of the recent increase in these conditions and their similarities to ADHD. Do not assume, however, that your child will necessarily develop any of them. The vast majority of children with ADHD don't have Asperger's syndrome, autism, or PDD.

The next chapter provides guidelines for obtaining a clear, accurate diagnosis and for establishing a smooth working relationship with each professional who may be involved in helping you and your family.

CHAPTER 3

Get the Best Professional Help

NO SINGLE FIELD of knowledge has all the answers about ADHD. Medical and mental health professionals can form the core, however, of a diagnostic and treatment team to provide the best possible help. Clearly, a physician is a very important part of your child's diagnostic and treatment team. Correct professional treatment for conditions causing apparent ADHD symptoms is crucial. If you choose medication for treating the ADHD, a prescribing psychologist or a physician will be needed to engineer the treatment and provide the proper medication and dosage.

Because ADHD is so pervasive and affects many aspects of your family's functioning—as well as your child's—a mental health professional is also a potentially valuable helper. Numerous other professionals can assist, depending on your child's specific needs. Your child might receive help from a psychometrist (a specialist in psychological testing procedures), neurologist, speech and language therapist, allergist, audiologist, Irlen screener, developmental optometrist, neurofeedback specialist, nutritionist, speech and language pathologist, occupational therapist, dietitian, learning disabilities specialist, or a combination of these specialists.

Does Your Child Have Multiple Problems?

The multifaceted nature of ADHD symptoms often requires several forms of intervention from medical, nutritional, psychological, and other professionals. Here's one mother's account of the problems her daughter experienced:

> Just before our daughter was 3 years old, we thought the terrible twos would never end. And they didn't until she was 7 1/2 years old and we were 10 days into treatment for her ADHD. Candace was impatient, irritable, impulsive, loud, and oversensitive. She had a short attention span, was disruptive at home and school, had an endless stream of physical complaints, and was severely depressed. She had also become chubby and very lethargic.
>
> We were a family in crisis. My husband and I were angry and frustrated with her and each other, and our other children were shortchanged because of our overattention to Candace's hourly outbursts and traumas. We dreaded picking her up from first grade every day because of the negative daily reports of her behavior. And her anger, tears, and frustration only added to her plummeting self-esteem.

Stay informed and confident of your ability to learn whatever is necessary to find the best assortment of measures to assist your child. You are the ultimate seeker and balancer of prescribed medication, dietary and toxinsulation measures, sensory integration procedures, specialized academic methods like the Irlen method, and any other of the approaches you decide to use. Don't be afraid to keep asking questions until you understand all the relevant options. An adequate information base increases your sense of personal control and effectiveness.

GETTING HELP FROM A PHYSICIAN

Some physicians rarely or never prescribe stimulants or antidepressants; others rely heavily on them. Some recommend nutritional and toxinsulation approaches, while others avoid mentioning these options. Some require lengthy series of unnecessary psychological testing beyond the customary teacher and parent reports and an exam and interview of the child. Others rely on skimpy data that is dangerously close to missing huge aspects of the diagnostic picture, collecting only information from parents and observation of the child in the office. Some decide if the problem is or is not ADHD simply on the inaccurate and misleading basis of how the child acts during a 10-minute office visit or whether the child ever sits still watching television. Research has shown that in four out of five visits to their physicians, these children do not show any visible signs of the disorder. Fortunately, these trends are changing as increasing numbers of physicians gain experience with ADHD.

> *Keep asking questions until you understand all the relevant treatment options. Adequate information increases your sense of control and effectiveness.*

Be prepared for the first visit to the physician. Rate your child, and have the teacher do the same, with the Taylor Hyperactivity Screening Checklist (see page 37). As a supplement to these observations, take a copy of relevant sections of chapters 1, 2, and 6 with all applicable sections and symptoms highlighted. Bring a list of any known allergies and sensitivities, relevant information from school files, and a brief summary of any social skills problems. Give the physician target symptoms, particularly those that are most troublesome.

You can use a convenient audiotape that gives 42 minutes of symptoms, aspects, and indicators of ADHD as an additional guide.[1] Simply jot down everything that applies and take that list to the physician. You have valuable knowledge and information to share. You are directly involved in getting your child's cooperation, maintaining the medication or dietary regimen, and monitoring the results.

It's crucial for the physician to rule out imitator disorders, detect associated medical conditions, and confirm the diagnosis of ADHD. The following conditions produce symptoms similar to ADHD that are *not* usually cured or reversed (but can sometimes be lessened) by physiological methods such as prescribed ADHD medications, toxinsulation, sensorimotor interventions, or dietary changes:

> *M*any other conditions produce symptoms similar to ADHD. It's important to rule them out.

- **Direct physical or biochemical insult to brain tissue** as a result of encephalitis, chorea, Reye's syndrome, a brain tumor, or a skull fracture. These types of tissue damage can cause forgetfulness, absentmindedness, memory problems, distractibility, and weakened control over emotions.

- **Diabetes** can cause temporary nervousness, hyperactivity, and a short attention span.

- **Thyroid dysfunction**—hypothyroidism and hyperthyroidism—can alter activity levels, sleeping patterns, and emotional control.

- **Medications**, such as bronchial dilators, antihistamines, and anticonvulsants, can cause inattentiveness and temporary increases in activity levels.

- **Seizure disorders**, such as temporal lobe epilepsy, can cause temporary states of agitation and confusion.

- **Hearing loss** can appear as inattentiveness or refusal to cooperate.

- **Vision problems** can result in facial grimacing, squirming, poor school performance, and irritability.

- **Sleep debt** caused by sleep apnea or physical discomfort interfering with sleep can result in hyperactivity, irritability, difficulty concentrating, forgetfulness, listlessness, bed-wetting, and school problems.

The following conditions produce symptoms similar to ADHD that *will* usually respond to the methods described in this book:

- **Iron deficiency** can lead to difficulties focusing attention, solving problems, and controlling activity, and in older kids it can drastically weaken the immune system. Various ADHD-like symptoms can occur as a result of poor immune function.

- **Heavy-metal intoxication** from storage of lead, aluminum, cadmium, mercury, or excess copper in brain tissue can cause inattention, tremor, and behavior control difficulties.

- **Protein/calorie malnutrition** can interfere with an infant's normal development of brain chemical processes.

- **Hypoglycemia** can cause shortened attention span, tremors, and inability to concentrate.

- **Physical discomfort**, such as breathing problems or an itchy skin rash due to allergies, can cause temporary irritability and decreased ability to concentrate.

FINDING EFFECTIVE PROFESSIONAL ASSISTANCE

Use care in selecting the professionals you want on your child's helping team. Keep hunting until you find those with whom you feel comfortable. They should inspire your confidence and earn your trust. They should be neither too optimistic nor too pessimistic and should sustain realistic hopes while not arousing false ones about the effectiveness of the treatments being considered and about the course of your child's disorder.

Doctors and other professionals should be sensitive to your child's capacity to accept technical information and should set aside a few moments to explain the options. They should talk directly with your child about ADHD and the treatments being used. They should give anticipatory guidance, outlining the expected developments regarding the treatment. From time to time, check to make sure you and they have approximately the same understanding of your child's progress.

Encourage clear communication. Don't camouflage stress. The office of any helping professional is not the place to hide trouble. Have your questions written down and be prepared to provide answers to all questions. If you have little opportunity to ask questions or are not able to formulate useful questions during the initial session, arrange for an additional session. Don't be afraid to admit that you don't understand something or that you need further explanation of some principle, idea, or procedure. Take notes or ask for a written summary of what has been discussed.

> *Encourage clear communication. Don't camouflage stress. The office of any helping professional is not the place to hide trouble.*

Be assertive without being offensive, insistent without being pushy, confident without being overbearing, and informative without lecturing. Remember that professionals wants to exercise their unique refined skills for the benefit of your child and family, and you must give them the freedom to do just that.

One of your functions is to use your expanding knowledge about your child to help prevent mistakes professionals might otherwise make. If circumstances warrant your sharing information about the many options discussed in this book, show relevant passages to them.

Your child's helping professionals have just as great a need for reliable help and information from you as you do from them. Your honesty, courtesy, punctuality, treatment follow-through, financial responsibility, and consistent feedback as to the effects of the interventions are important aspects of being a partner in caring for your child. Don't expect any professional to be universally knowledgeable. If you have doubts, express your concerns or frustrations without questioning the integrity or competence of the professional. Professionals understand misdirected anger dumped on them, yet they might react with some anger in return.

Remember that you and they have similar feelings when you are communicating with each other. Both of you may be just as frustrated, upset, unprepared, or burdened at the moment. Express empathy for their frustrations now and then and be aware of your common feelings.

If a continuing personality clash develops, say something like, "I respect your knowledge and experience, but I don't understand why you are recommending this particular procedure." This statement leads you to either a more successful partnership or a mutual decision to discontinue. If at any point you are not able to play out the correct balance between assertion and cooperativeness, learn from your error and improve your relationship with the next professional.

> *Don't expect any professional to be universally knowledgeable.*

GETTING HELP FROM A MENTAL HEALTH PROFESSIONAL

The more severe your child's symptoms, the greater the total impact on your child and family and the greater the need for help from a mental health professional. This person's primary services are to assist in diagnosis and to help counteract the stresses ADHD poses. As with most services, those of a mental health professional are more effective if sought early.

This person may be a counselor, psychologist, social worker, psychiatrist, or member of a similar profession. Mental health intervention usually starts with one or two sessions of information gathering on the nature of your child's behavior problems. Most experienced professionals will try to rule out ADHD-imitator disorders, confirm the diagnosis, assess comorbid psychological problems, and decide about counseling or therapy options.

In addition, those who are qualified to do so might want to administer some psychological tests to supplement the information gathered in the mental health interview. Psychological tests should be given only by persons who have sufficient training and experience in the complicated techniques of administering, scoring, profiling, and interpreting them. These skills are generally confined to psychologists and psychometrists, or to those from other professions who have been trained by a psychologist or psychometrist.

Conditions like the following feature symptoms overlapping those of ADHD and are best diagnosed by a mental health professional:

- **Profound conditions** such as autism, Asperger's syndrome, and childhood schizophrenia can cause extreme aggressiveness, difficulty relating to normal social signals, and profound distractibility and hyperactivity.

- **Distorted response** to misbehavior by adults, such as harsh punishment or emotional abuse toward the child, can trigger rebelliousness and noncompliance.

- **Overburdening** of a child who is being pushed to grow up too fast can result in impatience and distraction.

- **Appeals for attention** by a child can take the form of hyperactive-appearing misbehavior.

- **Frustrations** from learning disabilities can lead to irritability, depression, and refusal to cooperate at school.

- **Learning disabilities** symptoms, such as difficulty understanding verbal instructions, can cause confusion and apparent attention-control problems.

- **Conduct disorder and oppositional defiant disorder** include aggressiveness, conscience deficits, impulsiveness, contrariness, and poor school performance.

- **Developmental delays,** with or without accompanying mental retardation, can cause restlessness, confusion, and shortened attention spans.

- **Extreme emotional disturbance** because of a major stress or traumatic conflict can result in restlessness, inattentiveness, aggressive behavior, bed-wetting, and inability to focus.

- **Situational stress** such as extreme hunger, poor teaching, or educational tasks far above or below the correct difficulty level can cause misbehavior, loss of interest in performing, or anger.

- **Normal exploratory zeal,** particularly in toddlers and preschoolers, and the natural uninhibitedness of that age group can mimic the drivenness of true hyperactivity.

- **Intense boredom** during vacation periods or loosely supervised classroom activities can lead to restlessness, inability to sustain attention, discontent, and irritability.

- **Depression** can interfere with any child's ability to concentrate or produce sustained effort.

- **Anxiety** causes irrelevant comments, attention deficits, drivenness, and difficulty staying on-task.

INTEGRATING MENTAL HEALTH WITH OTHER INTERVENTIONS

In spite of medication or sensorimotor, dietary, or toxinsulation treatment, children with ADHD usually remain noticeably different from other children. The range of difficulties they experience often calls for other helpers in addition to mental health professionals. Children with ADHD who also have oppositional defiant disorder, conduct disorder, depression, anxiety disorders, obsessive-compulsive disorders, Irlen syndrome, and learning disabilities seem to have more severe difficulties than those without overlapping conditions. In general, children with ADHD who receive no special assistance beyond prescribed medication (discussed in chapters 4 and 5) or toxinsulation (discussed in chapter 7) do not succeed as well in school, in their relationships, in their overall emotional health and adjustment, and in their feelings of self-worth.

If problems remain, you should decide which resources would be most helpful. Think of your psychosocial assistance to your child as an aspect of your parenting that will continue for many years, along with any physiological methods you are using.

Mental health professionals can provide individual or family counseling or psychotherapy. Counseling explores options during face-to-face discussions. Group counseling is an option that may be particularly helpful. Participating children learn to better understand their feelings and thoughts and become reassured that they share challenges in common with other children. They gain emotional support, an arena for role-playing social skills, and helpful feedback from others.

Psychotherapy, a more intense approach, explores deeper difficulties expressed as angry outbursts, acute anxiety, or depression. It may also be indicated if your child has been abused or if diagnosis comes after years of abrasive relationships at home or school.

It is not always necessary for a mental health professional to be involved exclusively with the child. In general, these professionals can have as much impact working with parents as with children. If your child is enrolled in counseling sessions, stay abreast of what is happening and discuss progress frequently.

> *Regardless of how many professionals are involved with your child, never surrender your primary function as facilitator and coordinator.*

Although the training procedures given in this book involve sophisticated and effective forms of psychological help, you will probably be able to perform most of them without professional assistance. Many of them strengthen your child's self-control in situations likely to cause a deterioration in behavior.

Regardless of the types and number of helping professionals involved with your child, never surrender your primary function as facilitator and coordinator. Develop a team spirit and urge a frequent exchange and updating of progress reports among those professionals. Research and clinical experience consistently show that better results occur when a multifaceted approach is used, including social and emotional factors, school adjustment, and physiological treatment. The next few chapters detail the most effective forms of physiological treatment.

CHAPTER 4

Treat with Prescribed Medication

O F THE BIOCHEMICAL approaches to treating ADHD, prescribed medication is the most popular, most researched, and best accepted within the medical profession. Most often, the medications prescribed for individuals with ADHD are stimulants and antidepressants. At any given time, about one-third of children diagnosed with ADHD are taking stimulant medication. Three-fourths have received a stimulant at one time or another. Most surveys estimate that between 2 and 3 percent of elementary school children are taking a stimulant. In about 10 percent of office visits to physicians by children with ADHD, medication is prescribed.

Amphetamines (Dexedrine and Adderall, for example) and methylphenidate (Ritalin, for example) are the most frequently used stimulants. Antidepressants most commonly prescribed are the tricyclics amitriptyline (Elavil), nortriptyline (Aventyl), and imipramine (Tofranil), as well as fluoxetine (Prozac). Antihypertensives (Catapres and Tenex, for example) are also increasingly being used.

There is a recent trend to prescribe multiple medications simultaneously, and the antianxiety medications are also being more frequently employed.

You might wonder why stimulants would be used to create calmness in an overly aroused child. These medications stimulate the child's "brake pedal," whereas without treatment, the child is all "gas pedal." These drugs do not slow down everything the child does. Instead, they allow the child to do a more efficient job of choosing what to say or do. They also increase the ability to problem solve and to learn. They help the child become more alert and generally increase self-control.

Significant improvement occurs in about 70 to 75 percent of children with ADHD treated with stimulants. Experienced physicians and those affiliated with specialized centers for treating individuals with ADHD prescribe more accurately, with surveys indicating about a 90 percent success rate.

There is no surefire way of predicting whether a particular child will respond favorably to medication. Until recently, the standard procedure has been to try the medications one at a time, but the latest trend is to proceed with more than one medication for children with associated conditions. In general, highly anxious and highly aggressive children are less likely to show improvement from stimulants and antidepressants alone.

THE PHYSICIAN'S ROLE WITH PRESCRIBED MEDICATION

One of the most recent trends is for allied professions—most notably clinical psychology—to lay claim to legitimacy in joining physicians as medication prescribers. For ease of understanding, I will refer to the prescriber as a physician in this book, though your child's prescriber may be a member of a different profession.

The physician should gather detailed information about the history and course of your child's ADHD and occasionally conduct a complete physical examination. Be sure to mention any other medication your child is taking and report any outstanding emotional difficulties. During subsequent appointments, bring notes, journal records, observations about your child's symptoms, a recent Taylor Medication Effectiveness Report (see page 79), a recent Taylor School Medication Effectiveness Report from the teacher (see page 81), and a list of questions you may have. Ask what to expect from ingredients in prescription medications. If your child experiences any reactions, report them immediately. Inquire specifically about when your child should take the prescribed medication, rather than relying solely on the label instructions.

GETTING YOUR CHILD'S COOPERATION

No emotionally healthy, caring parent relishes the idea of having a child take prescribed medication for a long period of time. Most parents of successfully medicated children did not start out applauding the idea. You must be objective in noting results. The project must have your wholehearted support. Underusing a medication, underreporting its results, and deviating from the physician's prescribed regimen are three frequent forms of balking at medication treatment.

HOW MEDICATIONS WORK

The mechanisms by which these medications affect behavior seem to relate to the manufacture of neurotransmitters, chemical messengers within the brain. One of the chemical sequences most frequently cited for its ADHD involvement is the series of reactions leading to the manufacture of dopamine. After it migrates to the next nerve cell (at about 240 miles per hour), dopamine transforms into norepinephrine.

Research available at the present time indicates that the brain of an individual with ADHD does not manufacture these neurotransmitters in sufficient quantity. Very recent research has added a twist—there are some parts of the ADHD brain that contain too much dopamine, so the defects in protein metabolism have more to do with abnormal distribution of neurotransmitters than simply underproduction.

Serotonin, a chemical building block of these neurotransmitters, has been found to parallel behavior in children with ADHD. The lower the blood's serotonin level, the more symptomatic the child's behavior.

Brain chemistry is incredibly complex, and the exact mechanisms by which these medications work is the subject of considerable debate. A crude analogy would be to say that they fool the brain into thinking that the child has just eaten a protein-rich meal. The most common toxic effect they produce, for example, is premature satisfaction of appetite. They apparently increase the release of stores of several neurotransmitters. They order the brain to come up with more neurotransmitters but provide no nutritional support for obeying that order.

> *Brain chemistry is incredibly complex, and the exact mechanisms by which these medications work is the subject of considerable debate.*

Molecules of stimulants such as methylphenidate and the amphetamines are structurally similar to naturally occurring dopamine and seem to work by specifically increasing dopamine and norepinephrine. These medications probably produce several clusters of effects by affecting many chemical connections—called pathways—within the brain. Some, the expected clinical effects, are very desirable; others are unwanted toxic effects. Still others are so adverse they indicate intolerance (allergy or unusual sensitivity) to the medication.

NEUROTRANSMITTER BUILDING BLOCKS AND CAFFEINE

There has been little research on giving the chemical building blocks of the neurotransmitters—called precursors—to children with ADHD. Tyrosine, levodopa, and tryptophane have given encouraging results, however, in the few research attempts conducted so far.

Findings are controversial regarding caffeine, which was in widespread use prior to the development of Ritalin. It seems to have an ex-

---

Medications and Tourette's Syndrome

There is great controversy about the use of stimulants with children and adults who have Tourette's syndrome (TS). Stimulants appear to worsen symptoms in one-fourth to one-half of these individuals. In the vast majority of cases in which stimulants worsen tics, the administration of a different category of medication is helpful. Much success has been reported with the antihypertensives.

---

citatory, stimulating effect on the central nervous system, and it tends to reduce the body's anxiety-relieving systems. Its chemical effects on the body seem to be broader than those of the customary medications for ADHD. Drinking coffee is an obvious possibility, but there is great variability from one cup of coffee to the next in the amount of caffeine. For some individuals with ADHD, however, caffeine seems to magnify the effects of stimulants and reduce some ADHD symptoms.

HOW AGE AND OTHER FACTORS AFFECT MEDICATION TREATMENT

During its period of most rapid change—from the nine months in the womb through the first five years or so after birth—the developing human brain responds to artificial chemical stimulators with greater variability than afterward. So the effects of stimulants and antidepressants are less predictable in young children. Desired effects are achieved less often, and toxic effects occur more easily than in those over the age of 6. When your child loses those telltale two front teeth, the effects of medications become more predictable.

Children differ from one another internally as well as externally. Their biological systems responsible for absorbing, distributing, and using medications also differ. Predicting which toxic effects and which desired effects will occur is impossible prior to giving the medication to your child. The body is an extremely complicated system, and these medications can create reactions along several chemical pathways simultaneously. Of the six organ systems involved in ADHD, they directly address only one (the brain); they sometimes have toxic effects on at least two of the others (skin and digestive system). Always consider the balance between the benefits and the risks when making decisions about any of the main physiological treatments I recommend: diet, toxinsulation, and prescribed medication.

> *Predicting which toxic effects and which desired effects will occur is impossible prior to giving the medication to your child.*

Factors a physician will consider when deciding what dosage level to use include your child's history of disease, current medical status, age, weight, severity of symptoms, and previous reactions to medication. In general, the more severe the symptoms and the older and larger the child, the higher the required dosage.

The art in prescribing these medications is deciding which type to administer, how many times per day, the exact times, and what dosage level to create the desired effects with a minimum of side effects. Developing this skill takes considerable experience with patients who have ADHD and knowledge about the medications.

Show this chapter to your physician if there is any doubt about familiarity with this treatment approach for children with ADHD.

HOW MUCH IS ENOUGH?

Use table 4.1 as a rough guide for what to expect as an effective dosage of methylphenidate (Ritalin, for example). Feel free to share this information with the prescribing physician.

If the medication treatment is not working well, check to see that the physician is not making any of the following common errors in prescribing for ADHD:

Table 4.1 Methylphenidate Dosage Approximations Guide*

	Score on Taylor Hyperactivity Screening Checklist		
Child's Age	28–32	33–37	38–42
5	15	20	25
6	15	20	25
7	15	20	25
8	20	30	40
9	20	30	40
10	30	40	50
11	30	40	50
12	30	45	60
13	30	45	60
14	30	50	70
15	30	50	70
16	30	50	70

*Approximate effective dosage per day in milligrams of Ritalin (methylphenidate) for coverage throughout the day.

- Failing to consider nutritional and toxinsulation methods of enhancing the medication's effectiveness
- Providing an insufficient dosage
- Misdiagnosing the condition as not ADHD because low dosage doesn't stop the symptoms
- Misdiagnosing as not ADHD because behavior differs between home and school settings
- Providing insufficient coverage for all waking hours

- Providing medication for school hours only, leaving a lack of coverage during evenings and weekends
- Accepting the parent's conclusion that medication doesn't work because the parent sees the child only after wear-off of effective medication from school hours
- Providing insufficient early-morning medication
- Not manipulating type and dosage sufficiently to eliminate troublesome side effects
- Maintaining an arbitrary top limit of allowable dosage
- Maintaining an arbitrary top age for medication
- Misinterpreting the normal slight increase in required dosage that accompanies brain growth as meaning the child has developed a tolerance that makes the medication ineffective

Adjusting the Dosage

Most physicians familiar with treating ADHD start the medication at a low dosage and increase it gradually until the desired effects occur. This procedure, called titration, safeguards against accidentally causing an overdosage or triggering an allergic or sensitivity response. It is important to allow three to five days at each dosage level to obtain an accurate and consistent measure of a medication's effectiveness. The medication should provide symptom control throughout all waking hours unless you and the physician prefer a different arrangement.

Desired Effects

When the dosage is properly adjusted, the desired changes occur during the medication's period of peak effectiveness—usually a four-hour period for short-acting forms or a seven- to eight-hour period for timed-release forms. If the effects wear off before the next dosage, symptoms rapidly reappear. These rebound states can be lessened or prevented by careful timing of subsequent dosages and by giving a protein-rich snack toward the end of each dosage's period of effect.

When the dosage is at its proper level, clear improvement occurs in most or all of eight aspects of behavior. These improvements have titles beginning with the first eight letters of the alphabet—I call them the "A through H" effects.

1. Activity control. Overactivity subsides and coordination improves in the large and small muscle groups. Improved handwriting is, in fact, the most noticed academic feature of medication treatment at school. The child stops chattering, making intrusive and irrelevant comments, shout-

> *When the dosage is at its proper level, clear improvement occurs in most or all of eight aspects of behavior.*

ing out, and interrupting. Athletic coordination also improves, because large muscles as well as small-muscle groups come under increased control.

2. Brain in gear. The child is alert, asks questions, and uses clear expression in written compositions and sentences. Artwork becomes more creative, with a wider choice of colors and more attention to detail. The child is less impulsive, scatterbrained, and absentminded. The child displays abstract reasoning, an understanding of cause-and-effect relationships, and the ability to express ideas in a logical sequence.

3. Conscience. The child shows an improved sense of personal responsibility for mistakes or misbehavior, becomes better able to resist temptations and peer pressure, and is less attracted to mischief. The child respects boundaries and asks permission before doing things. Moral judgment improves, and the child becomes repentant and apologetic.

4. Diligence. The child becomes more earnest and serious about important matters, volunteers to help, does chores without coaxing, plays without breaking things, and works hard at school performance and grades. The child becomes concerned about neatness and tidiness.

5. Emotional control. Emotions have a normal range of expression. The child laughs and cries at appropriate moments. Irritability and impatience decrease markedly. The child is more at ease, controls anger, and can be teased without getting upset.

6. Focusing. The child pays attention to what is most important, is less distracted, completes tasks without supervision, and stops flitting from activity to activity.

7. Gentleness. The child becomes more cooperative toward adults and generally less stubborn. The child can be reasoned with, stops trying to win power struggles, listens to alternatives, accepts guidance, and respects authority.

8. Helpfulness. The child shows a genuinely caring attitude toward peers and siblings, reflected in politeness, generosity, forgiveness, kindness, empathy, and flexibility.

You might encounter several different degrees of effectiveness as various dosages are tried. If there is no effect whatever from the initial low dosages, the physician is probably on the right track. As dosage increases, the desired effects are likely to start appearing. This process should continue until the desired effects occur or side effects interfere.

> *During the first three months of treatment, an allergy or sensitivity can be triggered by the medication.*

Sensitivities and Allergies to Medications

During the first three months of treatment, an allergy or sensitivity can be triggered by a particular medication. If allergy indicators appear or if the desired effects are weak while toxic effects are prominent, ask the physician to consider switching to a different medication. About 2 to 3 percent of individuals with ADHD are considered highly allergic or sensitive to stimulants or antidepressants, resulting in headaches, hives, convulsions, or other complaints. The occurrence of these symptoms is usually not related to dosage level but to an intolerance to the medication itself.

Are Your Results Superlative?

I always hunt for superlatives from parents before concluding that the correct dosage is reached. Here is how the mother of an 8-year-old boy with ADHD described a typical blossoming of desired traits during the third week of medication treatment:

> Mark's Sunday school teacher said he had been a *real dream* for the last two Sundays. His leaders for the evening program said they had been *amazed* at how he had been handling problems in their classes for the last couple of weeks. His English teacher at school said she had *really* started to see improvement in his behavior and work. My brother, who had not seen him for months, said he *could hardly believe* how good Mark had been at a recent family gathering—no arguing or shouting at the table and he sat through the whole meal without getting up.
>
> My sister-in-law saw him several days later and said she was *amazed* at how grown-up he had become since she last saw him two months ago. She had always had a hard time dealing with his noise and constant demanding chatter.

Tolerance

Tolerance occurs when the same dosage of medication no longer has its characteristic effects. Some children with ADHD are helped with a certain dosage level for only a few weeks; then a higher dosage level is needed for a few weeks, then a higher dosage, and so forth. If an increased dosage results in a blossoming of desired effects in a series of two- to three-week plateaus, the physician should try a different medication because tolerance is developing.

A tolerance-like phenomenon as a child approaches adolescence is sometimes misinterpreted as being tolerance itself. Brain growth, which causes an apparent increased demand for the neurotransmitters, may require an increased total daily dosage for most children with ADHD.

If an older child no longer seems to benefit from medication, check first to make sure it is being taken as prescribed. Second, consider the brain-growth phenomenon as a potential explanation.

Finding the Best Dosage Level

I developed the Taylor Medication Effectiveness Report (TMER) to help you and your physician determine the most effective dosage of medication (see page 79). It provides a simple, quick rating of the A through H effects. The medications are having their full effect when all eight effects receive an A or a B. Until such a rating occurs, further adjustment is needed.

The form also lists toxic effects such as overdosage, allergy, and side effects. A parallel form for use by teachers (TSMER) provides the physician with information about effects observable at school (see page 81).

Another way to determine whether you have found the best dosage level is to ask yourself the "if-always" question: "Would I have sought professional help *if* my child had *always* behaved this way?" If the grades on the TMER are all As and Bs and the answer to the "if -always" question is no, the correct dosage level has been reached.

SIDE EFFECTS

Although methylphenidates had been considered among the least toxic of medications, recent chilling news of methylphenidate-induced cancers in laboratory animals has caused many to reconsider medication treatment. The prescription medications used for treating ADHD are associated with some toxic effects, referred to as side effects by the pharmaceutical industry.

Estimates of how often these toxic effects occur in successfully treated children range from 10 to 50 percent, and many occur only

TAYLOR MEDICATION EFFECTIVENESS REPORT

CHILD'S NAME: _____

YOUR NAME: _____

PHONE: _____

TIME PERIOD BEING RATED: From _____ (date) to _____ (date)

CURRENT REGIMEN:

_____ mg. of _____ taken at _____ A.M./P.M.

_____ mg. of _____ taken at _____ A.M./P.M.

_____ mg. of _____ taken at _____ A.M./P.M.

_____ mg. of _____ taken at _____ A.M./P.M.

1. DESIRED EFFECTS

Simply fill it out as a teacher would a Grade Report, with these grades:

Grade	Rating	*Percentage of times the child shows this trait, from among all opportunities to do so.*
A	Excellent—very pleasant	80–100% of the time
B	Good—okay, livable	60–80% of the time
C	Fair—barely tolerable	40–60% of the time
D	Poor—very unpleasant	20–40% of the time
F	Failure—not tolerable	less than 20% of the time

_____ *Activity control*. Mouth, hands, and feet well controlled; sits for normal length of time; not fidgety or squirmy; doesn't poke, touch, and grab; stays seated appropriately.

_____ *Brain in gear*. Asks thoughtful questions; understands and remembers clearly; not impulsive or absentminded, seems "tuned in," stops and thinks before taking action.

_____ *Conscience*. Considers moral aspects of decisions; doesn't lie, cheat, or steal; respects boundaries; asks permission before doing things; repentant and apologetic if caught in a misdeed.

_____ *Diligence*. Does things without being reminded or nagged; faces tasks and responsibilities head-on; wants to do a good and thorough job; earnest and serious minded rather than flippant; careful rather than careless; wants things to be orderly; concerned about neatness.

_____ *Emotional control*. Patient, not easily upset; can take frustrations in stride; doesn't have tantrums, can be teased; controls anger.

_____ *Focusing*. Normal attention span, pursues a goal without getting side-tracked, completes activities, not overly distractible, doesn't flit from activity to activity.

(continues)

_____ *Gentleness*. Doesn't argue or power struggle; obedient, cooperative, respects authority.

_____ *Helpfulness*. Polite, generous, courteous, kindhearted, doesn't demand own way with other children.

As and Bs in all eight desired effects signifies correct dosage for ADHD symptom control.

2. UNDESIRED EFFECTS

Indicate the levels that are happening:

0 = This effect is *not occurring* or is so small that adapting to it requires no effort.

1 = This effect is *mild* and manageable with just a small effort that is not inconvenient.

2 = This effect is *moderate*, causing some inconvenience but still tolerable.

3 = This effect is *severe*, causing great inconvenience and can't be allowed to continue.

Rating	Effect
_____	Groggy, overly tired
_____	Irritable, weepy shortly after taking medication
_____	Headaches
_____	Tics, jerking muscle movements
_____	Appetite decrease
_____	Stomach complaints
_____	Presleep agitation
_____	Other (describe): _____

3. OTHER CHANGES

Describe any other *negative* changes in behavior or performance since starting this particular medication arrangement, whether or not you think they might be directly related to this child's medication treatment: _____

_____

Describe any other *positive* changes in behavior or performance since starting this particular medication arrangement, whether or not you think they might be directly related to this child's medication treatment: _____

_____

4. OTHER CONCERNS OR MESSAGES

If you have any other concerns or messages, please indicate here and write them on a separate piece of paper.

Yes _____ No _____

Signed _____

Mail to:

TAYLOR SCHOOL MEDICATION EFFECTIVENESS REPORT

Child's name: _____

Your name: _____

Class/Period/Time of Day: From _____ to _____

Time period being rated: From _____ (date) to _____ (date)

Current regimen:

_____ mg. of _____ taken at _____ A.M./P.M.

_____ mg. of _____ taken at _____ A.M./P.M.

_____ mg. of _____ taken at _____ A.M./P.M.

_____ mg. of _____ taken at _____ A.M./P.M.

1. DESIRED EFFECTS

Simply fill it out as you would a Grade Report, with these grades:

Grade	Rating	*Percentage of times the child shows this trait, from among all opportunities to do so.*
A	Excellent—very pleasant	80–100% of the time
B	Good—okay, livable	60–80% of the time
C	Fair—barely tolerable	40–60% of the time
D	Poor—very unpleasant	20–40% of the time
F	Failure—not tolerable	less than 20% of the time

_____ *Activity control.* Mouth, hands, and feet well controlled; sits for normal length of time; not fidgety or squirmy; doesn't poke, touch, and grab; stays seated appropriately.

_____ *Brain in gear.* Asks thoughtful questions; understands and remembers clearly; not impulsive or absentminded, seems "tuned in," stops and thinks before taking action.

_____ *Conscience.* Considers moral aspects of decisions; doesn't lie, cheat, or steal; respects boundaries; asks permission before doing things; repentant and apologetic if caught in a misdeed.

_____ *Diligence.* Does things without being reminded or nagged; faces tasks and responsibilities head-on; wants to do a good and thorough job; earnest and serious minded rather than flippant; careful rather than careless; wants things to be orderly; concerned about neatness.

_____ *Emotional control.* Patient, not easily upset; can take frustrations in stride; doesn't have tantrums, can be teased; controls anger.

_____ *Focusing.* Normal attention span, pursues a goal without getting side-tracked, completes activities, not overly distractible, doesn't flit from activity to activity.

(continues)

_____ *Gentleness*. Doesn't argue or power struggle; obedient, cooperative, respects authority.

_____ *Helpfulness*. Polite, generous, courteous, kindhearted, doesn't demand own way with other children.

As and Bs in all eight desired effects signifies correct dosage for ADHD symptom control.

2. UNDESIRED EFFECTS

Indicate the levels that are happening:

0 = This effect is *not occurring* or is so small that adapting to it requires no effort.

1 = This effect is *mild* and manageable with just a small effort that is not inconvenient.

2 = This effect is *moderate*, causing some inconvenience but still tolerable.

3 = This effect is *severe*, causing great inconvenience and can't be allowed to continue.

Rating　　*Effect*

_____　Groggy, overly tired

_____　Irritable, weepy shortly after taking medication

_____　Headaches

_____　Tics, jerking muscle movements

_____　Appetite decrease

_____　Stomach complaints

_____　Other (describe): _____

3. OTHER CHANGES

Describe any other *negative* changes in behavior or performance since starting this particular medication arrangement, whether or not you think they might be directly related to this child's medication treatment: _____

_____

Describe any other *positive* changes in behavior or performance since starting this particular medication arrangement, whether or not you think they might be directly related to this child's medication treatment: _____

_____

4. OTHER CONCERNS OR MESSAGES

If you have any other concerns or messages, please indicate that here and write them on a separate piece of paper.

Yes ____ No ____

Signed _____

Mail to:

very rarely. Changing the dosage, type of medication, or times of administration usually reduces or eliminates the toxic effects. When the medications are prescribed by a physician experienced with them, these side effects prevent or seriously impair treatment in about 5 to 10 percent of children and teens with ADHD.

> *The most common side effect of ADHD medication is decreased appetite.*

The most common toxic effect is decreased appetite. Weight loss, stomach aches, cardiovascular stimulation resulting in a slight increase in heart rate and blood pressure, headaches (first five days *only*), nausea, weight gain, insomnia, nightmares, dizziness, dry mouth, skin rash, constipation, and hair loss also occur, though very rarely and almost exclusively at high dosage levels.

When toxic effects occur, here are nine alternatives, starting with those that require the least change to the medication program.

1. Ignore the toxic effects; they often decrease by themselves within the first three months.
2. Use psychological means to cope with the toxic effect.
3. Change the times of day and the amounts of medication taken at each time but maintain the same total daily dosage level.
4. Lower the total daily dosage level.
5. Give an additional medication to control the toxic effect.
6. Discontinue the medication temporarily, then reintroduce it (for imipramine skin rash but few other toxic effects).
7. Switch to a different medication.
8. Discontinue all medication if the child is very young and wait until the child is older.
9. Completely discontinue the medication.

In addition, there are numerous methods of compensating for side effects that go beyond manipulating medication. The following sections detail how to counteract the three most common toxic effects.

Presleep Agitation

Presleep agitation is a significant lengthening of the time spent trying to get to sleep. It involves many ADHD symptoms, usually because of a rebound effect from the wear-off of medication at bedtime. The average unmedicated child who has ADHD takes 40 minutes to get to sleep, which is twice the time children without ADHD take. As many as one-half of children with ADHD who are on medications report some presleep agitation, though its severity in the majority of these cases decreases as time goes on, and it does not represent a major stumbling block to treatment.

Here are suggestions for overcoming the presleep agitation side effect.

- **Regular bedtime.** Create and maintain a regular schedule for bedtime and tuck-ins. Have a set routine for bedtime preparations—bathing, brushing teeth, putting on pajamas, or getting a drink. Let the clock do the enforcing and have your bedtime companionship and services contingent on your child's accomplishing the necessary rituals by the time deadline. "It's 9:00 now" is all the reminder she needs.

- **Timing of meals and snacks.** Significant hunger can keep your child awake, particularly if there is an appetite loss side effect and the medication wear-off period occurs shortly before bedtime. Suddenly, your child feels very hungry when it is time for bed. The best solution is to honor his body signals and help him satisfy the hunger with a wholesome additive-free, protein-rich, low glycemic index snack. Follow the guidelines in chapter 6.

- **Bedtime medication.** You can fool your child's brain into thinking that you are providing protein needed to calm down by using a pharmaceutical substitute. Ask your physician to allow a small amount of stimulant medication 30 minutes before bedtime or an antidepressant a few hours before bedtime. I recommend the real protein snack over this option.

- **Mental focusing.** Help your child channel her thoughts by playing a tape recording of a bedtime story or music she enjoys. Some children prefer to read; others like to watch television or listen to the radio. The channeling of their thoughts and attention provides a comforting, relaxing experience. Even though not falling asleep quickly, the child is not bothering anyone else at bedtime.

- **Noise insulation.** Create a constant background noise that does not vary, such as from an air conditioner, humidifier or dehumidifier, air purifier, or have your child listen to tapes or music with earphones.

- **An active day.** Encourage your child to be vigorously active until about an hour before bedtime, so fatigue builds up. A nap during the day can worsen this side effect, especially in very young children. Mild activity before sleep tends to extend and deepen sleep, while strenuous activity too near bedtime has the reverse effect.

- **Gentle stimulation.** It is important that your child be calm and not overly stimulated during the last 30 minutes before bedtime. A warm shower or bath is helpful, as are washing and combing hair and sitting for a while in a rocking chair. Be careful about petrochemical exposure when selecting the soap (see chapter 7).

- **Pleasant room.** The ideal sleeping room temperature for most children is 64° to 66°F. Arrange the physical aspects of the room to provide comfort, calmness, and an assurance of safety. Adjust the night-light, window blinds or curtains, position of the door, and bedding in accord with your child's wishes.

- **Elaborate tuck-in.** Especially for the young child, an elaborate tuck-in procedure is well worth the effort and develops a calm and reassured state. Rubbing and affectionately touching him, praying together, playing simple games such as writing letters or numbers on his back, telling him a bedtime story, or playing quiz show with questions he is capable of answering can provide rich and rewarding moments of togetherness. Bedtime tuck-in should be pleasant but brief, coming to an end at a reasonable time without frustrating you. The entire procedure shouldn't consume more than 15 minutes. When tuck-in is over, give a good-night kiss or hug and depart quickly.

> *Especially for the young child, an elaborate tuck-in procedure is well worth the effort and develops a calm and reassured state.*

- **Adjustment of daytime medications.** Adjusting the time of day your child takes medication or the type and dosage can usually reduce presleep agitation. The longer-lasting forms of medication taken during the afternoon are less troublesome than the short-acting forms.

- **Day's review.** Bedtime affords an excellent opportunity to express love and talk tenderly with your child. Review the day's events with a focus on those that were pleasant and fulfilling. During this moment, express your love in a frank and honest way. This exchange at the close of the day is especially effective for a preadolescent or an adolescent.

- **Bright ideas notebook.** Give your child a notebook for writing down thoughts and ideas that are contributing to wakefulness during the presleep period. Getting the ideas on paper allows her to stop juggling them mentally and aids in preparing her for sleep.

Growth Stunting

Probably because of an interaction with growth hormones, this side effect occurs in children with moderate to severe symptoms who take moderate to high dosages for several years. When the medication is discontinued for about six weeks, growth rebounds rapidly, so the net result is little or no difference in final attained height and weight as an adult. My experience is that about one-half the children on high dosages over a period of several months experience a noticeable suppression of the rate of height and weight gain for that period.

Some physicians try to compensate for this side effect by taking the child off medication whenever possible; vacation periods provide the best opportunity. Most parents of children who discontinue medication annually for a two-month period during the summer report that the growth rebounds completely, and the child returns to a normal height and weight growth curve. Because this effect occurs in only *some* children on high dosages, I recommend close monitoring of height and weight before making any decision about medication-free periods. As in so many other circumstances with these children, the choice is between two difficult options.

> *Most parents of children who discontinue medication annually for a two-month period report that the child returns to a normal height and weight.*

Among those who are not given medication-free periods and who experience the stunting effect, the average amount is less than two inches. If stunting occurs and becomes an important psychological issue, choice of hair style and footwear can compensate.

Decreased Appetite

This side effect varies from a slight decrease in appetite to severe nausea, with most cases involving a minor but noticeable drop in appetite. Appetite returns after wear-off of the medication and usually recovers after a few weeks. Stimulants and antidepressants tend to create this side effect in one-quarter to one-third of those taking them. Appetite decrease is less of a concern when the child is already somewhat overweight. The basic approach for countering this side effect is to allow your child to eat whenever hungry, in order to compensate for any nutritional losses.

The choice of which food to offer can sometimes mean the difference between cooperation and conflict at mealtime. Avoid serving

"Those Pills Make My Tummy Feel Funny"

Sometimes slight nausea occurs when medication is taken on an empty stomach. The digestive tract is one of the six organ systems most often involved in ADHD, so it is important to solve this problem. Parents have reported success with these solutions:

- Accompany the tablet with some food.
- Give a papaya tablet 10 minutes before the medication.
- Give a capsule of digestive enzymes 10 minutes before the medication.
- Give an acidophilus capsule 10 minutes before the medication.
- Switch to a different medication.

meals when your child is overly fatigued. A short nap before a meal or a readjusted mealtime might better accommodate her natural cycles. Exercise that gently stimulates her without tiring her before a meal can sometimes help. Offering a smaller meal or snack during the day when appetite seems to recover somewhat can also be a useful maneuver.

Mentally and physically prepare your child for the upcoming meal. Give her a brief notice that the meal is about to be served. Just prior to a meal, the shift of attention away from other activities encourages your child to anticipate the meal with an aroused appetite. Use her favorite place mat, novelty drinking straw, personalized cup or mug, or other aspects of the table setting to encourage participation in the meal. Cutting or shaping food into interesting designs also helps.

Because nearly every child who has ADHD is somewhat malnourished and partially dehydrated, give your child's nutritional needs

Why Isn't the Medication Working Today?

Every child's brain chemistry varies from day to day and from situation to situation. The response of any two individuals to the same dosage level of the identical medication also differs. During a bad day, your child's brain is using up the medication at an unusually high rate. Seven factors are the most likely contributors to these bad days:

1. **Extreme emotional distress.** A family crisis, a visit to a noncustodial parent, abuse, or other emotionally draining experiences.

2. **Inadequate sleep.** A lack of sufficient sleep during the preceding 24 hours (probably the most common cause of bad days).

3. **Inadequate nutrition.** Insufficient nutrients for day-to-day functioning; the most likely deficiencies are of proteins, essential fatty acids, and minerals.

4. **Extreme emotional excitement.** A trip to an amusement park, a vacation, the birth of a sibling, a visit with playful cousins, or a similar event.

5. **Intense mental work.** Having a battery of academic tests throughout the entire school day.

6. **Vigorous play.** A three-hour soccer or football game, for example; expect problems if you see a sweat-covered shirt.

7. **Chemical exposure.** Ingestion of or exposure to a substance to which the child is highly reactive (see chapter 7).

high priority. Make sure that what he is able to eat is highly nutritious. Cut down on less wholesome foods and snacks. Get him to drink a nutritious beverage such as a homemade fruit smoothie with algae (tastes like a strawberry shake). Consider supplementing with a multivitamin and mineral tablet along with enough fiber to allow normal digestive processes. Carefully follow the nutritional recommendations in chapter 6. Of course, consult your child's physician or a nutritionist if you have serious concerns, but be sure to have her read chapter 6 before she gives her recommendations to you.

> *You can make medications work for your child, but keep monitoring them and make adjustments from time to time for maximum effect.*

If you arrange a separate mealtime for your child, don't prepare a separate meal. Simply put his portions of the regular meal into glassware containers and store them in the refrigerator. The meal can be conveniently reheated whenever his appetite returns.

While prescribed medication is the most commonly used form of treatment, its complicated nature tends to confuse and intimidate most parents initially. As you sift through the information—some of it false and some accurate—that you receive about medication treatment, you might feel somewhat overwhelmed and frustrated about the lack of consistency shown by helping professionals in their opinions about this form of treatment. Don't become sidetracked by that confusion. Good, user-friendly summaries of medication treatment are available.[1]

Stay in close contact with your physician and provide consistent, detailed information on the effects you are noticing. You can make medication treatment work for your child, but like any other important project, you will need to keep monitoring and make adjustments from time to time for maximum effect and minimum complications. Even though you may be quite pleased with the results, you face another set of challenges having to do with the attitudes of your child and others toward physiological treatment in general and medication treatment in particular. Chapter 5 prepares you to meet those challenges head-on.

CHAPTER 5

Sustain Cooperation During Medication Treatment

Y OU WILL PROBABLY receive raised eyebrows, frowns of dis-approval, doubts, and even outright criticism regarding any of the physiological treatment methods discussed in chapters 4, 6, and 7. This chapter details the various types of resistance you are likely to encounter from your child and others to medications, the most common form of treatment for ADHD. Your child might even raise some of these issues as a way of opposing treatment during the first few weeks.

MYTHS AND REALITIES

Following are some of the most common myths about medications, along with the corresponding realities.

Medications develop craving and addiction.   Physiological addiction usually occurs after the body is forced to accept an abnormally high amount of foreign chemicals. The body then adjusts by erecting chemical imbalances of its own. When the foreign substances are withdrawn, the body tries to readjust but finds the resulting state very unpleasant. When children with ADHD are medicated at proper dosage levels, however, there is no forcing of an abnormally high amount of neurotransmitters (chemical messengers within the brain) and therefore no basis for addiction. These medications don't cause a chemical "high" or loss of reality contact. In fact, many children with ADHD gradually oppose taking the medication or barely tolerate it.

> *W*hen children with ADHD are medicated at proper dosage levels, there's no likelihood of addiction.

Medications teach irresponsibility.   Taking the medication is an act of self-care that increases and strengthens personal responsibility. The effects include enhanced diligence and conscience.

Medications are a prelude to drug abuse.   Appropriately given, medication helps prevent the problems that would otherwise propel a person into the drug-abusing subculture. Children with ADHD who have taken correctly prescribed medication are *less* likely, not more likely, to become involved in drug abuse than untreated children with ADHD because their goal is to eventually discontinue the treatment.

Medications involve mind control and zombie-like states.   At proper dosage levels, there is no slowing down of mental processes. Properly prescribed medications strengthen independent and creative thought and help people with ADHD become more concerned, more serious, and more thoughtful persons than they were without the aid of medications. At proper dosage levels, they don't act as a chemical straitjacket. In overdosage, they create the zombie-like state. The Taylor Medication Effectiveness Reports (see pages 79–82) are designed to prevent that state from occurring.

Medications cover up the "real" child.   Treated children don't suddenly lose their personalities; instead, they become better able to follow through on their decisions. Their personalities become more expressive, not more hidden.

Medications are potentially harmful. Too many reports of liver damage have occurred about pemoline (Cylert), so it has recently been removed from the recommended list of medications for ADHD. The manufacturer of Ritalin sent out tens of thousands of warnings to physicians in 2000 acknowledging that there is significant scientific evidence of cancer risk from methylphenidate, based on careful studies using laboratory rodents. Of the objections to medications, this one is the most valid. Because of it, I recommend considering the other physiological options in this book before resorting to methylphenidate.

SHOW THE BENEFITS TO YOUR CHILD

Give your child realistic expectations for results from medication treatment. Be specific and concrete rather than making vague references to acting better or shaping up. The most important aspect of winning your child over is to show the strong contrast between life before treatment and life after treatment. I call this the pre- and post-treatment (pre-post) contrast.

One way to make a pre-post contrast is to *explain* to your child the differences between life before and life after treatment. Often, he's aware of such differences already.

Don't make exaggerated promises, such as that your child will feel or act perfectly, get straight As, never forget anything, and hit nothing but home runs in Little League. Indicate you expect improvement rather than cure. Avoid giving the impression that medication can change something difficult into something wonderful.

> *Give your child realistic expectations for results from medication. Don't make exaggerated promises.*

The most common observations by children with ADHD who are on successful physiological treatment programs are that their schoolwork improves, they get along better with other children, they feel calmer and more in control of themselves, and they get into trouble less often. Those with coordination difficulties notice improved coordination.

What Should You Tell Your Child?

Here is how to explain the anticipated results from medication. Modify the wording to fit your child's age and circumstances:

You'll be calm and less easily bugged or bothered by things. You'll feel more in control of yourself, as if you can stop and think and choose what you want to do, rather than saying or doing something first, without thinking about it, then being sorry and wishing you hadn't done it. Your memory might improve so that it becomes easier for you to understand and remember what your teacher talks about.

When these things happen, you should notice that I am not so aggravated at you, and your brothers and sisters aren't so mad at you. Basically, life will go better for you. The medication won't control you or make you do anything; it will only help you do whatever you want and try to do.

Usually the reasons for the child's opposition have little to do with the side effects of the medication. More often they reflect the following concerns.

Denial

Your child maintains that nothing is wrong and doesn't want any help in behavior control or academics. One good answer is to take a survey. Keep an accurate record of all instances of symptoms during the survey period, usually two to four weeks. At the end of the survey period, confront your child with the list. If ADHD symptoms abound, she has lost the denial line of defense. Invite her for at least an experimental start of medication treatment.

Another effective response is to have your child do a self-rating on the Taylor Hyperactivity Screening Checklist (see page 37), then compare it with ratings from parents and teachers. If the ratings are similar, the evidence is unanimous. If the child's ratings reflect denial, the evidence is still in favor of the existence of ADHD, which supports the need for at least an experimental treatment period.

Oppositionality

Another reason for refusing to cooperate reflects oppositional defiant disorder: Your child shows a "you can't make me" attitude. The more you try to force cooperation, the more resistance he shows.

Encourage opportunities for the exercise of free will and self-expression. Allow choices in other areas, including hobbies, participation in family meetings and discussions, and chores.

> *The more you try to force cooperation, the more resistance your child will show.*

Here is how to reinforce the idea of free agency, which is your child's ability to be the ultimate determiner of behavior. Modify the wording to suit your child's age and vocabulary:

> This treatment isn't making you do anything. It allows you to control your actions better. You get the credit for these changes. You are making very wise choices about how to act now that it is easier for you to stop and think about what to say or what to do. And you are choosing to be the New Calm Matt—playing quietly with your brother, doing your homework. Thank you for being the New Calm Matt.

Loss of "Self"

Children with ADHD are often concerned that they will no longer be their real selves: that medications will change them into sedate, goody-goody individuals. The slowing of their formerly rapid and chaotic behavior is so strange that they want to return to the untreated state. I have talked with children who have complaints such as "I can't be me. . . . Everything's too dull now. . . . I'm boring. . . . Nothing excites me any more."

It is important that your child does not feel she is being robbed of control over herself by becoming dependent on pill taking. Offer reassurance that the effect of the treatment is to improve her ability to stop and choose behavior rather than reacting on impulse. The treatment decreases her sense of drivenness and allows her more time and alertness for making more reasonable choices.

Emphasize that the assistance provided by medications is limited to supplementing her own efforts to accomplish genuine improvement in life at home and at school. Use the pencil-and-paper explanation:

> Whenever you write something with a pencil, the pencil helps you do the writing but can't write all by itself. It can write only when you want to write and try to write. Your treatment acts the same way. It helps you do things, but you must decide what you want to do and try hard to do it. Your medication will help you focus your mind on your work at school as long as you want to and try to. If you don't want to do your homework, the medication won't grab your hand and force you to start writing out your assignments against your will!

Fear of Being Different

Your child may be embarrassed and self-conscious about having to take medication. Point out that he is already different, in a negative way. Being different in terms of being calmer and better controlled may be novel and strange, but the rewards are plentiful.

Unfairness

Teach your child to accept the fact that not all things in life are fair and that everyone has burdens. Many children who have ADHD never receive treatment and remain unhappy and unsuccessful in school, in society, and within their families. Help your child realize that complete fairness in all aspects of life is unrealistic:

> Unfairness is a part of life, and everyone has a share of unfairness. You have a choice. You can either gripe about every unfairness every time it occurs throughout your life, or you can make the best of it and put

your effort into making your situation work the best that it can. You can't eliminate the unfairnesses, but you can choose to adjust to them.

If any of these concerns are interfering with your child's cooperativeness, find peer support. Locate another child with ADHD who is using medications successfully and arrange an interview with your child. This form of "buddy system" is quite effective. Emphasize the benefits of treatment and point out that the feeling of loss of excitement is only a temporary illusion. Life will become exciting again, but in a new and better way involving more social, personal, and academic successes.

> *Teach your child to accept that not all things in life are fair and that everyone has burdens.*

Sometimes a hesitant child will accept the idea of an *experiment* with treatment. Explain that you would like cooperation for at least the six weeks necessary to adjust the dosage level and to experience positive results. At the end of the six-week period, if things have not improved, you will agree to discontinue treatment and not bring up the topic again for a year.

YOUR CHILD'S RESPONSIBILITIES

Make it clear that there are unknowns about which types and amounts of medication are best or even whether a particular medication will bring about the anticipated results. State your need for cooperation in taking the medication until you determine whether the desired changes are happening. Several key responsibilities for practicing self-control after treatment has started are listed on page 99, "Is Your Child Observing Good Medication Etiquette?" These duties are paramount; they form the framework for all other responsibilities in your child's daily life until the treatment ends. Help your child meet these responsibilities by referring to them periodically. Try to obtain a once-and-for-all commitment from your child to cooperate with treatment. As in any other area of self-care, the goal is gradually to increase your child's share of personal responsibility for taking the medication. You have a greater responsibility for maintaining the treatment regimen, but you must determine the increasingly larger share to be given over to your child as time goes on.

MAINTAINING THE TREATMENT PROGRAM

After dosage is established, schedule an office visit every six months. If your child must take medication unsupervised, place the needed dosage, not the whole bottle, in a prearranged location where it will be safe from other children. Leave a reminder note if necessary. Give the child a reminder phone call at the time the medication is to be taken. Have him take the medication, then return to the phone to confirm that it has just been taken.

> *Try to avoid confrontations that appear to be challenges or power struggles when you remind your child to take medication.*

Forgetting to take medicine is usually the result of memory problems and has nothing to do with motivation or a lack of desire to cooperate. Supervision and structure can prevent forgetting.

Try to avoid confrontations that appear to be challenges or power struggles when you remind your child to take medication. For example, "It is time for your pill now" is preferable to "Take your pill now." Don't let your child maintain, however, that any forgetting to take medication is your fault because you didn't give a reminder on time. If needed, provide more than one reminder— for example, a chart indicating when the pills are to be taken, a check-off sheet showing they have been taken, and a note taped to the child's door.

During times away from home, such as camp, visits to the noncustodial parent, extended travel, and overnight visits, there are three basic choices:

1. Advise the caregivers to supervise the taking of the medication.
2. Let your child take the medication without mentioning that fact to the caregivers.
3. Let your child go off the treatment program while away from home.

Is Your Child Observing Good Medication Etiquette?

When taking prescribed medication, your child should:

- Not argue about taking the medication

- Watch for toxic effects and report them

- Watch for desired effects and report them

- Cooperate with your efforts to reduce toxic effects and increase desired ones

- Not deny the ADHD symptoms or the problems they cause

- Be alert for potential moments of temptation to violate the regimen

- Work at rebuilding a good reputation with friends, teachers, and others

- Not share medications with others

- Not discuss medications with others who have no need to know

---

Each of these options has its advantages and drawbacks, so your decision should be based on the specific circumstance. Generally, the first method is preferred.

DEMONSTRATING THE BENEFITS OF TREATMENT

There are going to be times when your child will need to explain and perhaps defend the treatment program, struggle with temptations to skip or stop the medication, or face ridicule about the treatment. To bolster against those moments, help him develop a deep conviction that the treatment works.

When you notice a particularly distinct difference between the medicated, symptom-controlled (S-C) state and the unmedicated symptom-reactive (S-R) state, use the moment for alerting your child to the benefits of the treatment program. The goal is that he recognize every S-R state, wear-off times of medications, and the effects of the treatment in bringing about S-C times.

If an S-R state is occurring, help your child understand the effectiveness of the medication. Position yourself for close eye contact, touch him on both shoulders, and use short sentences:

> This is one of those times when you are showing the Old Wild Michael. I want you to eat your protein snack now, because the medication is starting to wear off.

I strongly recommend that you offer a protein-rich snack at such a time. After your child has become calm, explain your reasons for intervening and once again draw the contrast between S-R and S-C behavior under the influence of the medication. It is much more effective to make these contrasts when your child is mentally alert and calm.

When you notice very controlled behavior, compare it with S-R behavior that would have occurred without the benefit of treatment:

> Usually at a time like this, you'd be unable to sit still so long, complaining that you are bored or teasing Andrew. It seems easier for you to control how you are behaving now, and your medication is probably helping you do that.

Children with ADHD usually express their awareness of the pre-post contrast in terms such as these, which reflect the kinds of insights that are important for sustaining your child's continued cooperation:

> The pills help me not fight with my sister. . . . calm me down . . . make me behave better . . . help me pay attention at school . . . make

Mom happier with me . . . make me stop being such a nuisance . . . make it so I don't talk as much.

The majority of children with ADHD who violate their pre-scribed medication regimens are aware that others can tell they have not taken their medications.

To help your child monitor the effects of medications, use a tape recorder to demonstrate the difference in how he acts during wear-off pe-riods. The goal is that he understand and agree with the need for medication. As far as possible, keep your child's role that of an informed partner

> *U*se a tape recorder to demonstrate the difference in how he acts during wear-off periods.

in the treatment. Though it may sound unusual to point out his be-havior in terms of training in pre-post awareness, do it anyway:

> You just sat down and answered all 10 homework questions without stopping. . . . You did both of your chores right away, and I didn't even have to remind you about them. . . . You stayed calm and didn't lose your temper with Julie tonight, even though she acted up the way she did.

There is no need to draw the pre-post contrast each time you comment favorably on your child's changed behavior. Give compli-ments for a few days, then summarize them as reflecting the impact of the treatment program.

The social impacts of your child's improved behavior—changes in the reactions of friends, teachers, siblings, and you—might be diffi-cult for him to perceive, even when quite obvious to you. Point them out in clear, simple terms whenever they occur.

After the effective dosage level is reached, help your child make comparisons between his own and others' behavior:

> Did you notice the way that child acted at the park today—yelling all the time, bothering his sister, being rude to those other children? I'm glad you're not acting like that anymore since your treatment started, and I'll bet you are too!

Of course, keep such comparisons in a light vein, never appearing critical and making sure your child understands you are not gossiping or making fun of others.

Find opportunities to portray what your child would have done prior to medication:

> Before your treatment started, you would never have been able to sit still for the 90 minutes this program took tonight. I'm so glad you can do that now. You can enjoy these programs more now!

The goal is that your child celebrate the joy of victory over the Old Wild Self, and part of the celebration is noticing the differences between the two selves. Your examples need to be specific and undeniable, because the pre-post contrast must not stay at a generalized level such as "I was bad; now I'm good." You want your child to avoid thinking in such self-condemning terms as being a bad person or a person who might accidentally become bad again.

With successful biochemical treatment of any kind—medications, toxinsulation, or dietary manipulation—children with ADHD gain better self-esteem and a new measure of success. The cycle of continuous frustration and discouragement is interrupted and replaced by a cycle of encouragement. They become aware of their increased academic and social efficiency.

> *The goal is that your child celebrate the joy of victory over his Old Wild Self.*

According to numerous research findings, after successful treatment of the child, adults improve their style of relating. Teachers become less intense and less controlling, talk slower, smile more, give more encouragement, and raise their voices less often. Parents become less directive and more likely to give affirmations and do favors for the child. These domino effects contribute to the encouragement cycle (see figure 1).

One parent of a 10-year-old boy with ADHD summarized the first four months of medication treatment: "We are so encouraged by the changes in behavior in Jared. It is like night and day. Just knowing

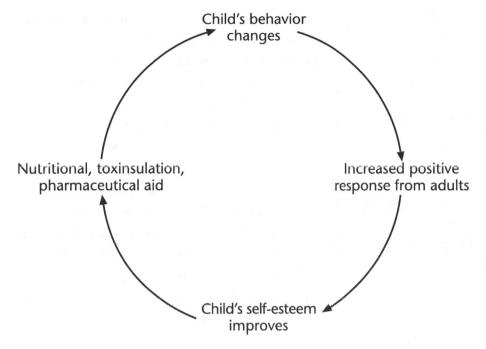

Figure 1—*Encouragemnet Cycle*

that the problem was ADHD and that it can be helped by medication has alleviated half the stress."

PREVENTING COMPLACENCY

When your child becomes less demanding and less disruptive with medications, teachers tend to be less alert to learning problems that might still remain. It is doubly important to monitor her schoolwork and academic performance carefully. Learning problems can remain even though behavior problems have decreased with treatment.

Another response to watch for—and prevent—occurs after your child cooperates with the treatment and symptoms are controlled. Self-confidence increases and leads to complacency and decreased diligence about following the regimen. Symptoms and difficulties suddenly increase. In this complacency cycle, your child weaves in and out of the prescribed regimen, first obeying it, then disobeying it. Prevent this cycle by urging constant diligence and by frequently monitoring whether she is taking the medication as prescribed.

> *Monitor your child's schoolwork and academic performance. Learning problems can remain even though behavior problems have decreased with treatment.*

Teach this self-reminder statement: "When I start to improve in my behavior, I need to be even more careful about taking my pills on schedule." Sometimes a complacency cycle is brought on by a parent. One child with ADHD told me: "When I'm acting good, Mom doesn't give me the pills so many times. She says I don't need them."

Your child should be concerned about any skipping of medication, but excessive wallowing in guilt won't be helpful. Help her strengthen her refusal skills and investigate how to eliminate temptation moments. Provide reminder notes and show your confidence that the deviations will decrease.

If your child violates the treatment program, the rest of the family should not have to experience the results of a chaotic and out-of-sorts child. When your child starts showing disruptive symptoms at the beginning of an S-R state, calmly send her to her room. Join her as soon as you are calm enough to discuss the situation and offer a protein snack.

TERMINATION AND OFF-MEDICATION TRIALS

Sometimes, physicians will want a medication-free period to test whether medication is still needed. The best time is after school has started and the child seems reasonably well managed. The off-medication trial period should last only long enough for the teacher and you to observe the presence or absence of ADHD symptoms. A variation of the off-medication trial involves making the child and teacher think the medication is still being given but instead substituting a placebo, a false pill. Medication holidays, which are periods of one or two days during which the child does not take any medication, also provide an opportunity to assess the need for continuing the medication.

Some physicians prefer that the teacher not be informed until the trial period is over. Denying the teacher the place of an informed ally, however, is an unnecessarily secretive approach. Left without knowledge of the off-medication period, he might conclude the sudden reappear-

> *Sometimes, physicians will want a medication-free period to test whether medication is still needed.*

ance of ADHD symptoms indicates the medication isn't working or is toxic. My experience is that it is better to keep the teacher informed, ask for close monitoring and objective judgment of the behavior, and have the teacher submit the Taylor School Medication Effectiveness Report form (see page 81) frequently during the trial period.

Keep these guidelines in mind:

- If a good blossoming of the A through H effects (see page 75) appears without medication, don't restart it.

- If your child's adjustment seems satisfactory without medications, continue to monitor how things are going but wait for deterioration in behavior before resuming medications.

- If stopping the medication caused deterioration in behavior, restart it.

- If the trial resulted in no appreciable change in your child, but there is not a full blossoming of the desired effects, the medication dosage was probably too low and may need to be adjusted upward.

All of these events need to be discussed with your physician. Discontinuing or restarting the medication should not be a decision made independently by you or your child.

There should not be an arbitrary age after which medications are no longer prescribed. The only way to know for sure how long a given individual will need to take medication is through consistent and thorough monitoring. Termination should be based on a biochemical change that results in a disappearance of symptoms, so that the medication is simply no longer needed. When high dosage levels are suddenly stopped, severe rebound effects can occasionally occur, including headaches, depression, profound violence, and suicidal thoughts.

> *There should not be an arbitrary age after which medications are no longer prescribed.*

One of the safest ways to terminate medication is to cut the dosage in half for three to five days, then in half again for an additional three to five days. Then give no further medication. The termination period for antidepressants should be somewhat longer, preferably around two weeks. The most common reasons given by adolescents for terminating their medication without their physician's knowledge or consent are:

1. A belief they would no longer have S-R states if medications were discontinued.

2. Unpleasant, poorly controlled side effects, such as stomach complaints, appetite loss, and presleep agitation.

3. A changed perception of the self, including feeling different from peers, feeling strange and unlike their "real" self, and feeling too juvenile.

4. Improperly prescribed dosages that result in an inability to maintain control, such as feeling drugged, numbed, depressed, lethargic, or "spacey."

Although embarrassment is one of the most common feelings noted by adolescents with ADHD who take medications, it is not one of the chief reasons to terminate treatment. To avoid having your teen stop taking medication against your better judgment, use the information in this chapter to demonstrate the fallacies of the four reasons given above.

Compensating for the many difficulties of people with ADHD does not stop when medications start. Nutritional, sensorimotor, and toxinsulation methods are always viable treatment options, whether or not medication is being used. When using more than one of these treatments along with medication, save reduction in medication as the last step, after you've seen good results from the other approaches.

CHAPTER 6

Use Nutrition Treatment Effectively

THIS CHAPTER REVIEWS some of the latest research findings with regard to how nutrients affect the six organ systems involved in ADHD. (These are the brain, the digestive system, the immune system, the skin, the body's fuel system—blood sugar—and the blood itself.) I've provided references for some of the key research. Large summaries of dozens of research articles are now available because of the flourishing research on the nutritional aspects of ADHD and related conditions such as autism.

To take full advantage of current knowledge in this fast-growing area of ADHD-related research, alter your thinking about nutrition. Here is a comparison between run-of-the-mill thinking and the most recent trend in ADHD wisdom.

Common Nutritional Teachings	ADHD Wisdom
Count calories	Count grams of carbohydrate
Fat is the culprit	Carbohydrates are the culprit
Keep proteins low	Keep proteins high
One egg per week	Four or more eggs weekly
Observe the food pyramid	Turn food pyramid upside down

Common Nutritional Teachings	ADHD Wisdom
Low-cal, low-fat is best	Low-cal, low-fat is often worst
Aspartame instead of sugar	Stevia instead of aspartame
Bread, pasta, potatoes daily	Avoid bread, pasta, potatoes
Food colors, additives are okay	Food colors, additives are culprits
Fruit and fruit juice daily	Fruit and fruit juice seldom
Margarine instead of butter	Butter instead of margarine
Skim or 1% milk	Whole milk

This list goes on and on, but you get the point. Beware of any dietitian or other professional who tells you that diet doesn't matter or that the only approach is to have a balanced diet, avoid fat, and observe the USDA food pyramid.

THE IMMUNE SYSTEM

Some of the most exciting new ADHD research provides startling insights about how the immune system is involved in creating ADHD symptoms and associated physical accompaniments. Recent research has shown, for example, that hyperactive children get more frequent head colds than their age-mates. A healthy, well-functioning immune system generally prevent colds, flu, frequent and numerous allergies, and a myriad of other problems for which children with ADHD seem to be at risk.

There are two-direction pathways between the immune system and the central nervous system, with each providing some regulation and control over the other. The anatomy of the human body appears to indicate that the brain could control immune cells and organs in much the same way as it controls other peripheral structures. There appears to be considerable alteration in neurotransmitter chemistry when an immune response occurs.[1]

Some of these immune responses involve allergies, with the net result of triggering a symptom-reactive (S-R) state in about 75 percent

---

All's Not Swell That Ends Swell

The classic immune response of histamine-based swelling has important purposes. But all that swelling comes at a price. That price is a terrible headache if the swelling occurs in the tissue lining the cranium. Or a cesspool pocket might form where new bacteria colonies can cause an earache.

Another price is that those hormones involved in orchestrating this process also affect brain chemistry. Individuals with ADHD are especially liable to experience further disruptions in their neurotransmitters, resulting in S-R states. Those bright-red cheeks and ear lobes shortly after a child with ADHD eats something he is allergic to usually spell trouble for his parents and classmates, at least for a few hours.

---

of children and teens with ADHD. Other immune responses involve genuine reaction to disease, with the net result of creating a period of unusual docility, quietness, and calmness in hyperactive children.[2]

Keeping the Immune System Healthy

Eating sugar in any form glucose, fructose, sucrose, honey, molasses, fruit juice—reduces immune function. This suppression of immune function can start within 30 minutes of consumption and last several hours, depending on the amount of sugars consumed, what they are consumed with, and the preexisting health of the immune system.

> *Eating sugar in any form reduces immune function.*

Having the digestive system do its job correctly is crucial to the functioning of the immune system. Over half of the immune system takes its signals from the digestive tract. In a sense, the digestive tract is itself an "early defense" part of the immune system.

To run an immune system requires considerable supplies of folate; biotin; vitamins A, D, B_6, and B_{12}; zinc; iron; and essential fatty acid derivatives. All of these nutrients must first come through the digestive system.

If antibiotics are used, replace the digestive organisms being destroyed by the antibiotics with live, vigorous acidophilus and bifidus bacteria (available in capsules) during the antibiotic use and for two weeks afterward. Acidophilus will implant and proliferate better if it is consumed throughout the day and accompanied by cold-processed freshwater blue-green algae.

Fatty acid deficiency increases the risk of viral infections, and a slight fever prevents viruses from multiplying. Providing good sources of essential fatty acids and avoiding the temptation to reduce mild fever are two additional strategies to use in preserving your child's health.

THE SENSITIVE-ALLERGIC CHILD

Research into why some children who have ADHD don't respond favorably to prescribed medications has unearthed a subgroup who have problems absorbing medications and various nutrients from the digestive tract. The inability of the medication to work its intended effects for these children apparently has more to do with abnormal digestion than with any special neurological processes.

> *Some children with ADHD don't respond favorably to medication because they have problems absorbing it and various nutrients from the digestive tract.*

These sensitive-allergic children (ADHD-sa) are also among the most chemically sensitive. Of all the organs, the brain is the most easily disturbed by a temporary overabundance or undersupply of any of its needed chemicals. An ADHD-sa child often shows symptoms such as these prior to age 2: difficulty nursing or accepting a formula, prolonged colic with poor sleep and frequent crying, little smiling, frequent spitting or vomiting, resistance to cuddling, prolonged and frequent tantrums, excessive perspiration, and excessive drooling.

The exact mechanisms by which allergens produce distinctive and dramatic increases in ADHD symptoms are not yet fully understood. Allergic responses mobilize the body's defenses against infection, namely the immune system. Skin rashes and hives are common indicators of allergic reaction. Treatment of allergies is generally a wise move for parents of allergic children to consider. Sensitivity reactions involve the body's misuse of chemicals that enter it, without triggering a response from the immune system. Tartrazine (yellow food dye), for example, has been shown to deplete zinc and thereby causes a worsening of ADHD symptoms without triggering an immune response.[3]

Asthma

Asthma is an allergic disorder featuring spasm of the bronchial tubes and excessive excreting of thick mucus in the lungs. The attacks range from mild wheezing to life-threatening blockage of the ability to breathe. All varieties of asthma, according to the latest research, are allergy related. Increasing consumption of water and essential fatty acids helps prevent or lessen the severity of asthma attacks.

The incidence of asthma has risen considerably in recent years, particularly in children, who comprise about a third of all asthma cases. More than 10 percent of all children in the United States have asthma; it is the most common disabling medical condition among U.S. children. The greatest increase in asthma-related hospital admissions has been for preschoolers. Children exposed to secondhand smoke and air pollution are, of course, at greater risk. Preborn children are also at significant risk if the expectant mother smokes. Being the child of a smoking parent is also a correlated factor in ADHD.

The research on the overlap between asthma and ADHD is inconsistent. Some studies show that children who have ADHD are no more or less at risk for asthma than non-ADHD children. Other studies indicate an apparent risk factor. Some studies show that the combination of the two occurs more often than chance among the near relatives of children with ADHD. The majority of children with ADHD who experience an asthma attack are likely to have an S-R state at the same time.

The American Lung Association is getting in on the act now, recommending many of the strategies in chapter 7. Even the Food and Drug Administration is echoing the importance of avoiding petrochemicals with asthmatic children, with its requirement that all foods laced with the food dye tartrazine be labeled as such because of the known risk to people with asthma.

> *Children with ADHD who experience an asthma attack are likely to have an S-R state at the same time.*

Migraine Headaches

A migraine headache usually reflects an allergy. There is swelling of the membrane separating the brain from the cranium and in additional areas surrounding the brain. The swelling is caused by the release of histamine, which is in response to immune system activity. According to some recent research, food intolerances can be the primary factor in initiating up to 90 percent of migraine headaches experienced by children.

The list of trigger foods for migraines is fairly well established. It includes foods that contain tyramine (such as ripening cheese, herring, all vinegars except white, alcoholic beverages, sour cream), anything pickled or fermented, nuts, bread that is hot and fresh, pods of broad beans, neurotoxins (such as monosodium glutamate), onions, canned figs, bananas, avocados, fermented sausages (bologna, salami, pepperoni, summer sausage), wheat, corn, soy, milk, eggs, chocolate, and chicken livers.

Foods marked "dairy free" usually contain hidden soy and MSG and may be triggers for some people. If consumed in excess, these foods also become triggers: citrus fruits (especially oranges), pork, tea, and coffee. Some trigger foods are heavy in caffeine, which dilates blood vessels in a way similar to tyramine.

Ear Infections (Otitis Media)

Ear infections occur as a chain reaction from allergy-based swelling in the middle ear. The swelling creates a pocket in which body-unfriendly bacteria can swarm and multiply. There is also some evidence that middle ear swelling can occur as a sensitivity reaction to the toxic phenols described in chapter 7. Whereas one-half of all babies in the United States have one ear infection prior to their first birthday, the rate for babies who later are diagnosed as having ADHD is probably over twice as great. One of the diagnostic markers that I use is whether a child has had three or more ear infections prior to her second birthday.[4]

According to research, a child exposed to cigarette smoke is nearly three times as likely to suffer from persistent otitis media as children whose parents don't smoke. The risk increases to fourfold if more than three packs a day are smoked in the home where the child lives. Smoke is most dangerous to children who have frequent nasal congestion and allergies. When such a sensitive child lives in the same home with a heavy smoker, the risk of ear damage increases by six times.

The issue for children with ADHD is that antibiotics wreak havoc on the body-friendly acidophilus and bifidus bacteria in the digestive tract, thereby unleashing body-unfriendly yeast, molds, and fungi to multiply unchecked. These organisms, especially candida yeast, release toxins and create disruption in the chemistry of the wall of the intestines.[5,6]

> *A child exposed to cigarette smoke is nearly three times as likely to suffer from persistent ear infections as children whose parents don't smoke.*

The aftermath of this kind of leakage of toxic products through the wall of the intestines is disruption of brain chemistry by an allergic involvement of the immune system. With the disrupted brain chemistry come those troublesome S-R states, which are flare-ups of ADHD symptoms.[7]

To prevent ear infections, prevent the swelling. Anything that reduces allergic reactions will likely decrease the frequency and severity of ear infections. Toxinsulation of allergens is a useful step (see chapter 7). If all milk, sugar, food additives, and fruit juices were eliminated from the diets of 100 randomly selected infants and toddlers with ADHD who frequently get ear infections, I believe that over 50 would show a rapid decrease or total elimination of the ear infections.[8]

Dust? You Must!

House dust is so allergenic that you should feel noble every time you run a vacuum cleaner. House dust contains more than molds and mites; it often also contains pesticides, solvents, lead, asbestos, and most of the nearly three dozen toxins in cigarette smoke if there are smokers in the house.

> *House dust is so allergenic that you should feel noble every time you run a vacuum cleaner.*

If your child is also dust allergic, make his bedroom a safe haven with a bare wood floor. Because most dust-allergic children who have ADHD are also phenol sensitive, my recommendations prevent exposure to phenols also:

- The bed frame should be metal or wood, without upholstering.
- Mattresses should be of solid foam, covered with barrier cloth.
- Pillows may be washable, nonallergenic, or solid foam.
- All bedding and blankets should be 100 percent cotton or wool.
- Wash the blankets and comforters every two months.
- Remove stuffed animals and other obvious hiding places for dust mites from the room. Avoid forced-air heating of the room from a furnace or heat pump.

As for air quality, keep plastics out of the room and place two toxin-absorbing plants (such as spider plants) in attractive locations to soak up airborne phenol molecules. Allow fresh-air ventilation if the outside air quality and pollens are not problematic. Consider an electronic air purifier if these precautions don't result in improvement.

Chasing After Allergies

The skin-prick test is suitable for judging the presence of allergies to house dust mites, fur, feathers, animal dander, pollen, grasses, and similar irritants. Unfortunately, it is very insensitive to allergic and sensitivity reactions to food and drink.

Cytotoxic tests, in which the examiner looks at a blood sample under a microscope, are not very reliable and vary in accuracy from one examiner to the next. The most likely error is to brand too many foods as unacceptable. Use results as a rough guide but test each identified culprit food for actual behavioral effects.

Vega tests work electrically on similar principles as acupuncture. They are painless, but their accuracy has not been sufficiently validated by science.

RAST tests use blood samples and are limited in accuracy to a few foods, specifically milk, fish, wheat, nuts, and peanuts, plus a few others.

None of these testing procedures is as accurate as a diligent parent who carefully monitors food intake and the child's behavior and hunts for correlations. Use the Taylor-Latta Diet Diary (see page 142) for this purpose.

FOOD INTOLERANCE AND ADHD

Food intolerances are caused by poor digestion. Incompletely digested food material gets through the wall of the intestine and into the bloodstream. The immune system reacts to these unrecognizable globs of foreign matter as if they are an invading organism. Histamine is released, bringing reddening and swelling in the form of skin rashes or rosy cheeks and ear lobes.

The numerous simultaneous reactions within the immune system are orchestrated by the brain and involve major alterations in the distribution of hormones throughout the body. Hormones drive protein mechanisms, and the already precarious protein mechanisms in the brain of the individual with ADHD become further out of balance. The result is a sudden and dramatic loss of behavior control or mental clarity. This sequence of events seems to occur in about three-fourths of children who have ADHD, according to numerous research articles in professional journals.

Allergy-based symptom flare-ups (S-R states) among children with ADHD are so common and so well researched that it is now possible to devise a list of the foods to which children and adults with ADHD are most likely to be food allergic: milk (the less fat, the more allergenic; skim is worst), wheat, corn, yeast, nuts, oranges, chocolate, eggs, soy, beef, and pork. Note that many of these allergenic foods are high in protein content. While it is beneficial to include a protein component in every meal and snack for most individuals who have ADHD, be sure to avoid the particular protein-rich foods to which that individual is intolerant.

> *Include a protein component in every meal and snack.*

Does It Help to Chase Down Food Allergies?

Here is one mother's answer:

> It's been about one year, and things are much better since I've removed milk, soy, corn, wheat, and chocolate from my children's diet. No more tantrums severe enough to injure a child; no more getting up
> 15 times every night to comfort a screaming infant; no more bruised-looking purple circles under their eyes; no more constant runny noses or recurrent ear infections. Yes, things are definitely better.

Conquering food intolerance is not an easy task. One mother summarized:

My son developed eczema in his first year, but it cleared when he was put on soy milk. He had no cow's milk until he was over 2 years old. At 3, he developed rhinitis. He also had frequent ear infections requiring antibiotics every few months. He developed a slight hearing loss in one ear, and his behavior was quite appalling—tantrums, aggressiveness, and difficulty getting to sleep.

With expert medical advice, we went on a dairy-free diet. In a few months, his hearing was normal, his behavior had improved markedly, and he was sleeping better. At school, his concentration improved. We have also found he reacts badly to sugar in any form, so this is kept to a minimum.

Ideally, you should eliminate everything your child might be intolerant of and notice improved behavior. Then test each suspect item one at a time for behavioral effects or physiological effects such as runny nose, puffy or rosy cheeks, skin rashes, or headaches. Use the Taylor-Latta Diet Diary to help identify problem foods.

> *Use the Taylor-Latta Diet Diary to help identify problem foods.*

Can You Use Diet and Toxinsulation Together?

In one of the most important and scientifically rigorous studies in the ADHD field in recent years, researchers tested the effectiveness of toxinsulation combined with avoiding food allergens to assist children with ADHD.

Seventy-six children with severe hyperactivity were placed on a carefully controlled diet that excluded milk, chocolate, citrus fruit, wheat, grapes, cheese, tomato, fish, pork, beef, corn, tea, oats, melon, ham, bacon, pineapple, peanuts, eggs, soy, and sugar. Their consumption of the food additives tartrazine and benzoic acid was also reduced. Sixty-two (82 percent) responded with improved behavior as measured by raters who did not know about the dietary manipulation.

Twenty-eight of those 62 participated in a second double-blind phase, and the majority were rated as significantly better behaved

Does Your Baby Have Colic?

If your baby has colic, you have several options. Cold-processed freshwater blue-green algae (Cell Tech brand) mixed with acidophilus can be used for soothing a colicky baby. Many mothers report success from breaking open a capsule and putting half of the algae-acidophilus mixture on the baby's tongue. Expect a quiet, calm baby in about five minutes.

Make sure your baby's digestive tract is not being assaulted by petrochemicals in the form of artificial ingredients in vitamin drops or medicines. Confine sweeteners for him to stevia and tiny amounts of table sugar.

Carefully inventory all the food and food-lacing chemicals you are consuming, especially the artificial additives. Read labels and switch

when on the allergen-free diet than when they were covertly fed the food to which they were apparently allergic.[9]

Yeast and Food Allergies

Food allergies are caused by faulty digestion, not by tainted food. The whole story starts with the population of "guests" who are taking up residence in your child's digestive tract.

Yeasts are microorganisms found just about everywhere in nature. They live in human intestines and are kept under control by body-friendly bacteria. When antibiotics are given, the body-friendly bacteria are killed right along with disease-producing ones for which the antibiotics were prescribed. The result is overpopulation by yeasts, which can grow out of control rather quickly, increasing by as much as 200-fold in one year. It's not the yeasts but their by-products—called fungal metabolites—that actually do the damage to

away from brands containing petrochemical additives. Join the Feingold Association of the United States and follow their guides.

Nursing with human breast milk is generally the ideal way to feed a baby. It is most likely to prevent the development of ADHD, according to research. Formula-fed babies are more at risk for a host of difficulties, ADHD included. Nothing manmade compares with the balance of essential fatty acids in mother's milk. The closest substance in nature is cold-processed freshwater blue-green algae.

Discontinue caffeine from tea, coffee, and chocolate. Studies have shown that caffeine can be secreted from breast milk and can circulate in a baby's plasma for several days after being absorbed. Take acidophilus and bifidus supplements. Avoid gas-forming vegetables like broccoli, cauliflower, and cabbage, even though these vegetables will later become among the best to feed your child.

brain chemistry. Those metabolites include opiate peptides, arabinose, and tartaric acid, all of which are normally present in only very low concentrations and confined to the interior of the intestines.

As the yeast colonies grow unchecked, their metabolites are absorbed into the bloodstream, from which they cause disruption of brain chemistry. The body tries desperately to get rid of them and eventually succeeds in getting them into urine.

Food allergies are caused by faulty digestion, not by tainted food.

There are even laboratory tests now for these metabolites, so that yeast overgrowth can be assessed conveniently and accurately. The disruption of brain chemistry can cause symptoms along the entire continuum of brain toxicity disorders (introduced in chapter 1), from depression all the way to autism. Diarrhea and a general worsening of allergies usually are also a part of the picture when candida or other yeast overgrowth is occurring.

In a worst-case scenario, if yeast overgrowth remains undetected and untreated, the candida yeast shifts into a fungal form that develops roots (rhizoids) that can grow into the intestinal wall, literally creating tiny holes in it. Toxins and undigested proteins then get into the bloodstream. The immune system senses these foreign bodies in the bloodstream and manufactures antibodies against them. From that point onward, your child will have a food allergy to whatever proteins slipped through the intestinal wall.

Also parasites such as pinworms and hookworms thrive in a candida-infected intestinal tract. Basically, the only good news about a yeast overgrowth in your child's digestive tract is that it can be prevented by following the recommendations in this chapter.

THE DIGESTIVE SYSTEM

A healthy, well-functioning digestive system will produce the following results. Children who have ADHD are at risk for defective performance of all six functions:

1. Complete breakdown of foods into their smallest components
2. Rich population of body-friendly bacteria and other microorganisms (called flora) in the bowel
3. Minimal growth of body-unfriendly flora in the gut
4. Intact interior lining and walls of the intestines
5. Timely, smooth processing of foods and discharge of feces
6. A "golden banana" of soft feces per day

Heroes of the Gut

If there were an award for the most important and heroic assistant for your child's ability to extract nutrition from food and avoid food allergies, that award would go to the little bacterium with the long name—

Lactobacillus acidophilus. This delightful little creature populates the human intestine by the billions and performs these services, among others:

- Creates lactase to digest milk sugar
- Replaces beneficial bacteria when antibiotics are killing them off
- Produces vitamin K
- Helps keep the interior of the intestines clean
- Helps correct faulty elimination processes
- Produces several B vitamins
- Helps assimilate calcium from foods
- Helps keep blood cholesterol at the proper level
- Produces agents that provide an intestinal environment that is somewhat toxic to body-unfriendly flora, thus keeping them in check
- Helps reduce body odor—nature's internal deodorant
- Aids in the production of digestive enzymes
- Helps reduce flatulence (gas)
- Helps prevent bad breath from digestive outgassing
- Cleans and beautifies the skin
- Adds shine to the hair
- Counteracts toxic and hazardous substances that arrive in the intestines

That's the good news. The bad news is that most children with ADHD probably don't have enough acidophilus in their intestines. The net result, of course, is faulty performance of the digestive system, leading ultimately to many of the digestive complaints common among individuals with ADHD: excess flatulence and gas, constipation, and easily upset stomach. And even worse news is that food allergies become much more likely to occur when there is insufficient acidophilus in the intestines.

One of the best steps to take if your child is showing any of these digestive problems, including suspected food allergies, is to provide acidophilus capsules daily for four weeks. Your child can take one or two capsules with each meal. It is almost impossible to overdose because the problem for children who have ADHD has to do with underpopulation in the first place. In the unlikely possibility of an overdose, diarrhea would result.

Another hero is bifidus, which performs most of the functions of acidophilus. There are about 20 other "good guys" in the gut, most of whom are sloppy eaters that squirt out extra enzymes while attacking food particles. Those enzymes prevent poisoning and malnutrition. Any undigested food in the digestive tract will interact with the bacteria present in the gut to produce toxic chemicals and gasses that can damage the gut wall and actually start killing off the good guys.

Improving the Digestive System

Gut-friendly food habits include:

- Chewing foods well
- Drinking liquids 30 minutes before a meal, not during or after
- Eating fruit only 30 to 60 minutes before a meal
- Avoiding any food to which the child is allergic
- Avoiding alcoholic beverages
- Avoiding aspirin and ibuprofen
- Snacking on pumpkin seeds
- Consuming cold-processed freshwater blue-green algae
- Consuming lecithin or phosphatidylcholine
- Consuming quercitin

> ## Is There Scientific Evidence for Diet Treatment?
> In a double-blind placebo-controlled study, researchers tested a diet free of wheat, corn, milk, chocolate, and most of the other allergenic foods. They found that 74 percent of a group of children with ADHD showed significant behavioral effects from being either exposed to or deprived of the allergenic foods.[10]

- Consuming L-glutamine (*not* monosodium glutamate)

- Consuming foods rich in essential fatty acids

- Taking digestive enzymes (capsules) 30 minutes before a meal

- Avoiding all of the toxic substances discussed in chapter 7

- Consuming fibrous foods

- Consuming foods that are fresh, raw or minimally cooked, whole, thoroughly cleaned, and free of pesticide residue

- Avoiding large amounts of sugar in any form

- Avoiding neurotoxins and petrochemicals, including food additives

- Consuming a half gallon of fresh, pure, bacteria-free, chlorine-free, fluoride-free (filtered) water daily

FAULTY LIPID METABOLISM IS A CORE PROBLEM

One of the most frequent medical complaints for which children with ADHD are taken to their pediatricians is skin rash. The skin problems of these children are a reflection of their difficulty with lipid metabolism. Basically, the bodies of most children with ADHD have lost some natural moisturizers in the form of essential fatty acid derivatives and are suffering from a form of dehydration. The skin reflects this dehydration by becoming itchy and developing rashes. Sometimes, you will notice tiny red dots underneath the upper arms of infants and children who have ADHD. Sometimes, their hair and nails will be dry and brittle.

If I were asked to state what the ultimate or core cause of ADHD is, my answer would be faulty protein and lipid metabolism. I believe that, ultimately, ADHD reflects a problem with the handling of protein metabolism, primarily in the brain. Intimately intertwined with this problem, however, is a second one—faulty handling of fats.

> *Ultimately, ADHD reflects a problem with the handling of protein metabolism, primarily in the brain.*

The brain is over 50 percent fat, and its tissues need constant replacement with building blocks in the form of fatty acids. The body normally makes its own supply but requires two sources from food, called essential fatty acids (EFAs). Researchers have recently discovered that children with ADHD typically experience a shortage of several derivatives from essential fatty acids. Many brain proteins have specific interactions with EFAs in cell membranes. Left without its needed supply of fatty acids, the brain becomes less efficient at sending its signals among the neurons and shows some ADHD symptoms. In fact, EFAs are so crucial to brain functioning that some authorities now say their effect on the human brain is more pharmacological than nutritional.

The classic symptoms of body dryness associated with EFA-derivative shortages are common among individuals with ADHD: excessive thirst, sweating during sleep, digestive complaints, dry skin, itchy skin, skin rashes, numerous allergies, disorganized immune processes, and brittle nails.[11–14]

The best way to solve skin problems is from the inside out. Make sure your child consumes essential fatty acids daily and avoid giving him food that sabotages fatty acid metabolism.

Have your child use soaps that are mild, white, and hypoallergenic and that have very little or no petrochemical dyes and perfumes. Filtering the shower or bath water is a good idea.

Good Fat and Bad Fat

Essential fatty acids are found in all plants that have not been cooked, and they are especially concentrated in seeds and nuts. Oils extracted from seeds are excellent, such as flaxseed oil, evening primrose oil, nut oils, and hemp oil. Flaxseeds (soaked overnight to soften), sunflower seeds, and pumpkin seeds are excellent snacks.

All nuts are good, walnuts being the best nut to feed to a child with ADHD. Peanuts are actually beans. While most beans are desirable food for individuals with ADHD, I don't consider peanuts a good choice for a variety of reasons. I strongly recommend walnut, almond, pecan, or cashew butter as an alternative to peanut butter for children who have ADHD.

Algae and seaweed are rich in EFAs, with cold-water algae being the richest source. Cold-water ocean fish that consume large amounts of algae store essential fatty acids, and we refer to them as oily fish. What is called fish oil is actu-

> *All nuts are good, walnuts being the best nut to feed to a child with ADHD.*

ally algae oil stored in fish tissues. Capsules of fish oil are excellent sources of EFAs, as are the fish themselves. Salmon, tuna, mackerel, and sardines lead the list. EFAs will be sabotaged if the child is not getting enough zinc, magnesium, B vitamins, and vitamin C.

Fake fats like Olestra and hydrolyzed fat substitutes are not good ideas for children with ADHD. It is best simply to have your child consume the "good fats," and some amount of saturated fat is quite tolerable.

Fats that have been hydrogenated tend to disrupt the metabolism of the good EFAs. To make a long story short, hydrogenated and partially hydrogenated fats are undesirable and will contribute to your child's dehydration problems. Margarines are hydrogenated fats, but butter is not. Common vegetable oils are hydrogenated, but cold-pressed olive oil is not. There is no harmless deep-frying fat; keep deep-fried foods to a minimum.

MINERALS AND ADHD: IT'S LATER THAN YOU ZINC

According to recent research, the majority of children who have ADHD are deficient in calcium, zinc, magnesium, and/or iron.[15]

Giving inorganic salt minerals in standard vitamin-mineral tablets is an insufficient method of mineral supplementation. The ideal way for your child to obtain needed minerals is to consume minerals that have been naturally chelated by plants raised in mineral-rich and petrochemical-free soil or water. The second-best method is to consume the needed minerals through supplements in which the minerals have been artificially chelated.

> *The majority of children who have ADHD are deficient in calcium, zinc, magnesium, and/or iron.*

Relying heavily on zinc and magnesium, the human brain actually needs the 19 minerals branded by the U.S. government as "essential," plus many more. It is almost impossible to overdose on minerals, and many parents have noticed favorable results when they provide their children with about four times the RDA (recommended daily allowance) of artificially chelated mineral supplements daily. Freshwater blue-green algae is very mineral dense, all of the minerals being chelated naturally by the algae.

PROTEINS AND ADHD

A simple and effective way to reduce symptoms in most individuals with ADHD is to trickle feed proteins throughout the day. Think in terms of providing a protein component at every meal and every snack—a grand total of seven times per day. This maneuver provides an abundant supply of building blocks for making neurotransmitters and helps to keep the body's energy system stabilized.

Protein-rich foods from the plant kingdom include soy, tofu, seeds, nuts, whole grains, beans, peas, legumes, lentils, mushrooms, seaweeds, and algae. Protein-rich foods from the animal kingdom include dairy products, egg whites, white and red meat, and fish. Often protein-rich food also contains essential fatty acids and/or saturated fat. But fats are not culprits; high glycemic index carbohydrates are, especially if unaccompanied by protein and essential fatty acids. (See page 133 for examples of foods with a high glycemic index.)

FOOD CRAVINGS

The third most widely craved food category by children with ADHD is salty or highly seasoned food. They are probably craving the minerals. The vast majority of children who have ADHD are mineral deficient, which contributes to many of their symptoms.

The second most widely craved food among children with ADHD is cheese. They are probably craving the proteins. ADHD probably involves both faulty lipid and faulty protein metabolism.

The most commonly craved food (actually more of a nonfood) is sugar. Probably because the brains of most individuals with ADHD are not receiving sufficient amounts of blood sugar as fuel, there is a natural tendency to crave more fuel. However, the body is not prepared to accept large amounts of sugar into the bloodstream; instead, the body sends insulin to escort any ingested sugar into muscles, keeping the blood sugar level constant. The brain never does get increased fuel from driving the child to pig out on sugar. The result? Continued craving for more sugar.

> *A* DHD probably involves both faulty lipid and faulty protein metabolism.

The best way to respond to these common food cravings among children who have ADHD is to listen to what their bodies are saying.

Abnormal Blood in Children with ADHD

Examining samples of blood has yielded mixed results in terms of drawing connections between blood status and the behavior of children with ADHD. Numerous studies have shown that the level of methylphenidate in the blood, for example, is almost useless as an indicator that the correct dosage level has been reached.

There appear to be numerous factors affecting the behavior of children with ADHD, and blood status is increasingly being considered one of them. Much of this line of research comes from live-cell analysis with dark-field microscopes. So far, these mostly have been informal observations by microscopists working outside of university research settings.

Provide minerals with mineral-rich, naturally occurring foods, or with manmade chelated mineral supplements. Provide proteins by trickle feeding protein-rich food several times each day. Keep blood sugar at a correct level by the same method—trickle feeding of proteins—and never allow a lot of sugar to be eaten without being accompanied by protein. Knock out sugar craving by providing a wide variety of minerals, serving somewhat more fruit and fruit juices temporarily, and allowing small amounts of stevia or sugar, accompanied by proteins.

> *The best way to respond to common food cravings among children who have ADHD is to listen to what their bodies are saying.*

FOOD AVERSIONS

The fussy, picky eater syndrome that occurs in about 40 percent of children with ADHD is one aspect of their sensory integration difficulties. It also reflects their nutritional imbalances.

A typical blood sample of a healthy child without behavioral or medical problems, examined under a dark-field microscope, shows a predominantly dark background and clear separation or only slight contact among the red blood cells. The essential fatty acid derivatives are providing the correct amount of slickness to the cell walls, and there are no fat deposits floating in the plasma.

A typical blood sample of a child with ADHD shows a much lighter background, indicating excess fat particles in the blood—probably a reflection of the faulty lipid metabolism that I believe is central to most instances of ADHD. Also, the restacking of red blood cells is probably in part from faulty essential fatty acid processing and probably impairing the blood's ability to carry oxygen to the brain.

Encourage a broader range of foods by involving your child in menu planning, grocery list preparation, shopping, label reading, food preparation, cooking, and serving. To the extent that your child has a personal investment in the outcome, her interest in expanding her food options will increase. Children like the adventure of comparison shopping and label reading. Hunt for the brands that contain the right nutrients and that are free of petrochemical additives.

WHAT TO FEED YOUR CHILD

Careful review of current scientific findings reveals great increases in our understanding of the effects and physiological roles of nutrients. Taking into account the importance of addressing all six organ systems likely to be involved in ADHD, it is now possible to develop a list of the best foods to offer a child or teen who has ADHD.

Anything rich in essential fatty acids, naturally chelated minerals, vitamins, phytochemicals, bioflavonoids, chlorophyll, natural enzymes, or protein is a good choice. Eggs are great, including the yolks; choose jumbo size and serve several per week. Vegetables (except potatoes) are better than fruits, and the best vegetables are cauliflower, kale, brussels sprouts, broccoli, asparagus, celery, and cabbage. Fresh vegetable juices are excellent. About the only good use for fruit juices is to mix them with vegetable juices so that your child will drink the vegetable juice. I recommend no more than one fruit every two days, confined to the whole raw fruit, served with a glass of pure water. Fruit juice ranks right up there with soda pop as far as its effect on a child with ADHD is concerned. For a rough overall guide, turn the USDA food pyramid upside down. Emphasize essential fatty acids and nonhydrogenated oils, proteins, and vegetables. Minimize the carbohydrates such as potatoes, fruit juices, bread, and pasta.

> *Fruit juice ranks right up there with soda pop as far as its effect on a child with ADHD is concerned.*

The grand prize from the animal kingdom has to go to salmon, with its massive amounts of protein, chelated minerals, and algae oil in the skin and flesh. Second prize goes to other deepwater fish that store algae oil—tuna, cod, mackerel, and sardines.

First prize from the plant kingdom goes to cold-processed freshwater blue-green algae, with its rich content of over 100 nutrients, including essential fatty acids, chelated minerals, bioflavonoids, phytochemicals, enzymes, chlorophyll, digestible RNA, beta-carotene, B vitamins, and about 40 natural antidepressant nutrients.

Second prize goes to manmade formulations combining extracts from vegetables, bioflavonoids, the skins and bark of plants rich in phytochemicals, and other nutrients. Most of the really good products are not available in stores and must be obtained from consultants and distributors. For contact information, log on to www.add-plus.com.

Count Glycemic Index, Not Calories

Glycemic index is the rate at which a food increases the level of blood sugar. The higher the index, the more disruptive the food is to ADHD brain metabolism, especially if consumed in large quantity all

Table 6.1   Common Foods with Low or High Glycemic Index

Food	Low	High
Cereals	Oatmeal, bran (no raisins)	Corn flakes, crisped rice
Pastas	Egg fettuccine, spaghetti, meat ravioli	Taco shells
Grains	Oats, bulgur	Short-grain white rice
Shortbreads	Banana bread, sponge cake	Croissant, bagel
Breads	Stone-ground whole wheat, whole-grain pumpernickel	Rye, supermarket "whole wheat," white
Cookies	Oatmeal, tea biscuits	Graham crackers, vanilla wafers
Vegetables	Carrots, sweet potatoes, beans, peas, lentils	White potatoes, pumpkin
Fruit	Watermelon, cherries, grapefruit, apricots, apples, peaches, pears, plums	Cantaloupe, dates, pineapple
Dairy	All, except ice cream	Ice cream
Juices	Orange, apple	Sports drinks
Snacks	Dried roasted nuts	Corn chips, pretzels
Sugars	Fructose, lactose	Maltose, glucose
Meat	All	None
Fish	All	None
Poultry, eggs	All	None

at once unaccompanied by lower-index food. Table 6.1 provides samples of common foods with a low or high glycemic index.

SUGAR AND ADHD

The research on sugar has largely been funded by the food industry and is very suspect for that reason. What is known scientifically is that

30 to 40 percent of parents of children with ADHD strongly believe that sugar causes their children's behavior to deteriorate.

Some of the available studies on sugar, biased as they are, do yield some interesting conclusions. One of the most heavily publicized of the food industry–sponsored studies designed to exonerate sugar, for example, involved giving a moderate amount of sugar in limited dosages throughout the day. The children were kept on a protein- and nutrient-rich diet that also eliminated most petrochemical food additives. The results? Of course, the sugar did not cause problems. Too bad those researchers didn't simply call me and ask me how to administer sugar in a way so that it won't cause problems for children with ADHD. I could have saved them a lot of trouble.

Forget cholesterol and calories. Count carbohydrate content instead. Remember, fat is not the culprit. Anything that changes quickly into sugar upon entering the digestive tract is a culprit, especially if unaccompanied by protein. Glycemic index is the information you are interested in, not calories. In fact, if the food is marketed as nonfat, low-fat, or "diet," it is probably likely to cause problems.

> *F*orget cholesterol and calories. Count carbohydrate content instead.

Carbohydrates in general are not particularly helpful. High glycemic index carbohydrates such as potatoes and other starchy foods, breads, and pastas should be kept to a minimum or, better yet, never served. If you serve them, try to use the whole-grain varieties and accompany them with rich protein foods. Coarse chewy breads are much less troublesome for a child with ADHD than mushy supermarket white bread.

Avoid grains with a high glycemic index, such as white rice, and keep in mind that the glycemic index of a rice cake is higher than that for many candy bars. The glycemic index of white flour is extremely high. In order, the best-to-worst grains are oats, wheat, corn, rice. An easy way to remember some of this information is that white things are bad and dark things are good. Avoid white rice, white flour, and white sugar. Use dark grains and dark whole-grain flour.

For sweeteners, the darker the better. Honey and molasses satiate quickly—your child stops with a spoonful. Artificial sweeteners derived from petrochemicals are very neurotoxic and should never be offered to your child. The ideal sweetener for individuals with ADHD is stevia, derived from a South American bush and used as a natural sweetener for centuries. It is available at health food stores. All three of these recommended sweeteners (honey, molasses, and stevia) are dark in color.

Get away from narrow concepts of what food can be eaten when. At bedtime, consider a bowl of oatmeal or a poached egg on whole-grain toast. For breakfast, consider creamed tuna on whole-grain toast or a beef patty. For after-school protein, save a small portion of a main dish your child likes and store it in the freezer for reheating. Avoid microwaving proteins or fats; microwaving is acceptable for carbohydrates.

The next chapter provides details on toxinsulation against irritant chemicals that are likely to create ADHD symptoms by altering brain chemistry, digestion, and immune function for children and teens with ADHD.

CHAPTER 7

Insulate from Toxic Exposure

❧

ONE APPROACH TO helping children and adults who have any of the disorders on the continuum of brain toxicity is to limit or, better yet, eliminate their exposure to toxic substances that are causing symptoms. An associated approach is to detox any heavy metals already deposited in brain tissue. The key questions are:

- Which toxins?
- How can I insulate my child from them?
- How can I detox heavy metals already lodged in my child?

Most individuals who have ADHD are at risk for major problems with six organ systems: the brain, skin, digestive tract, immune system, body fuel (blood sugar) system, and blood. To get on top of ADHD, toxinsulate your child against anything that worsens the function of any of these systems. Simply put, that means limiting or preventing exposure to potentially harmful or toxic substances.

What will worsen the body dehydration problem that leads to all those rashes on your child's skin? Anything that sabotages the synthesis and metabolism of essential fatty acid derivatives. That means margarine and vegetable oil in your kitchen, for starters. It also means copper, which is toxic to the majority of children with ADHD and which interferes with the precious zinc their skin needs to stay soft and supple. The copper comes from water pipes when there is no filter at the tap.

What will worsen the classic ADHD symptoms of flatulence, constipation, and incomplete digestion of food that leads to food allergies? Alcoholic beverages, caffeine, chlorine in drinking water, too many high glycemic index carbohydrates, antibiotics, aspirin, ibuprofen, and most petrochemical food additives.

What will weaken the immune system? Consuming too many foods to which the child is allergic as well as consuming carcinogenic and mutagenic food contaminants, food additives, copper, and sugars.

What will make the body fuel system less efficient? Monosodium glutamate and too much consumption of high glycemic index carbohydrates unaccompanied by protein.

What will make the stacking of red blood cells worsen and contribute further to the high incidence of fat globules in the plasma? Anything that sabotages essential fatty acid derivative synthesis and metabolism.

To make a very long story very short, the central message of this chapter is to avoid anything that is:

- Carcinogenic (causes cancer in lab animal experiments)

- Mutagenic (disrupts DNA messages in lab animal experiments)

- A toxic "-ite" or "-ate" (such as nitrite, nitrate, sulfite, sulfate, MSG, aspartate in aspartame, phosphate)

- An aromatic phenol (perfumes, swimming pool chemicals, smoke, white-board marker odors, perfumy soaps)

- A petrochemical (pesticide residues, artificial flavorings, food dyes, artificial food preservatives)

- Laden with any of the following five heavy metals children with ADHD are at risk for storing in their brain tissue, which lead to various disruptions in brain chemistry

Lead (from water pipes, auto exhaust, air pollution, house dust, home remodeling, tobacco smoke, lead paint)

Cadmium (from burning metal, welding, auto exhaust)

Copper (from water pipes)

Aluminum (from deodorants, cooking in shiny aluminum cookware, and some innoculations)

Mercury (from tooth fillings, tainted shellfish, and some innoculations)

- Designated "artificial" on a food or beverage label
- Neurotoxic (as demonstrated by killing nerve cells of animals)

HOW TOXINSULATION WORKS

The theory behind toxinsulation is that the brain of a child with ADHD is experiencing a chemical sensitivity reaction—not an allergy—to the offending chemicals. The toxinsulation method involves eliminating

---

Toxic Substances and ADHD

Avoid artificial *anything* added to foods and beverages. Read labels carefully, join the Feingold Association of the United States, and carefully follow the excellent guidelines they send as part of your membership.

Excellent summaries of the growing body of research on petrochemical toxins and their effects on autistic children and children with ADHD are now available.[1,2]

In animal studies, one way researchers create rat equivalents of hyperactive babies and children is to expose their pregnant mother rats to nicotine. Other ways are to feed their pregnant mothers MSG, aspartame, or artificial food colorings. To create research rats with the equivalent of Alzheimers, MSG does the trick.

contact with chemicals commonly added to food products, cosmetics, and medicines, as well as exposure to airborne or skin-contact sources of offending chemicals for some individuals. The ADHD-sa subgroup represents the extreme of those who are sensitive to these chemicals. Available data indicate the vast majority of individuals with ADHD are probably sensitive to some of these chemicals, though their reactions are not as obvious as those of the ADHD-sa group.

USING THE FEINGOLD PROGRAM

Few issues are more controversial in the field of ADHD than the proposal that controlling chemical exposure can reduce ADHD symptoms. Developed in the early 1970s by pediatrician-allergist Benjamin Feingold, M.D., the Feingold program identifies the chemicals to which most children with ADHD are sensitized. Virtually all are low molecular weight, unstable, phenol-based compounds, and many have been found to be carcinogenic. Children who are very sensitive to them usually reflect other sensitivities and allergies that put them in the ADHD-sa group.

Estimates of success rates by those familiar with the program range from 50 to 70 percent for those children whose exposure to the suspected chemicals is correctly controlled. Those estimates match well with recent scientific studies of its effectiveness. The desired A through H effects on the Taylor Medication Effectiveness Report forms, summarized in chapter 4, are the same for this method as for prescribed medication.

> *For most children who have ADHD, major offenders are synthetic food dyes, artificial flavors, flavor enhancers such as MSG, and preservatives.*

The first phase of the Feingold program involves eliminating exposure to many of the chemicals commonly added to foods and beverages for cosmetic purposes. For most children who have ADHD, and especially the sensitive-allergic ones, major offenders are synthetic food dyes (petroleum- or coal tar-based), artificial flavors, flavor enhancers such as MSG, and preservatives such as BHA, BHT, and TBHQ.

In addition, the substances from the categories listed in appendix D, "Sources of Chemical Exposure," are minor offenders for the typical child with ADHD but can represent serious problems for those in the ADHD-sa subgroup. Contact with these substances must usually be decreased. After contact with the offending chemicals is eliminated, ADHD symptoms decline or disappear in about 75 percent of children. Label reading of food products, while helpful, is not always the best way to guarantee toxinsulation from exposure to chemical irritants. I therefore recommend the helpful materials available from the Feingold Association.

There are naturally occurring phenols that apparently sometimes cause problems for children who have ADHD. They are the salicylates found in certain fruits. Most children with ADHD seem to be sensitive to only a few of the salicylates. After eliminating high-salicylate foods, the next step involves gradually adding them back into the child's normal diet. Provide the foods one at a time, so any sudden flare-up in symptoms can be traced to a specific food.

To assist in this process, the Taylor-Latta Diet Diary (see page 142) provides a method of double-checking the ups and downs of symptoms in response to the reintroduction of potentially offending salicylates. (The salicylates are summarized in appendix E.) The involvement of salicylate sensitivities with ADHD symptoms is one of the least researched areas of toxinsulation. Most of the available data comes from the informal observations of parents.[3]

Maintaining the Treatment

One toxic exposure can trigger ADHD symptoms.

The Feingold program is a viable alternative to prescribed medication for the majority of individuals with ADHD; it tends to work especially well with small children, whose intake of food chemicals and exposure to airborne chemicals are easy to control. Snack and

TAYLOR-LATTA DIET DIARY

TIMES: Arise_____   To Bed_____   Asleep_____

Breakfast_____   Lunch_____   Dinner_____

Time Period	Food and Ingredients	Amounts	Notes	Symptoms and Traits
Nighttime Before Arising				
Arising Through Breakfast				
After Breakfast Through A.M. Snack				
After A.M. Snack Through Lunch				
After Lunch Through P.M. Snack				
After P.M. Snack Through Dinner				
After Dinner Through Bedtime				
After Bedtime Until Asleep				

From Jonn Taylor and Sharon Latta, *Why Can't I Eat That! Helping Kids Obey Medical Diets*; Salem, Oregon: A.D.D. Plus, 1996.

convenience foods are permitted, and there is no prohibition of sweets. Alert label reading and a grocery shopping list help prevent accidental exposure to synthetic additives.

Monitoring and supervision are vital. It is necessary to make advance preparations for extended visits away from home, car travel, camping, and school lunches. The discussion in chapter 4 about gaining your child's cooperation, encouraging increasing responsibility for maintaining the treatment program, and making a strong pre-post contrast applies equally to this program.

Concerns About the Feingold Program

Toxinsulation against phenols is one of the most effective methods for dealing with ADHD. Especially for a young child, it is one of the most reliable first steps to take. Opposition to it arises from the food and food chemical industries and those who believe the public relations information promoted by them. Most opposition falls into two categories: claims that it doesn't work and excuses for why it does.

Advantages and Disadvantages

The Feingold program works for all age levels, including babies. It involves no deviation from wholesome and balanced food selection, keeps

> *The Feingold program is a viable alternative to prescribed medication for the majority of individuals with ADHD.*

you alert to nutrition, and teaches your child self-care habits. There is no worry about side effects or the unknowns that accompany the use of medication.

A commonly reported observation from parents is that if they also follow the program, their own allergy and sensitivity-related problems decrease. This finding is particularly striking because most parents don't expect or look for such changes.

One accidental exposure to an offending chemical can trigger an S-R state within minutes. Two or three such contacts per week can

Myth Versus Fact About the Feingold Program

Research is now validating the approach of insulating against toxic chemicals as an ADHD treatment option. Anti-Feingold propaganda has slowed this progress but can't prevent the forward march of science.

Myth	Fact
It is a fad diet.	It is neither a fad nor a diet.
Food additives are safe.	Food additives are very potent creators of S-R states.
Disruption of food shopping and preparation create chaos.	Increased order about food is what occurs.
There's no scientific evidence for it.	Many scientific studies now verify it.
Scientific studies prove it doesn't work.	Propaganda studies from the food industry claim it doesn't work.
It deprives the child of vitamin C.	It doesn't deprive the child of any nutrient.

keep some children with ADHD in a constant S-R state. The fact that minor alterations of chemical exposure through additives in food can switch the ADHD symptoms on and off is reassuring and proves the accuracy of this approach. The challenge is to inoffensively provide the needed structure. A thorough winning over of the child to a commitment to self-care is increasingly important as he grows older.

If you are following the program stringently and ADHD symptoms are still occurring, there is a strong likelihood your child is intolerant of some of the foods he's eating. The search for allergens, again incorporating the Taylor-Latta Diet Diary, should then overlap the effort to avoid chemical exposure.

Myth	Fact
It works by giving the child extra attention.	The child usually receives less attention.
Results come from the placebo effect.	It works even when no placebo effect is possible.
It works by creating increased order and structure at home.	It works in restaurants, the school cafeteria, when visiting, etc.
It works by decreasing sugar and empty-calorie food.	It's not a no-sugar program; desserts are allowed.
Additive-free food is too expensive.	Parents save money and avoid overprocessed junk food.
Exotic food from health stores is needed.	Parents can shop at regular supermarkets.
The child becomes isolated from his peers over food issues.	The child can have fast-food hamburgers, pizza, desserts, etc.

Identifying environmental irritants can be challenging. One mother of a 2-year-old boy who has ADHD summarized:

> A guest used Brian's bed for a rest. She remembered afterward that she had hair spray on, and I said I'd change the pillowcase but forgot all about it. That night, Brian had trouble falling asleep and woke several times saying, "I'm sick, I'm sick." Then I remembered the hair spray. I changed the pillowcase, and he slept soundly the remainder of the night.

It helps if the entire family can make some switch in food brand choices. Rebellious adolescents are poor choices as candidates for this program, because they too often and too easily allow chemical exposure when not supervised.

Some parents, particularly those near emotional bankruptcy, simply do not have the necessary energy to provide the occasional home cooking and relatively constant dietary supervision needed. The elimination of salicylates, even when simplified and streamlined by using the Taylor-Latta Diet Diary, represents too large a project for some distraught parents. The replacement foods are introduced during symptom-controlled times, and the repeated flare-up of symptoms that accompanies the testing of substitute foods is too stressful an accommodation. An alternative is to start the child on medications, then slowly apply the Feingold program.

Preventing Chemical Exposure When Others Are in Charge

To prevent outsiders from offering off-limit food brands to your child, explain the program on a need-to-know basis. When your child is temporarily under the care of other adults, specify the exact guidelines. People usually respect firmness, a positive attitude, and determination cushioned with courtesy. Lists of acceptable foods and beverages are better than lists of restricted items.

Preventing Chemical Exposure When Traveling

For extended travel, keep at least two days' supply of approved foods, with an emergency snack always available. Restaurant dining can be tricky. Cafeteria-style restaurants have the advantage of allowing inspection of each item prior to its purchase. Menu items that are closest to their natural state have the most predictable content and least likelihood of chemical additives. A bit of fresh lemon juice squeezed on salads avoids all questions about ingredients in the salad dressing. It is best to order a plain food item, using acceptable condiments and other foods from your own supply to round out the meal.

Restaurant personnel are likely to cooperate if you don't put them on the defensive. Show by your attitude, statements, and actions that you intend to patronize the restaurant, plan to enjoy the meal, and assume the meal suits your family's needs. Make it clear, however, that you must double-check certain aspects of the menu because of important medical considerations. State that you need information about a dish's ingredients before you can place your order. Use a statement such as: "My child has some allergies and can't eat food that contains certain chemicals." Then follow up with the request, "Can you please tell me whether this item happens to have (the ingredient) in it?"

Enlisting a Total Effort

A child's involvement in the Feingold program, like any other project, goes more smoothly when the parent-child relationship is solid, and the child perceives the program as desirable. You will need to teach your child some refusal skills for moments when off-limit food with chemicals in it is offered. A suitable standard statement that works for most children who have ADHD is "Thanks, but I'm not allowed to have that type of food. Do you have any (permitted chemical-free item)?"

Avoiding chemical exposure involves more than label reading at the supermarket. If a product lists "spices, seasoning, or flavoring," for example, the substances could include salicylates. "Natural flavorings" can mean pits and leaves of salicylate fruits as well as MSG. Many substances used in food processing remain in the product but are not listed on the label.

Many parents briefly attempt the program but give up when no noticeable behavior changes seem to occur within a week or so. They usually have tried to prevent chemical exposure merely by label reading and have overlooked nonfood chemical exposures or have experienced allergies that create confusion. It is imperative to obtain the Feingold Association's reference materials, including the shopping guide and newsletter giving updated food chemical information.

> Some parents give up too quickly on the Feingold program if no noticeable behavior changes occur within a week or so.

As with any other aspect of helping your child, the keys to success are arrangements that prevent problems from occurring and supervision

Why Does "Andrew" Act So Hyper?

This is the first generation in which each morning "Andrew" uses shampoo that **smells like strawberries** and uses soap that **smells like a rose garden** and is **colored blue and green**. Then he applies more phenols to his hair with **scented hair spray**. He applies **aluminum-containing** and **petrochemical-scented** deodorant kept a pretty color by **petrochemical dyes**. Then he dresses in clothes that smell springtime fresh from **scented laundry detergent** and **scented chemical dryer sheets**.

He walks across the carpet and breathes residue of **flea killer** and **shampoo.** His parents smoke, so he smells the phenols and various toxins from **cigarette secondary air**. His parents cover up the cigarette smell with **scented room deodorizer**, which Andrew also smells as he walks to the kitchen. As he passes through the living room, he smells the **phenols from the fireplace.**

Once in the kitchen, he pours himself a bowl of Rainbow-Colored Krispie Krunchie Yummies, made from rice (**instant sugar in his stomach**) kept colorfully crunchy by **petrochemical dyes** and **petrochemical preservatives**. On the cereal, he puts some **neurotoxic** aspartame and skim milk that contains **BHA** as well as **herbicide and pesticide residue** from the grass eaten by the cow. He also has some white-flour toast (**instant sugar**) spread with a thick layer of margarine containing **artificial flavorings, artificial coloring**, and **preservatives** as well as **trans-fats**, which further dehydrate him.

Then he has a pancake made from white impoverished flour (**instant sugar**), fried in margarine, then coated with more margarine. Over all those **petrochemical flavorings, colorings, and preservatives**, he pours pancake syrup containing **artificial flavor, artificial coloring, preservatives,** and three different forms of **sugar.**

For his breakfast beverage, he chooses a concoction labeled "10 percent real fruit juice" and containing **neurotoxic** aspartame and assorted petrochemicals in the form of **artificial flavorings, colorings**, and **preservatives**. For protein, he has some sausage, containing **sugar** and assorted phenols in the form of **erythorbates, nitrites, preservatives**, and **artificial smoke and maple flavorings.**

After breakfast, he walks across that **fragrant carpet** and through the **perfumed** and **phenol-laden air** again, back to the bathroom, where he brushes his teeth with toothpaste that is **colored** and **flavored** with petrochemicals. Then he uses a mouthwash that is **colored** and **flavored** with more petrochemicals.

Ready at last, he leaves home and walks across the lawn, which has **pesticide and herbicide residue** on it. As he awaits the school bus, he breathes **auto exhaust** from passing traffic. When the bus arrives, he enters and sits down. On the way to school, **auto exhaust** enters every time the doors open and shut.

Once at school, he notices the smell of **fresh paint** on one of the walls. During first period, he goes to art class, where he uses assorted **paints** and **glues**. During second period, he has wood shop class, during which he cuts into **particle board (50 percent glue)** and coats wood with **varnish**. After second period, he starts to get thirsty, so he stops at the soda machine and selects **artificially flavored, colored, and preserved orange** soda pop, which contains the greatest amount of petrochemicals of any flavor of soda pop. For lunch, he has a **school lunch** replete with **artificial flavors, artificial colors, preservatives, starches**, and **sugars**. Those are some of the reasons Andrew acts so hyper.

along the way. Parents experienced with the program generally find it reasonable, powerful, and practical; they don't complain of difficulties shopping, and they typically persist in preferring it over using medication.

Detoxing Heavy Metal Deposits

Over a dozen scientific articles in professional journals have recently been published indicating that children with ADHD are at risk for retaining heavy metals in their brain tissue. The best method for getting rid of these deposits falls under the broad category of chelation therapy. In theory and in practice, anything rich in chlorophyll, enzymatic activity, and sulfur-containing amino acids will flush out these heavy metals. Of all the chelating (flushing) agents, algae is one of the most effective.[4,5,6]

Probably the most effective of all is cold-processed freshwater blue-green algae. The Cell Tech brand even comes in child-usable forms (fruit smoothies, gummy bars, chewable wafers). Currently, all other brands use heat in their processing, which weakens or destroys the enzymatic activity of the algae products.

Addressing ADHD from various directions is an important strategy. Using the physiological measures discussed in this and the three preceding chapters will go a long way toward helping your child. The next chapter describes an additional tool kit to consider using.

CHAPTER 8

Use Sensorimotor Treatment Options

I LIKE TO conceptualize the four major avenues of intervention to help children with ADHD as consisting of four tool kits, each with a different name. They are the academic, psychosocial, physiological, and sensorimotor tool kits. In this chapter, I describe the two most universally applicable methods from the sensorimotor tool kit. Two other sensorimotor methods—use of Irlen lenses and visual training—are more limited in the scope of symptoms addressed. They are discussed in chapter 12.

SENSORY INTEGRATION

Long before today's neuroimaging techniques vastly expanded our understanding of brain mechanisms, occupational therapist A. Jean Ayres formulated methods of assisting children who had difficulties related to auditory language functions, form and space perception, left-right orientation, and touch defensiveness. In the mid-60s, she proposed that higher functions of performance are dependent on adequate organization at the more primitive brain levels. The target of intervention was to improve the organization of brain stem and midbrain functions, rather than aiming specifically at higher cognitive functions such as reading.

In essence, sensory integration means that the brain assigns correct relative importance and a different level of response to each message coming to it from the various senses, muting some messages while magnifying others. To have sensory integration (SI) disorder means that the brain does not perform this kind of sorting out of incoming messages. Instead, it is as if the brain attempts simply to give equal prominence to everything coming in. The result is abnormal handling of the various sensory inputs. What should be muted ends up being magnified and vice versa. The child is acutely aware, for example, of any touch on his skin but seemingly unaware of internal signals about hunger or bowel needs.

> *With sensory integration disorder, the brain mishandles sensory input. A child may be acutely aware of any touch on his skin but oblivious to hunger pangs.*

One mother described her observations of her child who had SI disorder:

> I finally realized why my son needed a separate desk; part of his brain that was supposed to filter irrelevant stimuli wasn't functioning properly. The other student tapping his pencil got the same amount of my son's attention as the teacher giving instructions. His tactile sensations were not as sensitive as a normal child's. As a result of the diminished sensory input, he went out of his way to aggravate situations that would produce excessive stimuli.

TOUCH DEFENSIVENESS

Tactile defensiveness, one of the SI problems that most highly overlaps with ADHD, involves trouble differentiating between a touch that is gentle and one that is threatening. Light touch seems like an irritating tickle, and a gentle pat is painful. While a heavy touch with slow strokes and deep pressure is tolerable, the child is ticklish and literally

Does Your Child Have Sensory Integration Disorder?

Many indicators of sensory integration (SI) disorder also occur in ADHD, Asperger's syndrome, and autism. A child with SI disorder is likely to:

- Physically remove herself from others

- Avoid eye contact

- Be lethargic in expressing emotion

- Overreact to stimulation from light, sound, or touch

- Underreact to pain

- Be overly aware of all stimulation and therefore very distractible

- Be driven, aggressive, and abnormally high in activity level

- Be unable to calm down without help

- Not handle transitions between activities calmly

- Have a low, sluggish activity level

- Make rocking movements (in bed or a chair)

- Avoid touch

- Dislike certain clothing items

- Have eye-hand problems (tying shoes, writing, buttoning, using zippers or scissors)

- Avoid or resist daily hygiene (brushing teeth, bathing, applying deodorant)

- Overreact to odors, fragrances, or food smells

- Be accident prone, clumsy, or awkward

afraid of being touched. He avoids being touched on the face and mouth, may be a picky eater because of food textures, dislikes having his hair or nails cut, and shuns back rubs and hugs. He avoids being physically close to others and dislikes going barefoot, getting his hands dirty, or touching soft-textured art materials.

Children with tactile defensiveness have trouble differentiating between a touch that is gentle and one that is threatening.

One mother reported: "It would take both of us to give Michael a bath because he hated it so much—his body would just tremble."

Sensory integration therapy generally aims for symmetry and balance by incorporating combing and brushing, rocking, twirling, use of a therapy ball, rubbing and wrapping with a soft towel, balancing activities, trampoline, swinging, and squeezing the body with emphasis on joints. Typically performed by occupational therapists, this form of treatment is effective at any age, from infancy through adulthood.

Unfortunately, there is little written about sensory integration and not much in the way of scientific research in professional journals to support it. In my opinion, the evidence is slowly mounting that this form of intervention can be a genuine help for many children with ADHD. There has been some research on deep-pressure touch in children at risk for ADHD. Prematurity is one of those risks. Preterm infants given 15-minute massages three times a day for 10 days while in their hospital incubators displayed increased growth and development, as well as increased levels of norepinephrine and epinephrine, compared with babies who didn't get the massage.[1]

Another ADHD–risk group is comprised of babies born to early-adolescent girls. In one study, massage was compared with rocking. Forty full-term infants born to teen mothers were given 15 minutes of either massage or rocking for 12 days over a six-week period. The massaged babies were more active and alert, cried less, were more contented and less stressed, gained more weight, showed better improvement on measures of temperament, responded more normally

Is Your Child Touch Defensive?

Touch defensiveness is a serious problem that severely hampers social and academic adjustment. Here are some suggestions for helping the child who is touch defensive.

- Increase her consumption of zinc and magnesium.

- Avoid light touch (patting, gently stroking, back rubbing); don't try to "desensitize" her to touch.

- When approaching the child, proceed slowly from the front and explain what you are doing.

- Confine all touch to firm and direct contact, such as a gentle squeeze.

- Maintain physical contact; don't keep breaking it off.

- Give the child permission to pull away and assure her that you will stop if anything doesn't feel good.

- Involve movement exercises such as slow swinging, rocking, compression (gentle pressure), or stretching.

- Have squeezable, soft objects (felt, sponge, rubber ball) available.

- Seek the services of a skilled occupational therapist.

during face-to-face contact with their mothers, and developed higher levels of serotonin (a key neurotransmitter-building protein).[2]

Babies born to cocaine-addicted mothers almost always have an ADHD-like syndrome. In one study, cocaine-exposed infants who were massaged showed better weight gains and development of muscle control than nonmassaged cocaine-exposed infants.[3]

In one study, researchers compared autistic children who received deep-pressure massage with others whose teachers held them and showed objects to them. The massaged autistic children were quite unopposed to treatment despite their pronounced touch defensiveness, probably because the treatment involved deep-pressure touch rather than light touch. Compared with the other children, the massaged children displayed marked improvements in their social relatedness, decreased off-task time, and decreased eruption of autistic stereotyped behaviors.[4]

The effects of the type of touch used in sensory integration treatment can be far reaching and can involve various body systems. Among the many connections between the immune system and ADHD is the incidence of asthma among children who also have ADHD. One study compared asthmatic children before and after parent-administered deep-pressure massage, 20 minutes per day for a month. The levels of body stress hormones and anxiety decreased, as did the frequency of asthma attacks. The children also displayed various improvements in pulmonary functions and uplifted mood.[5]

> *The massaged babies were more active and alert, cried less, were more contented and less stressed, gained more weight, and responded more normally during face-to-face contact with their mothers.*

How does deep-pressure touch work? A partial answer may lie in its ability to increase vagal activity and parasympathetic nervous system arousal. Increasing vagal activity lowers physiological and stress hormones such as cortisol. Decreased cortisol brings improved functioning of the entire immune system. Arousal of the parasympathetic system has been shown by research to be associated with decrease of various ADHD symptoms.[6]

NEUROFEEDBACK

Neurofeedback training can be described as high-tech yoga. The ultimate goal is to train the child to suppress slow-wave (4 to 8 Hz) theta waves and increase fast-wave (16 to 20 Hz) beta waves when attempting to learn or concentrate. When the brain has all the nutrients it needs, neurofeedback works better.

Can Massage Help Your Child?
A recent fascinating study compared deep-pressure massage with relaxation training on a group of teens with ADHD for 10 consecutive school days. Compared with the relaxation-trained group, the massaged teens showed a greater decrease in fidgetiness after the sessions, spent more time on-task, and experienced a greater decrease in their overall level of hyperactivity at school.[7]

This painless training involves putting electrodes on the surface of the skull. It is pleasant and empowering to the child, who takes an active role while watching a computer monitor. The age range for effective treatment is approximately 7 through adulthood. Forty to sixty sessions are usually given, with some progress usually being demonstrated by the twentieth session. In the future, with faster signal processing and improved technology, neurofeedback treatment will probably entail fewer sessions.

ADHD symptoms that seem most responsive to this form of intervention are lack of attention focusing, poor organization and task completion, impulsiveness, and fidgeting.

Research has clearly demonstrated that the inattentiveness, hyperactivity, and distractibility of ADHD children is associated with excessive theta wave activity, whereas beta wave activity is associated with reversal of these three symptoms. Some research has demonstrated that neurofeedback training enhances performance on tests of attention, information processing, concentration, and even IQ.[8–13]

The four graphs in figure 2 illustrate typical results from subjecting children with ADHD to various toxic substances. Notice the shift downward for beta waves and upward for theta waves when exposure is to airborne or ingested phenols. Five minutes of exercise, however, oxygenates the brain and brings a temporary state of elevated beta waves and heightened alertness.

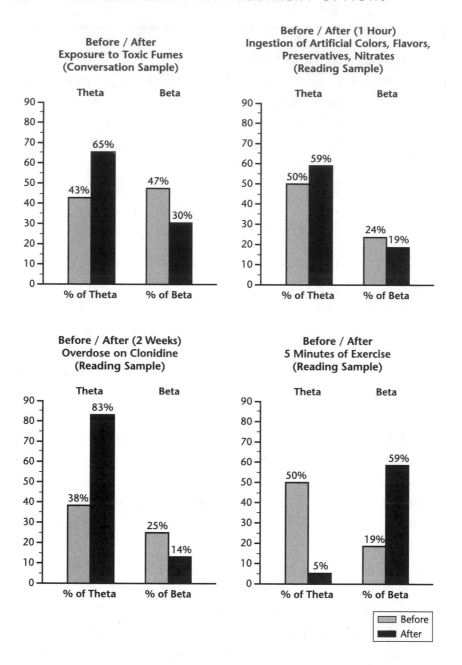

Figure 2—*Change in Theta (Nondiligent) and Beta (Alert) Brain Waves in Four Children with ADHD.*

CHAPTER 9

Uplift Self-Esteem

I HAVE HEARD PARENTS of children with ADHD say that their child's self-esteem is not only low, but "horrible . . . dragging on the floor behind him . . . abominable . . . as if he is an absolute nothing . . . as if she can't do anything right . . . nonexistent."

OVERCOMING ADHD TRAITS

This tragic loss of the most basic sense of self-worth results from the child's sense of being driven, confused, victimized, rejected, uncontrolled, angry at others, and angry at himself. You can help your child overcome these feelings of low self-worth and then nurture his self-esteem by offering encouragement, helping him develop time-management skills, and teaching him how to learn from his mistakes.

Being Driven

The most common wish of hyperactive children with ADHD is that they stop misbehaving. They want to do better. I have asked this question of hundreds of hyperactive children: "If you had a magic wand and could wave it and change something about yourself, what

159

would you change to make life go better for you?" The most common answers have the same general theme: stop misbehaving.

Here are some examples: "I'd wish for being able to stop acting up. . . . not be so bad . . . stop bugging my sister . . . control my temper better . . . stop making Mom and Dad mad at me . . . stop getting into trouble."

These children's drivenness makes them appear senseless, excessive, automatic, and intrusive. They have a genuine fear of being out of control and feel helpless to prevent their impulsive acts, even though they know better than to commit them. Sometimes, they think of themselves as being two people—a calm self and a wild self. I often use this awareness in therapy as part of self-control training after physiological treatment. It becomes the starting point for rebuilding a sense of self-control. The child can, often for the first time ever, actually choose whether to act like the Old Wild Self or the New Calm Self.

For many people, trying harder means working faster on a task. For the hyperactive child, however, it's often the opposite. Encourage self-reminders such as "If I want to do well, I need to slow down. . . . Stop and think: what do I need to do next? . . . Sit on my hands and think."

Teach your child my four-step KITE decision-making procedure (see page 161).

Being Confused

Children and adolescents with ADHD vary greatly in their degree of insight and awareness into how they affect others and how well they are doing in school. You can assess their level of insight by having them fill out the Taylor Hyperactivity Screening Checklist (THSC; see page 37) and comparing their answers with adults' ratings.

To improve your child's insight, give her convincing and undeniable feedback that problem behaviors are occurring, along with an explanation of ADHD. Help her understand the connection between

---

Let's Fly the Decision-Making KITE!

To encourage better self-control and wiser decisions, guide your child through these four steps:

1. **Know the problem:** Who else has had this problem? What did they do?

2. **Identify the choices:** Evaluate the pros and cons of each.

3. **Try the best one:** Select what seems to be the best option and do it.

4. **Evaluate:** What did you learn for next time?

ADHD behavior and negative responses from other children and supervising adults.

Explain the diagnosis and its physiological causes to your child. Say that everybody has special challenges, and your child's particular symptoms represent her cluster of challenges.

Use this explanation, modifying the wording to suit your child:

"You know your body makes its own liquids—tears, blood, and saliva, for example. Your body isn't making enough of certain liquids (chemicals). Because of that, you . . . [give examples of ADHD symptoms your child agreed to from the TIISC]."

Tell her that most other children's natural tendency is to act like column A on the checklist, whereas her natural tendency is to act like columns B and C. Explain the reason for this difference as the presence of ADHD symptoms.

If your child wants to know the location of the liquids, acknowledge that they are in the brain. Refer to ADHD as a uniqueness, not a disease. Explain that problems with brain chemicals do not mean mental retardation, mental illness, or infection or germs in the brain. Give only as much information as your child seems ready to accept.

Being Victimized

Untreated children and adolescents believe that much of what happens to them is unfair, in part because they don't clearly note their own contribution to their difficulties. Assuming a victim stance, they conclude that others are out to get them or are picking on them. Assuming a victim's perspective increases the likelihood for delinquency as an adolescent.

Being Rejected

Even though bossy, impatient, or critical, the child doesn't connect these ADHD traits with the fact that other children don't want to play with her. If fact, the most common complaint made by children with ADHD about their lives is "I don't have enough friends."

Teach your child exactly what to do in a situation where there is a risk of rejection. Rehearse proper behavior to prepare her for the possibility of rejection and encourage broadening social contacts and experiences.

Being Uncontrolled

Faced with a constant stream of negative reactions from others, your child might take the path of least resistance and decide those who criticize are correct. The result is the adoption of a troublemaker or brat role. Prevented from being the best, your child may choose to become the best worst, with an "I don't care what you think" attitude.

Where there's a brat, there's usually an angel nearby. Be aware of the total situation whenever your child seems to be receiving a negative reaction from other children. Notice their special interest in tattling on, or comparing themselves favorably with, your child.

Notice others' reactions to your child based on his reputation and urge them to react instead to the current, improved behavior. Watch for any tendency of your own to jump to conclusions about "who did this?" If your child must go on trial, let the trial be conducted on evidence, not on reputation!

Being Angry at Others

Hyperactive children with ADHD often are angry because of the combined effects of the self-awareness traits discussed thus far. Typically, these children are irritable, short-fused, and volatile. They punch holes in doors and walls, tear curtains from their mountings, break windows, throw things, yank drawers out of dressers, and toss dressers over. They attack adults as well as children with fists or kicks,

---

Is Your Child Depressed?

About one-third of children with ADHD become depressed at one time or another. Be sure to get professional help if depression occurs. Here are nine indications to watch for:

1. Irritability, loss of emotional control.
2. Decreased interest or pleasure in nearly all activities.
3. An apathetic "I don't care" attitude about most things.
4. A decrease in appetite and loss of interest in eating (not caused by medication).
5. Disturbed sleep (not caused by medication).
6. Fatigue and insufficient energy for normal activities.
7. Feelings of worthlessness and talk of escape by running away.
8. Marked indecisiveness and inability to concentrate or think.
9. Frequent sobbing or crying.

and they sometimes threaten with blunt objects or knives. Verbally, their anger takes the form of needling, harassing, name-calling, cussing, and picking on other children and adults.

Like most highly competitive persons, they are poor winners and poor losers. If they win, they make fun of the loser and flaunt the victory. If they lose, they demand a rule change, quit the activity, accuse the opponent of cheating, or attack the victor. These wholesale problems with anger control are generally much more pronounced in those who have an overlapping conduct disorder (ADHD-cd subgroup).

Because dealing aggressively with others is unacceptable, your child must learn how to solve problems and get her wants and needs met through cooperative relationships. The suggestions given here are effective for teaching anger control:

- **Keep it a "little anger."** Teach your child to separate the notion of the "little anger" of frustration from the "big anger" of rage by labeling situations for their anger-arousing potential. Have her ask herself if this is a red light, yellow light, or green light situation for her.

  Green means, "Go—proceed because I'm not likely to get angry in this situation."

  Yellow means, "I'd better stay calm and stay in control."

  Red means, "Zip my lip, turn around, and leave as soon as possible."

- **Tell an adult.** Your child goes to a trusted adult for advice in resolving the situation whenever anger starts to develop.

- **Blow off steam.** Pounding a sturdy punching bag, doing jumping jacks, and running are ways to vent anger safely.

- **Leave the scene and breathe.** Your child takes 10 long, slow, deep breaths while using the self-reminders "stay in control" and "relax."

- **Cool off and calm down.** Your child leaves the scene of conflict and listens to music.

- **Say "stop."** Your child announces clearly and honestly the need for the other person to stop. I've developed a useful three-part message for this purpose:

  1. Please stop [irritating action].

  2. Please do [alternative action] instead.

  3. If you do [alternative action], I'll do [this favor] for you.

- **Fun-run.** Have your child run around to decrease her anger.

- **Get a cool drink.** Your child can leave to get a drink of water, algae smoothie, milk, or juice.

- **Write it down.** Your child can write the incident in a concerns notebook. Later, you can have a calm discussion about the matter.

- **Stay in control.** The self-reminders "stay calm" and "stay in control" are more helpful than "don't get angry."

- **Zip the lip.** "Zip my lip, turn around, and leave," is a useful self-reminder.

- **Count to 10.** Perhaps the most famous of the emergency anger-control procedures, this ageless remedy also works for children who have ADHD.

- **Talk it out.** Teach your child to negotiate rather than have tantrums. Developing conflict-solving skills is a good long-term anger control method.

Each of these suggestions has its benefits and drawbacks. Teaching your child to leave the scene when angry doesn't permit her to practice using negotiation skills. It is, however, a starting point. Venting anger also doesn't teach good social skills. The best long-range solution is to teach your child how to negotiate when potential conflict situations arise. The "please stop" three-part confrontation message is ideal for that purpose.

Training your child how to react constructively to stress ensures better cooperation with treatment attempts, better harmony in the family, and much better symptom control, thus leading to increased self-esteem. Pinpoint the pressures occurring in your child's life. If you suspect she is having a particularly difficult day, suggest possible sources of stress. Once specific stressors are identified, they can be dealt with more easily.

Rest breaks are very important. Mental fatigue from a restrained situation or academic task decreases the ability to cope. Invite your child to exercise the option of leaving any stressful situation temporarily.

Provide a location at home (not to be confused with a time-out place for discipline) where your child can have refuge from stressful situations. Her bedroom may be the best choice. Encourage a quiet activity she enjoys from the fun idea list discussed in appendix F.

> *Relaxation procedures can help some children with ADHD. The best ones are usable on the spur of the moment in a wide variety of situations.*

Relaxation procedures can help some children with ADHD. The greatest benefits lie in increased control of emotional expression, better tolerance of frustration, and decreased aggressiveness. The best relaxation procedures are usable on the spur of the moment in a wide variety of situations. Twenty minutes of meditation is not as helpful as a two-minute procedure. Slowing the rate of breathing increases calmness. Your child should take 10 long, slow, deep breaths for relaxation within a couple of minutes. As an added measure, instruct her to think of relaxation words, such as *calm* when breathing in and *quiet* when breathing out.

Being Angry at Self

Some children with ADHD have terribly low self-esteem and are just as angry at themselves as they are at others. They gradually become adept at thwarting most positive messages, discounting and explaining away high grades or successes. Wallowing in self-hatred, they can become bitterly pessimistic and unhappy about life.

Will Regular Exercise Help Your Child?

Regular exercise almost always uplifts the mood of a child or teen with ADHD.

It doesn't have to be grueling, competitive, or boring to be effective. Here are some guidelines I've developed from talking with hundreds of children and teens:

- Is the exercise *self-regulatory?* Can your child determine how long or how fast to exercise? Can it be accomplished one step at a time?

- Is it *interesting?* Is it fun and will your child enjoy participating?

- Is it *convenient?* Can your child do the activity at or near home at convenient times?

- Is it *appropriate* to your child's needs? Is the activity in concert with his age, state of health, physical condition, and activity preferences?

- Is it *gradual?* Hyperactive children have a way of overdoing almost everything they attempt. The biggest danger is getting involved in complex exercises too early

HOW TO REALLY UPLIFT SELF-ESTEEM

Healthy *self* esteem is healthy *other* esteem. Encouragement is the process through which a person becomes more aware of his capabilities and of a sense of belonging. An encouraged child feels good about himself and about others. Children who feel and act unlovable need the most encouragement; those who feel and act lovable receive and accept encouragement most easily. The backbone of your ability to deliver love to your child is your ability to provide encouragement.

Few gifts are more precious than your gift of encouragement. Here are some guidelines for establishing an encouraging atmosphere in your family:

- **Set realistic goals.** Help your child establish suitable goals. Those that are too simplistic and too easily attained offer no challenge; reaching them would be only hollow victories. On the other hand, goals that are too challenging are usually not accomplished and result in discouragement. The goals can be in various areas on which you and your child agree, such as social, educational, or athletic goals.

> *Healthy* self *esteem is healthy* other *esteem.*

- **Talk with, not to, your child.** Talking *to* your child allows no choice. It is one-way communication in which you preach and demand unthinking obedience. Talking to the child destroys harmony and is discouraging. Talking *with* your child means having a two-way conversation.

- **Adjust your help.** When you give assistance, do not give too much. There are two basic methods:

  1. Help is available but withheld. Your assistance is offered but is not forced on your child. "I will help you if you think you need it, after you've tried."

  2. Help during part of the activity. Your assistance is offered only during the beginning, or the middle, or the end of the task.

- **Show faith in your child's ability.** Give "You can do it!" messages.

- **Help your child over hurdles.** Give a supportive reminder to start or to continue the activity: "Start now and we'll see how it goes" or "All beginnings are difficult."

- **Show empathy for stresses.** Give statements such as "I know this seems difficult to you" and "This is hard for you, isn't it?"

- **Emphasize your child's gains.** For example: "Look how much your skill has improved since you first started" and "It's becoming easier for you, isn't it?"

- **Help use mistakes wisely.** Mistakes confront your child in a never-ending parade, but they need not cause lower self-esteem. They are an opportunity to strengthen his self-esteem and for him to grow psychologically from struggling to make fewer errors and to achieving a greater degree of competence.

- **Teach satisfaction with small gains.** Even the longest journey starts with just a single step. Mountain climbers never run up the mountain; they always take one small step at a time.

- **Show casual appreciation of quality.** Train your child away from perfectionism. Appreciate high skill but don't put excessive emphasis on it. Comment on the completion of some of the task, without mentioning the quality level. Quality will take care of itself as long as your child is showing serious effort and enjoys the activity.

- **Emphasize your child's strengths.** Say "I like the way this part was done" and circle all the correct answers in red.

- **Encourage identification with others.** Your child might enjoy reading about successful individuals with ADHD. Thomas Edison, for example, created a work environment where he was free to develop his own hours and work at his own pace. He slept four hours per night and developed nearly 1,200 patents, including the phonograph, mimeograph, and electric light bulb. Other prominent people often regarded as having ADHD or learning disabilities include Winston Churchill, Eleanor Roosevelt, Albert Einstein, Michael Jordan, Robin Williams, and Louis Pasteur.

Having few friends is the most frequent complaint children with ADHD make about their lives. The next chapter gives several ways to bring new hope to this crucial area of your child's functioning.

CHAPTER 10

Develop Better Interpersonal Relationships

M ANY CHILDREN WITH ADHD have a hard time establishing smooth and cooperative relations because other children resent the intrusion on their time, their activities, their personal space, and their property. Children with ADHD are apparently poor at reading body language. They have trouble telling whether others are annoyed, tired, offended, bored, or hurt. This chapter highlights the most common difficulties in their relations with those who live, study, and play with them.

HOW TO REDUCE SIBLING RIVALRY

The most common complaint from siblings is that the child with ADHD won't stay out of their rooms and won't leave their belongings alone. Insulate the siblings by providing them with their own separate rooms with a lock on the door.

Parents often treat children with ADHD differently from their siblings. Even before the parents realize what is happening, siblings can often see a pattern of overinvolvement developing. They consider the adults too supportive of the child with ADHD, who apparently is exempt from rules, refuses to cooperate with established routines, and in other ways tries to claim special privileges.

Make sure each child senses your unique and special concern. Try to help siblings understand the plight of the child with ADHD. Jealousy will be reduced when they realize her apparent privileges come at great cost and are evidence of difficulties rather than success in life. Let them know of your frustrations and assure them of your desire that the child with ADHD not continue to violate routines, disobey rules, or demand further exemptions.

Use Realistic Consistency

Suppose you promise a trip to a favorite store in the evening, but your child misbehaves during the day. Which type of consistency do you show? Do you follow through on promises, treat all children with the same consequences for misbehavior, or reflect your true feelings by going back on your promise? In your attempt to avoid favoritism, you might be tempted to pursue these misguided attempts at consistency:

- **Evenness of mood, moment-to-moment and day-to-day.** *"I will always smile and be pleasant to all of my children"* (even though my sleep, nutrition, and stresses vary greatly, and the children's behavior fluctuates).

- **Values and beliefs about right and wrong.** What is unacceptable behavior in one child is also unacceptable in any other: *"If it is wrong for Billy to do it, then it is wrong for Amy to do it"* (even though Billy and Amy handle responsibilities entirely differently).

- **Follow-through and determination.** *"Because I promised that I would do this favor for Sheila, I'll do it"* (even though I don't feel like it anymore because of the way she acted after I made the promise).

- **Universality of rules and their enforcement.** The same rules and consequences apply for all the children: *"Since I won't let*

Matt climb on it, I won't let James climb on it either" (even though James uses great care and won't hurt it).

- **Maintaining order and routine.** *"We don't do what Candi is asking for. We've never done it before, so she can't do it now"* (even though this circumstance is a unique opportunity for Candi).

- **Pairing certain actions with certain consequences.** *"Every time Tyrone does that, this will happen to him as a consequence"* (even though the circumstances and his intentions are different).

- **Equivalence.** *"What I do for one child, I will do for all"* (even though some may not want it done, and others are desperately seeking it).

- **Parental agreement.** *"We must always agree on every aspect of raising our children"* (even though we differ in hundreds of other ways and seldom have the same understanding of a situation).

In contrast to those misguided forms, two types of consistency actually *work*. Manage consistency with congruent and contemporaneous treatment of your child. He will receive useful feedback about the impact of his behavior on others.

- **Congruence.** Matching feelings and actions, parents act according to how they feel, giving a direct and honest indication of their response to the child's behavior or to their own circumstance: *"This is how I feel, so this is what I am going to do. I feel this way in part because you acted the way you did." "I know I promised to take you shopping, but I'm just too tired right now. I'll rest a bit and try to arrange to take you later today or tomorrow. I'm sorry."*

- **Contemporaneous treatment.** Treating according to readiness, parents provide guidance needed by a specific child at the moment, regardless of whether a similar action would have been taken with a different child: *"I'll let you go over to Sam's* *house because you have been so helpful to me with Sara, even though we don't usually let anyone from our family visit Sam at this time of day."* Discourage demands by siblings for equal privileges. Substitute instead the concept of *equally special* privileges that are uniquely suited to each child. The safest, most reliable consistency is to provide whatever each child needs and is ready for.

Watch for the Carousel Effect

Most siblings of children with ADHD who respond to the various physiological interventions I've been discussing are pleased with the improvements that occur and quickly forgive the child with ADHD for his past misdeeds. They launch a close, loving, mutually appreciative relationship with the treated child.

> *The safest, most reliable consistency is to provide whatever each child needs and is ready for.*

Some, however, react negatively to the positive changes that occur in the child with ADHD. The two children then become like two animals on a carousel, such that as one rises, the other lowers. The self-esteem of the other children in your family is in part based on their comparison of themselves with the child who has ADHD. The carousel effect involves sudden deterioration in the behavior of a sibling when the child with ADHD shows improved behavior. The sibling who was formerly in a favored position suddenly no longer seems so angelic because the child with ADHD is no longer so devilish. The children trade roles, and a new family brat emerges.

The best solution for the carousel effect is to give the formerly better-behaved siblings new ways to be angelic that allow them to reclaim the specialness lost when the child who has ADHD improved. Special helper roles provide a new importance and circumvent the need to take over the position of "best worst" in your family.

Decrease competition. Competition and sibling rivalry go hand in hand. Children who are jealous of each other quickly become competitive. To decrease sibling rivalry, decrease competition in your family. Interpersonal competition—one person against another—is very destructive.

Emphasize individuality. To the extent that each child feels affirmed as a unique individual, there is less need for her to be treated the same as siblings.

Encourage kindness. Support any of your children's actions and statements reflecting courtesy, negotiation, sensitivity, sharing, and cooperation.

Encourage sharing. Counter all egotism and selfishness about time, ideas, or material objects. Encourage the sharing of skills, knowledge, ideas, and objects.

Teach assertion skills. Train your children to discuss and settle issues by mutual consent after exploring each other's wants, rather than by bullying or competing. Encourage them to ask directly for what they want, rather than screaming, whining, hitting, or grabbing.

Defuse volatile situations. Your child might misbehave simply to gain attention from other children. Give any pestered child some simple ways to defuse the situation so intense conflict doesn't have a chance to develop. If one child starts being a nuisance, the other child has three alternatives:

1. Leave the scene.
2. Get the child with ADHD to stop being a nuisance.
3. Agree to pay attention to the bothersome child.

Telling the annoyed child to ignore the antics of a bothersome child who has ADHD often doesn't solve anything and goads the misbehaving child to intensify attention seeking.

"But I Don't Like Him, Mommy!"

Being the sibling of a child with ADHD is the world's best training ground for practicing the art of forgiveness. One of the best ways to reduce sibling rivalry is to give the sibling a "special helper" role. It involves several key aspects:

- Helping the child with ADHD recognize the improvements from treatment
- Assisting in interpreting for others the fact that the child has changed
- Standing up for the child in stressful situations
- Helping you monitor the effectiveness of the treatment program
- Reporting to you about the occurrence or absence of ADHD symptoms
- Reporting to you about side effects if medications are being used
- Reminding the child to be his "new calm self" at choice points

If siblings still find it difficult to turn their relationship in a positive direction to coincide with the improvements in their sister or brother, seek professional counseling.

HOW TO IMPROVE RELATIONSHIPS WITH PLAYMATES

Playmates and classmates often reject a child with ADHD and take advantage of him. In games such as tag, the child with ADHD becomes "it" most of the time. Following are methods I have found useful for improving the social relationships of children and teens with ADHD.

Recognize Areas of Need

Hyperactive children often suffer peer difficulties because their intrusive, impulsive, obnoxious behavior and poorly developed social skills make them unattractive. The inattentive subtype children are often underassertive, shy, and too timid. Among the most common difficulties for children and adolescents with ADHD are the following:

- **Reciprocity.** Entering an ongoing conversation, interrupting courteously when interruption is necessary, joining group activities, waiting for one's turn in line or in a game, being a participant without dominating.

- **Handling negatives.** Accepting criticism, accepting a no answer to a request, responding to teasing, losing gracefully in a game—being a "good sport," disagreeing without criticizing.

> *Hyperactive children suffer peer difficulties because their intrusive, impulsive, obnoxious behavior and poorly developed social skills make them unattractive.*

- **Self-control.** Handling peer pressure, making decisions without assistance, resisting temptations.

- **Communication.** Understanding and following instructions, answering questions, conversing well, being an alert listener, using eye contact, showing empathy.

- **Affirmation.** Giving compliments, encouraging others, being a friend, inviting others to play, noticing and commenting on the good news in others' lives, doing favors, giving thoughtful gifts, lending, sharing, being hospitable, showing interest in others.

- **Tact and courtesy.** Showing gratitude, developing hello and goodbye skills, apologizing, honoring others' "boundaries," being courteous, using polite language, self-disclosing without bragging.

Give Social Skills Training

There are three basic social skills training methods. The *mentor method* involves learning from an older child who has refined social skills and would be a suitable model. Arrange for this child to give your child feedback and suggestions for improvement after observing some moments of play or other interaction.

The second is the *counseling method*, which involves enrolling your child in group or individual counseling that includes discussion and practice of social skills.

The third is the *instruction method*, which allows you to give your child experience at refining her social skills within the protective and encouraging confines of your home. Select a day, time, and location that afford privacy. Confine the training sessions to a maximum length of 15 minutes. This method consists of six steps, the first letters of which spell *scored*.

1. **Show.** Demonstrate how to perform the skill by acting it out.
2. **Coach.** Describe the skill step-by-step; instruct how and when to use it.
3. **Offer self-reminders.** Provide self-reminding statements to remind your child how and when to use the skill.
4. **Rehearse.** Let your child perform the skill by role-playing in a realistic simulated situation.
5. **Encourage.** Comment favorably on your child's attempts and correct any aspects needing refinement.
6. **Debrief.** Encourage your child to apply the skill to real-life situations then discuss the results with you.

Counteract a Bad Reputation

Peers are generally rather slow to accept the idea that a child can change dramatically during physiological treatment. The disappearance of disruptive behavior doesn't necessarily bring with it the degree of social polish that makes your child an enjoyable partner in peer activities or attractive as a potential friend.

Your child may have developed a reputation that interferes with his peers' willingness to accept him as a friend. I call this phenomenon the wake effect. Think of your child as a speedboat and ADHD as the motor. When the motor stops, the boat no longer moves across the water, but the wake catches up with the boat and rocks it. In the same way, his bad reputation will continue to plague your child long after his troublesome ADHD symptoms have stopped.

A classic example of this wake effect occurred with a 9-year-old boy with ADHD, whose mother reported:

> I take each day as it comes, not knowing what it will hold. I even received an anonymous clipping in the mail with no return address: "Pointers on How to Raise Juvenile Delinquents." Josh can't even breathe without everyone jumping on him.
> Everything that happens is all Josh's fault.

Your child needs to undo the wake effect. The moment his symptoms start to become controlled, the burden is on him to demonstrate to all that things are going to be different. I've known children with ADHD for whom it took over a year to undo their reputations, replace

> *P*eers are generally rather slow to accept the idea that a child can change dramatically during physiological treatment.

friendships, and revise their peers' and teachers' expectations about their behavior. Switching to a different classroom or school is also an option that opens new friendship possibilities if all else fails.

Assist by talking individually with adults who regularly see your child. Explain the wake effect to them and tell them of the improvements that are occurring. Ask them to help undo the wake among your child's classmates and playmates. Explain the wake effect to your child and offer ways to undo it:

> Other people expect you to still act like the Old Wild Matt instead of the New Calm Matt. Even your teacher expects you to still be like

The Eight A's of Apology: How to Do It Right

All eight aspects of a true friendship-rescuing apology just happen to begin with the letter A. Use all eight when you apologize:

1. **Admit.** Admit you did the offending act.

2. **Account.** Explain what you were trying to accomplish or what you were thinking at the time.

3. **Acknowledge** the wrongness. Indicate you are aware of the pain, hurt, or inconvenience you caused.

4. **Apology statement.** Say you are sorry that you caused this offense and hurt.

5. **Ask forgiveness.** Say that you hope the person will forgive you.

6. **Affirm the relationship.** Indicate your desire to maintain or improve your relationship with the person.

7. **Amends.** Do a favor, bring a gift, do chores for the person, or invite the person to do something fun with you.

8. **Adjust.** Think about what you can do differently next time so that you won't repeat the mistake. Change something to prevent it from happening again.

Old Wild Matt. You need to convince them you are now the New Calm Matt. Tell them, "I don't do that anymore," whenever they act as if they expect you to still be Old Wild Matt. You might want to say something else along with it, like "I would like to be your friend, and I don't do that anymore."

Teach Your Child How to Apologize

A crucial part of your child's overcoming the wake effect is learning to backtrack successfully after offending someone. I have developed a

How to Make and Keep More Friends

I have developed this list of friendship principles for children who have difficulty making friends:

- Talk to them rather than remaining silent.
- Talk about what they want to talk about.
- Ask questions so they will talk to you.
- Do what they want to do.
- Let them say when to start and stop an activity.
- Let them control their half while you control only your half.
- Smile.
- Exchange small gifts and favors.
- Show you understand how happy they are.
- Talk about the potential friends rather than yourself.
- Get them to talk about themselves.
- Invite them over and be a friendly host.
- Let them have first choice of what topic to talk about, game to play, movie to watch, or food to eat.

powerful, easy-to-remember guide to help children and adolescents undo their social blunders. The eight "A steps" represent the eight aspects of a true friendship-saving apology. A begrudging, mumbled "sorry" is not sufficient, nor is the false apology "*If* I lost your toy, I'm sorry." Rehearse with your child and consider collapsing some of the points if giving all eight steps is too cumbersome.

Cultivate Friendship Skills

Your child will never learn social skills by pretending to be a hermit. Don't support his attempts to reject other children. Instead, assist him

How to Prevent Children's Fights and Conflict

Here are 16 suggestions I have developed with children and teens who have ADHD for reducing or eliminating conflicts, arguments, and fights. In general, avoid deep emotional entanglement and drain the fight of its power over you and others. Encourage conflict solving, always working toward a win-win solution for the future.

1. Tell your children that you are now generally going to stay out of their fights.

2. Deprive the fight of an audience—and of power—by leaving the area.

3. Maintain routines and continue whatever you were doing.

4. Stay minimally emotionally involved. You don't know who started it, and you don't want to know.

5. Calmly discuss at a later time the results of, and alternatives to, fighting. Start with "When you are fighting, are you happy?"

6. Have a discussion about fighting at the next family council meeting.

7. Arbitrate a win-win solution at a later time, perhaps at the next family council meeting.

in rebuilding stressed relationships or developing new ones. Show him how to ask questions to discover areas of overlapping interest and experience with prospective new friends—how they spend time, where they have lived, interesting places they have visited, and their hopes for the future.

Don't let your child become a couch potato. Look for activities and new skills to develop. Take advantage of common interests your child shares with other children. Lean toward activities in which he wants to excel or already does well.

8. Stare at the fight and invite the children to continue. Say "I'm watching you fight; go ahead." Be totally unimpressed by their fight but keep staring at it.

9. Have a regular time to discuss issues and conflicts, in addition to family council meetings.

10. Invite the children to use a punching bag. I recommend the duffel bag size, not the football size.

11. Set up a ring and have a foam pillow or marshmallow fight.

12. Move both fighters out of your sight: "Go into the backyard with your fight."

13. Separate the combatants briefly. Assign them a joint project of presenting you with a single written account, signed by both, of the problem they are trying to resolve.

14. Intervene neutrally, without playing favorites, and suggest a win-win solution.

15. Make the audience assume some responsibility: "Because there was a fight in this room, all of you must go outside now."

16. Express confidence in the children's decision-making and conflict-solving abilities: "I'm sure you can work out a win-win solution."

Emphasize honest ways of relating, being a true friend, and showing sincere interest in other children. You are not trying to train your child to be phony or political. Instead, you are teaching him how to be genuinely kind—the essence of increasing his attractiveness as a candidate for friendship. The best way to accomplish these goals is to invite individual children as guests in your home for brief periods. This method also encourages everyone to regard your home as the center for fun activities and opens the door for your continued assistance.

Teach your child how to strengthen friendships with genuine gratitude. Suggest specific wordings for giving sincere compliments without sounding phony or patronizing. Sincerely expressed gratitude also prevents others from feeling they are being taken advantage of. Teaching the simple technique of eye contact will help refine your child's concentration and listening skills. Tell him to look directly into the eyes of whoever is speaking.

Your child needs basic guidelines for various circumstances. Overstate and simplify principles rather than drawing fine distinctions or being too technical.

Help Your Child Resist Temptations

If friends are leading your child into trouble, train her in the skills needed to refuse invitations to mischief.

Label temptations as cheap tricks. "They say, 'Everybody does it . . . you are chicken if you don't . . . we won't get caught . . . just this once would be okay.' What are some other ones?"

Provide self-reminding statements. "They are trying to control me—I won't let them. Stop and think, what should I do now?"

Practice refusal statements. "No thanks . . . absolutely not . . . you can get into trouble if you want to, but not me."

Invite a once-and-for-all decision. Ask your child to make a decision never to get into particular types of trouble and not to follow the lead of a certain troublesome peer.

Two no's, then leave. "If you have to say no twice, turn around and leave."

Teach two rules for harmony when playing. The *50/50* rule is that choices are to be distributed evenly ("First let's play what you want, then we can play what I want"). The *freedom-to-stop* rule is that either child is free to depart at any time, and all participation is voluntary.

Determine what your child does that creates problems in relating to other children. Whenever you bring up a negative, offer a positive, such as a suggestion to help make things better next time.

Prevent Conflicts and Fights

If a friend disagrees with your child, teach the art of friendly disagreement. Point out that nobody wins an argument. A damaged friendship is much worse than an agreement to disagree peaceably. Also ask how each could have prevented the fight or could have made things less hostile. Use the "what would happen next time if . . ." approach:

"Next time, what would happen if you stop and think about what else you could do?" "Next time, what would happen if you invite your friend over to our home?"

To deal with teasers, take the teaser and victim aside and analyze the incident. If the teaser is actually fishing for more contact, suggest better ways than harassment.

Counteract Undesirable Friendships

If you have concerns about peer influence, gently set limits on the relationship. Insert yourself as a sieve between the two children, filtering and supervising the amount and type of contact they have with each other. You might want, for example, to confine contact to infrequent visits to your home and only when you are present.

Involve your child in other, new activities that exclude the undesirable peers. Encourage more wholesome relationships by inviting potential new friends over to your home. Ask the teacher to plan activities that pair your child with prospects for wholesome friendships. Don't force the issue but plant the seeds so your child will consider standards for whom to befriend. State your intention not to try to stop any friendships unless absolutely necessary but say that you want your child to consider these matters very carefully.

You can reduce sibling rivalry by giving brothers and sisters meaningful new roles to fulfill and minimizing competition. By strengthening your child's social skills, teaching the eight As of apology, cultivating friendships, and guarding against undesirable peer influence, you can give him dozens of useful techniques for more successful interpersonal relationships. Chapters 11 and 12 focus on how to solve the many stresses the ADHD syndrome imposes on all the relationships within your family.

CHAPTER 11

Understand Your Own Feelings

AS THE PARENT of a child with ADHD, you have the distinction of being a member of the most misunderstood, overburdened, and underhelped group in the world. The emotional stresses you face are beyond what most people can comprehend. They represent strange contortions and twistings of your psyche and clashes of basic sensibilities such as wanting to love and protect your child, yet feeling incredible rage against your child's behavior.

Many times, the parent of an energy-draining child with ADHD starts out with naive expectations that a little bit of parenting effort will solve things. One mother related:

> As a parent, I was determined that nothing was going to make me put my son on pharmaceuticals unless I absolutely had to. He got on my nerves, but my plan was to just be patient with him and keep on disciplining him and make him play outdoors more. Anyway, at that time, I believed that ADHD was just an excuse for having undisciplined kids.

THE EARLIEST EMOTIONAL STRESSES

Even before birth, the child with ADHD can manage to stir up negative reactions in his parents. Hyperactivity in the womb keeps the mother-to-be awake at night, which makes that long-awaited birth process even more taxing. The numerous signs of disrupted body chemistry during infancy bring with them urgent demands for continual parental attention, which further drains both parents. The colicky, unsoothable baby creates physical and emotional stresses that often take months to unravel.

The key to emotional survival during the infancy of a severely symptomatic child is to arrange rest breaks and time away from the burdens of caring for him. Try rotating baby-care duties or get help from a relative, friend, or paid caregiver. Also, of course, follow the recommendations for toxinsulation and dietary and food allergy control in chapters 6 and 7.

LATER EMOTIONAL STRESSES

The feelings many parents of children with ADHD experience represent an emotional roller coaster. Typically, they appear in this approximate order, each step leading to the next:

1. Feeling misunderstood and criticized.
2. Feeling guilty and inadequate.
3. Feeling the need to serve and protect.
4. Feeling angry.
5. Feeling emotionally bankrupt.

Feeling Misunderstood and Criticized

The two most prominent criticisms the parent receives are that the child is not receiving enough love and that the child is not receiving

UNDERSTAND YOUR OWN FEELINGS

enough discipline. If the parents would just shape up, everything would be solved.

The parents understandably feel undersupported and criticized. They soon become aware that others really don't understand what it is like to raise this child. One parent expressed this feeling to me in this way:

> If they could have my child at their home just one evening—even just one hour—they wouldn't say the things they've said to me about how I should be calmer and "boys will be boys." I'd like to see how calm they'd be when he attacks their children, has tantrums when you make a reasonable request, turns off the TV when everyone is watching, and can't remember anything you tell him for longer than 30 seconds.

After diagnosis of ADHD and comorbid conditions, a new volley of criticisms can occur. Your uncovering of the correct diagnosis may be condemned and regarded as prejudicial labeling and scapegoating.

As if all of these attacks aren't enough, once you start any of the physiological treatments, you open yet another source of complaints from outsiders. Whether you are using dietary changes, prescribed medication, phenol toxinsulation, or any combination of the three, you will be criticized by misinformed, judgmental people from the helping professions as well as from the general public.

React to these people as if they need more information—which indeed they do. If they genuinely want to help, give them more information, such as by referring them to relevant sections of this book. Illustrate your awareness of the concern shown by the other person:

> Thank you for your interest in my child's welfare. I know you mean well and have his best interest at heart. People have many different opinions. I am very aware of these issues and have thought them out already. The bottom line is that the best help for my child right now is to use this treatment.

Ask them to respect your stewardship over your child; then ask for whatever specific help you desire from them.

Feeling Guilty and Inadequate

If the barrage of criticism takes hold, feelings of failure, helplessness, and self-pity can evolve into a defensive anger against the child, for which the parents then feel guilty. The result is often conflicting feelings of:

- Intense resentment of the child
- Guilt over that resentment
- An urge to protect, love, and help the child
- Guilt about not having been a caring parent

The gripping tentacles of guilt are illustrated in this parent's confession about dealing with her 4-year-old prior to starting treatment:

> Each day is a giant struggle, and I pray for patience all the time. Every morning when I wake up, I tell myself: "Today I will be calm and loving." And before I am through the morning, I've already failed.

It has been my privilege to provide many parents with the first authoritative ADHD diagnosis after a review of the child's and family's history, checklist results from home and school, and observation and interview of the child. There is a great lifting of the burden of guilt when a cause is finally recognized. This joy was captured by a mother who heard me discuss ADHD on a nationally broadcast interview:

> I had never imagined that hyperactivity might be our problem. I listened to the list of 21 behavioral characteristics of the hyperactive child [the Taylor Hyperactivity Screening Checklist, page 37], and by the end of the list, my mouth was open in shock. . . . Our son manifests each of them. At last, to know what it is that we're dealing with; it's such a relief! It has helped to ease the guilt that I'd heaped on myself and has given me determination to deal with the behavior in a constructive way.

Of course, every parent who suspects ADHD should seek an appropriate professional diagnosis rather than relying on media shows and a checklist. The feeling of relief this mother expressed, however,

Do You Think You're at Fault?

Feeling guilty, inadequate, and at fault is the most common negative feeling experienced by parents of children with ADHD. As one mother explained:

> For the first year of his life, they doped him with phenobarbitol and called him "hyperirritable." At a year, they put him in a hospital for tests. Five days and $2,000 later, they had no answer. I went to a psychiatrist to see if it was me. It wasn't. At 3, we put him in a Montessori preschool, but after six months, they asked us to take him out. He was unteachable. I went back to the psychiatrist again, to be sure it really wasn't me. It took six months to convince me this time.

is typical of that experienced by parents of children with ADHD when the diagnosis is finally established.

Feeling the Need to Serve and Protect

Partly in an attempt to compensate for guilt feelings and partly out of a realistic concern for the child's difficulties, parents of children with ADHD often overdo their attempt to run interference. Brothers and sisters witness and resent this seemingly excessive service, devotion, time, energy, and concern.

Six types of overinvolvement often develop between parents and their children who have ADHD:

1. Overprotecting. The parents feel a need to intervene so that no misfortunes occur, and they develop the habit of automatically defending the child. As the mother of a boy with ADHD explained:

> I know I am way overprotective, and I do take up for Kevin. But if I don't stand up for him, who will? When he was younger, before being

diagnosed hyperactive, I was afraid to answer the phone or door for fear of what Kevin had done now.

When parents place restrictions such as, "Don't climb the ladder; you might fall off," or, "Don't go outside without a jacket, you might catch a cold," they rob their child of the opportunity to learn how to cope with difficulty or responsibility.

2. Nagging. The child's lack of diligence—combined with a short memory for verbal messages—leads parents into issuing an endless string of directives, reminders, commands, and suggestions. Nagging is probably the most common error made by parents in general and by parents of children with ADHD in particular.

My worst case of this nag cycle involved the mother of a 7-year-old hyperactive boy who claimed that, on the average, she repeated each request or command 17 times before her child would respond!

3. Spoiling. Overindulging the child means trying to shield her from every frustration. One father indicated this tendency to spoil with this motto: "You just breathe; I'll do all the rest for you!"

4. Hypervigilance. The parent is in a constant state of alert, asking "Where is my child now? What is he doing now?"

5. Pitying. The parent overly sympathizes and allows harmful little violations of medication or nutritional treatment. One mother expressed this feeling:

> I was on tranquilizers, but nothing was strong enough to blunt the sadness of seeing my little girl in such turmoil. She used to roll and roll on the floor, in an effort to get rid of some of the frantic energy going through her little body. She was sure that God hated her because He would not let her mind her parents.

6. Infantilizing. In response to their need to run interference, the parents perform so diligently that the child can also fail to develop ordinary social and personal coping skills.

To encourage your child's efforts, give her help without excessive service. Reduce stresses without taking away her opportunities to learn to face challenging situations. Refuse to be tricked into guilt-motivated servitude to your child. "If you were nicer, you would do this for me." Be alert to such a manipulation and do the opposite.

Your child cannot learn to swim by sitting on the shore and watching you swim. Avoid the "I can do it faster and easier" trap. Your child can learn far more by being unsuccessful at completely mastering a difficult situation than by simply watching you master it.

Concentrate on reducing the number of verbal directives you give, putting the emphasis instead on setting up the structure and routines to support what you want your child to do.

> *Your child cannot learn to swim by sitting on the shore and watching you swim. Avoid the "I can do it faster and easier" trap. Your child can learn far more by being unsuccessful at completely mastering a difficult situation than by simply watching you master it.*

Feeling Angry

Anger can be one of the most difficult and potentially destructive emotions within a family. Parents may discover they cannot be alone as a couple without interruption and pressure from their child. They may feel like his prisoners, obliged to supervise him constantly and unable to leave him alone for fear of what might happen.

They might feel manipulated and used by the child. They may defend him in public in a certain situation, only to discover that he suddenly acts calm and orderly, making their concern appear foolish and excessive.

Most parents of a child with ADHD sense an invisible psychological wall or barrier between the child and others, including themselves. They are aware of never having truly made contact in the sense of closeness of spirit or emotional intimacy. Parents can become angry about this barrier.

You create your own anger. "I'm getting angry as I listen to you talk" is a much more accurate statement than "You are making me angry by what you are saying." Accepting that the source of your anger is within you brings it within your grasp and potentially under your control. Anger directed inward can turn into self-pity, self-criticism, or depression. Everyone has problems in life. There is no particular injustice in the fact that you are facing this problem. The answer to "How could this happen to me?" is "Very easily, because it *is* happening!"

> *D*ifferentiate between the child and the behavior: The ADHD, not your child, is the culprit.

Differentiate between the child and the behavior: The ADHD, not your child, is the culprit. If your child had the measles, you would hate to see the red spots but would still love your child. "I'm frustrated because I don't know what to do" is more accurate than "You are frustrating me."

Feeling Emotionally Bankrupt

The parents of a child with ADHD often end up feeling completely defeated, drained, and at the end of their rope. They may have been faced with the medical stresses, feelings of guilt and inadequacy, and the emotional exhaustion of overinvolvement in efforts to save the child from impossible situations. There may have been disruption in the family, bombardment with destructive criticisms from outsiders, and a barrier between themselves and the child.

They may feel as if they are trying to put 60 jigsaw puzzle pieces together to make a picture that requires only 50. Every time they make a move in one direction to get something to fit, some other situation needing their attention pops up. Their daily lives may become an endless struggle for peace, quiet, and calmness for themselves and their family.

Emotional bankruptcy occurs after the parents have exhausted the usual range of child management methods. Ordinary techniques for showing love and giving effective discipline don't work. Relying on ordinary sources and standards for child rearing, such as how their friends handle their children or what their parents did in raising them, does not work. As I point out in chapter 6, even ordinary criteria for a wholesome diet can't be applied to children who have ADHD.

The parents try everything and find that nothing works. There may be "How many times do I have to tell you?" lectures, coupled with endless nagging. A sure sign emotional bankruptcy has been declared is the parents' sense that they've run out of options. They give up and start to feel defeated and depressed.

One parent may then react by trying to dump parental responsibility onto the other parent or to legally remove the child from the home. Neglect and abandonment of the child can sometimes occur. The parents may stop trying to exert influence on the child, expressing their sense of helplessness with a "what's the use" attitude.

A tragic reaction at this stage is child abuse. Hyperactive children are overrepresented among the victims of all types of child abuse: verbal, emotional, physical, sexual, and ritual. The likelihood that a hyperactive child will be abused increases if one or both parents are hyperactive, have a character disorder, or abuse drugs or alcohol.

Verbal abuse includes excessive bossing, criticizing, swearing at the child, name-calling, use of sarcasm, threatening, insulting, belittling, yelling, dwelling on weaknesses and failures, unfavorable comparisons to other children, and undermining the child's sense of worth.

Emotional abuse includes withholding love. The parent who will not do favors for the child, who avoids affectionate touching, who is spiteful, who does not provide gifts when gift giving is expected within the family, or who gives "I hate you" messages is committing emotional abuse.

Physical abuse includes hitting, slapping, strapping, kicking, hair pulling, throwing, biting, shoving, burning, spraying, shaking, excessive twirling, excessive tickling, or excessive spanking. These actions are not always abusive. They become abusive when they are nonaccidental, excessively frequent or severe, or have a destructive effect on

Anger, Anger, and More Anger

The anger that parents of children with ADHD feel can rise to mountainous proportions and is often directed inward as well as outward. One parent who came close to abusing her child summarized:

I felt that Crissie's behavior problems were all my fault. I knew nothing but frustration. There were times when I would lock myself in my bedroom so I wouldn't risk hurting her.

the child. For example, almost every parent feels the urge at times to spank or slap the child. When these impulses become excessive and sadistic, they constitute child abuse. More extreme and bizarre forms of physical abuse amount to torture and similar acts of brutality.

Sexual abuse includes forcing, tricking, or persuading the child to witness or participate in sexual activity. Hyperactive children are also overrepresented among sexual offenders to other children. They are not only more likely to be molested but also more likely to molest than are children who are not hyperactive.

Ritual abuse includes all of the other categories and typically is performed as part of cult activity.

Overcoming Emotional Bankruptcy

If you are at the end of your rope, separate yourself from your child and from your routine surroundings. Take a brief weekend away, alone or with a friend. You need to regain your sense of emotional balance, self-respect, inner calmness, and personal strength.

Emphasize controlling yourself and your own emotional reactions to the child's behavior, rather than controlling the child. When you have less investment in making the child act differently, he will have less need to prove to you that you can't do it.

It is much easier to *prevent* emotional bankruptcy than to get rid of it. Eliminating the feeling of desperation and returning to a calm and productive way of dealing with your child is next to impossible to do by yourself. Seek professional counseling if emotional bankruptcy is occurring.

The key to regaining your emotional composure about your child's behavior is to keep the condition's effects as minimal as possible. Follow through with the three physiological treatment options of nutrition, toxinsulation, and pharmaceuticals. Employ techniques from the sensorimotor tool kit as needed, and practice the additional psychosocial and academic methods outlined in this book.

Remember that there is light at the end of the tunnel. You will be able to experience a joy similar to what most parents of children with ADHD know when they use the techniques in this book. As one mother summarized:

> I was so *pleased* with the improvements I saw! I could actually carry on a conversation with my child, and we didn't get into a fight! I actually *enjoyed* sitting at the table with him, something I had hated to do because of the constant disciplining I would have to do.

Don't be afraid to obtain the services of a skilled therapist or counselor for your own sake and that of your family. Professional assistance in unblocking your built-up feelings through counseling or psychotherapy will be a beneficial and wise investment of your time and energy. Be determined not to let negative emotional responses sabotage your efforts to make life work for your child, for you, and for your family.

> *Don't be afraid to obtain the services of a skilled therapist or counselor for your own sake and that of your family.*

CHAPTER 12

Rebuild Family Harmony

Y OUR MARRIAGE IS the foundation of all other relationships in your family. The ways you settle conflicts with each other, express affection toward each other, handle difficulties together, and talk with each other teach your children important lessons. One of the greatest gifts a child can ever receive is happily married parents.

ADHD can be a dangerous threat to any marriage. It usually exerts a heavy stress in many ways. The constant change in both partners, caused in part by reactions to the child's symptoms, puts additional strain on the marital relationship.

RECOGNIZING DESTRUCTIVE PATTERNS

I have found 12 patterns that consistently develop in families with ADHD. Many evolve so slowly the partners don't realize they are developing. These patterns are:

1. Partial denial. One spouse denies the ADHD, while the other recognizes and tries to deal with it.

2. Joint denial. The second parent joins the first in denying. Together, they remain ill-equipped to help the child, whose behavior becomes increasingly out of control.

3. Partial abuse. One parent becomes abusive and may blackmail the other parent by threatening to cease all parental functions if the nonabusive parent complains.

4. Joint abuse. Both parents abuse the child verbally, emotionally, or physically. When the abuse comes to the attention of social agencies, such couples often move out of the area rather than face the risk of losing their children.

5. Partial overinvolvement. One parent becomes overinvolved with the child. The other parent often wants to correct the situation, and the resulting conflict puts additional strain on the marriage.

6. Joint overinvolvement. Both parents become overinvolved and overprotect, spoil, nag, pity, or infantilize the child, who is catered to by two energy-drained parents.

7. Partial emotional bankruptcy. One parent declares emotional bankruptcy, forcing the other parent to assume the total burden of parental responsibility.

8. Joint emotional bankruptcy. Both parents declare emotional bankruptcy. They attempt to unload their parental responsibility onto an external source by trying to give the child away, abandon her, or offer her to a social agency. If the child remains in the home, there may be gross physical and emotional neglect.

9. Partial one-up. The second parent feels self-righteous and superior and labels the first parent inferior, inept, uncaring, ignorant, weak, or sick. Both parents allow the primary burden of child rearing to fall on the first parent, who suffers not only from the burden of dealing with the child but also from the critical attacks of the second parent.

10. Mutual one-up. When the first parent counterattacks after being criticized by the second parent, the two parents can't negotiate mutual decisions about child rearing. Each considers the other weak, incompetent, abusive, and unfit. Both assert that everything would be all right if only the *other* parent would change.

11. Divided and conquered. Primarily through lack of communication, the parents are deceived by the child's manipulations. The situation deteriorates so that the child needs to deal with only one parent rather than both. The parents are first divided, then conquered, by the child. Hyperactive children are particularly good at bulldozing. They learn that if they nag and yell all day, they can wear out one parent and get their way.

> *Hyperactive children are particularly good at bulldozing. They learn that if they nag and yell all day, they can wear out one parent and get their way.*

The child may also bully the conquered parent by threatening with physical assault, destroying property, or hurting others. The child may goad the parent in a "go ahead, see if I care!" fashion. Often she does not have to announce the blackmail weapon. The parents may already know it exists and may apply it to themselves with little or no provocation from the child. The parents may tell themselves: "If I don't give in, she will [destroy my things, scratch the paint on the car, attack her sister, steal what I won't buy for her]."

Sometimes the child's manipulation involves taking unfair advantage of a conflict that already exists. If the parents cannot agree on a child's allowance, for example, she will approach the more generous parent for money.

12. Overcompensation. The excess of one parental trait in the first parent is responded to by the second parent, who develops too much of the opposite trait. Each time the child is treated softly, the firm parent will become more firm; each time the child is treated firmly, the soft parent will become more soft. At any specific moment, the child is treated either too firmly or too softly.

OVERCOMING DESTRUCTIVE PATTERNS

The first step in dealing with these destructive marital behaviors is to recognize them. Regardless of how pressured or discouraging the situation is, there is always hope for improvement as long as you are aware of what is occurring.

Hunt for the good.   Don't let ADHD dominate your family. Identify and emphasize all the positive aspects of your family. Help your spouse appreciate all family members. Although your glass may seem half empty, remember that it is also half full.

Don't expect a perfect solution.   Realize and accept that there is no perfect answer to the many difficulties your family experiences. Find the best available method for any specific situation and accept the fact that none will be perfect.

Seek constant improvement.   The more confident you are as parents, the more confidently you can respond to the stresses of your child's ADHD. Everything you can do to increase your parental and marital skills and knowledge will help. Attend workshops, classes, and retreats on parenting and marriage enrichment. Read instructive materials. Sometimes, it is best to seek assistance from a mental health professional who is knowledgeable in family relationships and ADHD.

Defend against criticism.   One mother of a hyperactive child expressed her thoughts this way:

> Negative responses are like negative fields of energy—they can't do any harm if they remain grounded. I try to latch on to all the positives—friends who are understanding, a success for my child, realizing nobody is to blame when I know I've tried my hardest. If people criticize my parenting, I have begun to realize that this is *their* problem; it has nothing to do with me.

Acknowledge your anger.   Whenever you feel frustrated, write down your thoughts and arrange to discuss the matter with your partner at a later time. The use of anger as a weapon will decrease when you both can frankly acknowledge it is self-generated.

Recognize manipulations.   Notice your child's attempt to play one parent against the other. Consider the events that occurred just before you entered the situation. Find out what happened with the child and with your spouse during these moments.

Avoid overinvolvement.   Don't run excessive interference between your child and others. Let others deal directly with him. Be available but don't smother your child. Stand united as a couple *behind* your child, not protectively in front of him.

Expect differences in approach.   Accept the fact that you are both trying to do what is best for the child. Even if your approaches to a particular situation differ, support each other's effort without trying to pin blame. Deal with the specifics of the situation in a spirit of mutual respect and acceptance. The important question is "What is the best type of parenting for the child now?" rather than "Who is the better parent?"

Switch parental duties.   To aid your understanding of how your spouse feels, exchange roles for at least one full day. This measure is especially useful when one parent is near emotional bankruptcy. The spouse can take over while the overstressed parent receives much-needed relief. Switching duties is a cooperative adventure, never to be done with resentment or as part of one-upmanship.

Be willing to negotiate.   Remaining blindly rigid is the beginning of many destructive marital patterns. When one parent loses flexibility, the other may overcompensate in the opposite direction or fall into a one-up pattern toward the inflexible partner. Try to come to a mutually negotiated agreement, especially in a disciplinary situation.

Use co-parenting.   The principle of co-parenting is one of the most useful tools. Check with each other before giving an answer to the child's request. Find a mutually agreed-upon solution, developed by quick negotiation between both parents. The negotiation should take place immediately and in private. If you can't arrange an instant discussion, set a time of day as a deadline for giving the child an answer.

Co-parenting protects each parent from being canceled out by the child's manipulations. Playing one parent against the other suddenly becomes impossible. This technique is excellent for situations in which the child is likely to try to manipulate. Discuss with each other ahead of time those areas that can be decided individually without the need of co-parenting.

Arrange for time away.   Being a 24-hour-a-day, 7-day-a-week parent of an child with ADHD is a giant energy drain. Rest breaks, vacations, nights out, and similar opportunities to relieve stress are crucial for your emotional survival. Without them, you run the risk of becoming depressed and emotionally bankrupt. Visit friends, develop a hobby, or become active in church or community work. At a minimum, take an occasional bubble bath, sit in a comfortable chair with your eyes closed, and listen to music you enjoy.

> *It is far better to use a sitter for a few hours each week than to have your children in the care of emotionally exhausted parents.*

At least once each week, spend a few hours with your spouse in an enjoyable activity. The quality of time spent together is very important. Try to have a relaxing and intimate talk, along with periods of recreation. The most crucial part is the sharing of feelings in a romantic, mutually appreciative spirit.

Don't worry about leaving the children at home. It is far better to use a sitter for a few hours each week than to have your children in the care of overstressed, overcompensating, emotionally exhausted parents who have no opportunity to strengthen their love for each other.

Have regular business meetings.   Reserve your weekly private time together for its intended purpose—romance, not problem solving. Decisions about time schedules, meals, shopping, home improvements, and dozens of other matters have to be made almost daily. At regular intervals, discuss with your spouse the routine problems and make the decisions that constitute family leadership.

REBUILDING HARMONY THROUGH INCREASED LOVE

As you overcome destructive patterns and strengthen your marriage, family harmony will improve. Love and discipline are the twin bases for effective leadership. If there is too much or too little for each child, the family relationships become strained and children's misbehavior increases. Of the two, love is the primary need. It is the rock on which sound discipline must rest. Without love, discipline can be unauthentic and uncontrolled to the point of child abuse. The most successful method of restoring harmony in your family is to provide judicious, balanced discipline as well as genuine love to all of the children. Effective parents are very firm *and* very loving. Rebuilding harmony through effective discipline is the topic of chapter 16.

As your child's behavior improves, your approach, and that of relatives, teachers, and friends, must also change. Improvements must be acknowledged and appreciated. Be ready to discontinue your old habits and responses. Harshness or anger that formerly may have seemed necessary, for example, will become excessive. There will be fewer moments in which a raised voice or an angry look will be appropriate.

The expectation that the child with ADHD will be the primary source of irritation in most family conflicts is a difficult habit to break. As you follow the guidelines throughout this book, you will be able to see more clearly the roles of others, particularly brothers and sisters, in creating family stresses. The temptation to rely on punishments as solutions to conflict, the tendency to nag and scold repeatedly, the habit of ignoring the child's behavior, the habit of expecting the child to oppose you whenever you ask for cooperation, and readiness to have a parent tantrum are all responses that must be toned down and eventually eliminated.

> *The expectation that the child with ADHD will be the primary source of irritation in most family conflicts is a difficult habit to break.*

Injecting more love-energy into the family will be much easier if both parents share this goal. Any improvement in the marital relationship will, of course, promote family-wide love and harmony. The following activities will also help promote harmony in your family by increasing everyone's sense of being loved.

Express gratitude.   Find occasions to thank your children for doing things. Too often, children hear about the things that they *don't* do or don't do correctly. Even little acts like bringing in the newspaper or feeding a pet can be noticed and appreciated. Doing small favors provides ways for everyone in the family to show love for each other on a daily basis.

Use holidays wisely.   Make every holiday a chance for the entire family to discover more ways to enjoy each other. Show family movies, videos, and slides. Assemble picture albums and family scrapbooks. Involve your children in making greeting cards for loved ones.

Celebrate your family.   Have pictures of family members on the walls of your home. Do genealogical research together and discuss family heritage. Be alert for opportunities to give all family members a greater sense of unity and togetherness.

Conduct cooperative ventures.   Work and play together with the common goal of cooperation and companionship. The project should involve something for the entire family: planting a garden, sprucing up the lawn, cleaning out closets, cooking several meals in advance, pitching a tent, painting something, or having a picnic.

Talk about feelings. Have conversations in which family members take turns talking about gaining new insights, avoiding self-defeating behavior, being fulfilled and excited, having a success experience, or similar good feelings.

Thank each other. Expressions of gratitude sustain love. Have a thanks-sharing circle, in which the family sits in a circle and each person gives a sincere message of gratitude to another family member. Variations on this theme are endless. One family has a love message center consisting of large envelopes with pockets. Family members write notes of appreciation to each other and deposit them in the envelopes; the messages can then be read privately or shared at the weekly family council meeting.

Arrange a gift exchange. Gifts can be tangible or can involve a service or activity such as playing a game, giving a back rub, or doing a favor. The custom of giving gifts on holidays is a form of love-gift exchange.

Have special days. Give each family member a day to be "king" or "queen" and to do just about anything, including being free of the usual responsibilities and obligations. The child can have a special table setting to eat from, wear a special hat, have favorite meals, and choose family fun activities for that evening.

Pair off together. Each parent should spend some time alone with each child, who basks in the undiluted love and attention of the parent. Do a high-energy activity together that is recreational in nature and suited to the child's interests.

Competition Doesn't Belong in Your Family

Outsiders, and even your own children, may try to justify encouraging competition between siblings in your family. Here are my rebuttals to people who try to maintain that competition is somehow healthy or desirable, which it isn't:

- Human beings "herd" together and gather in groups naturally, not to show that they are "better" than each other, but to cooperate for mutual goals.

- Competition may be "necessary" in our society because of our economic system, but it is necessary only in a corporate sense. Even corporate competition requires interpersonal cooperation.

- Some "competition" is more "cooperation" than competition. Lawn games, table games, and athletics are usually more enjoyable if the competitive element is minimal.

- Interpersonal competitiveness by an individual within a group makes that person unpopular and alienated rather than an effective group member.

- The majority of economic trade activities are actually not at all competitive, but are cooperative. There is an exchange of inter-

Use surprises wisely. Weekly notes describing pleasant surprises can be included in each child's lunch box or given in some other way. The surprises can include favors and privileges, such as lunch in a restaurant of the child's choice.

Emphasize cooperative play. A regular playtime has several advantages for parents as well as for children, as discussed in chapter 17. Cooperative games can be a great help in rebuilding harmony in your family.

dependent services, groups help each other, credit and money handling procedures are cooperative, there is division of labor so that each person contributes a skill or service and has needs met by others.

- The most insecure place to be is "king of the mountain" or "number one."

- The encouraged, noncompetitive person is more likely than the discouraged, competitive person to produce "good quality" work and thus be successful in life.

- The encouraged, noncompetitive person can better withstand the blow to the self-concept when he or she doesn't "win" than can a competitive person.

- Competition breeds poor winners who egotistically lord their success over others and selfishly use their skills for self-aggrandizement.

- Competition breeds poor losers who want to quit if they can't win or who start violating the rules in a desperate attempt to win.

- Overly competitive persons are not enjoyable to play with.

Cooperative games differ from competitive games in that the factor of persons being pitted against each other is minimized or absent. Instead of a winner who defeats a loser, all players work toward a common goal. All players win if the goal is reached, and all lose if the goal is not reached.

The goal might be that all players finish their parts of the game at the same time. In cooperative Chinese checkers, for example, all players try to place their last marbles into home place on the same round. In cooperative sentence writing, the players take turns adding a new word to the sentence. Players do not communicate with each other about what the sentences will say. Any player can add punctuation in addition to a word. The sentences that result can be read aloud for everyone's enjoyment. In cooperative picture drawing, each person makes a pencil or crayon stroke during each turn, with no communication between players.

Tell a story-in-the-round.   Storytelling is a delightful family activity. The children can take turns acting out the story being told, or they can take turns adding segments to the story.

REBUILDING HARMONY THROUGH THE FAMILY COUNCIL

The family council is one of the most powerful tools for building and maintaining a new level of harmony in your family. It allows your children a voice in family affairs while providing you with a useful avenue for exercising your leadership. The family meets at an appointed time to discuss issues, make plans, voice concerns, solve problems, agree on solutions, and celebrate their love for one another. A typical family council meeting has this kind of schedule:

> *The family council is one of the most powerful tools for building and maintaining a new level of harmony in your family.*

- **Review of last week's activities.** The pleasant activities during the preceding week are discussed to refresh memories and to bring everyone up-to-date.

- **Notes from the last meeting.** Notes from the preceding meeting are read aloud. They include the issues discussed as well as the agreements, decisions, and plans that were made.

- **Personal schedules.** Transportation, child care, meals, and similar routines may need to be modified during the upcoming week. All members know where everyone is going and, in general, what everyone is doing.

- **Family projects.** The group discusses family recreational activities as well as work projects. Decisions are made about how the family will spend the upcoming weekend.

- **Chores and routines.** Any family member can make suggestions for changing daily or weekly routines about clothing, meals, housework, lawn care, pet care, car care, room cleaning, and related issues.

- **Concerns and negotiations.** Items dealing with long-range family plans, such as vacations, job changes, moving, holidays, or household remodeling are discussed. Any difficulties or conflicts that any family member is experiencing can also be discussed.

- **Recording of agreements.** One person takes on the secretarial duty of writing or tape recording the agreements and the plans made during the meeting.

- **Lesson.** A lesson involving religious, moral, or social values and including visual aids or other entertaining features is presented on a rotating basis by the various family members. Usually, the lesson consists of a presentation followed by discussion.

- **Allowances.** Financial matters are discussed, and allowances are distributed to the children.

- **Celebration.** The council meeting closes with games, singing, storytelling, refreshments, or some similar celebration of family life. With a little advance planning, the celebration can become a basis for regular parent-child togetherness for the purpose of preparing and cooking the refreshments.

Getting the Most from Your Family Council

Guard each person's right to express concerns and opinions, so your children sense their growing impact on the family's decisions. Encourage a spirit of inquiry: What is the situation? How does it look to each family member? What would be best for the whole family?

Maintain respect for everyone's viewpoint and everyone's right to make choices. As the children learn that their opinions are valued, they will put more thought into them.

The decisions in the family council are agreements; unanimous or by consensus, with each family member participating. Consensus differs from majority rule, in which those who disagree are outvoted. Agreement occurs only when all family members, not just the majority, can go along with the proposed plan of action. If no agreement occurs, postpone decisions until the next family council or use an experimental decision temporarily.

One way to help ensure a high level of openness of communication is to rotate the positions of chairperson, secretary, refreshment preparer, and lesson giver. Don't let your family council deteriorate into a gripe session. Each person expressing a complaint should present one or more suggested solutions. The emphasis is on what the *family as a whole* can do to prevent a certain difficulty from arising in the future.

The first few family council meetings should be oriented toward making plans for pleasant activities, such as deciding about weekend projects or vacations. In this way, the family can become accustomed to the concept of regular meetings without having to face difficult or touchy negotiations.

> *Through an open forum where each child feels free to communicate needs and desires, you can prevent misbehavior and rebuild relationships.*

Provide a notebook or bulletin board on which family members can write the concerns and issues they wish to discuss. Gradually the family council meetings will reduce contention among family members.

All members are invited to participate, but attendance should be voluntary. The best way to lure an uncooperative family member into participation is to conduct effective and interesting meetings. Eventually, the member will participate, out of curiosity if for no other reason. Even preschoolers can participate to some degree in family council meetings. Certainly, the younger children can help prepare or serve the refreshments. With the aid of a tape recorder, a nonreader can serve as secretary for the meeting.

By being vigilant for opportunities to encourage acts of love and caring among your children and by minimizing competition, you can strengthen the fiber that binds your family together. By maintaining an open forum where each child feels free and safe to communicate needs and desires, you can prevent misbehavior and further rebuild the relationships that make for harmonious family life.

THE CHALLENGES OF BEING THE CUSTODIAL PARENT

The struggles of the single parent of a child with ADHD are basically the same as those of other single parents, though some of the difficulties are magnified. Single parents with primary responsibility for a child with ADHD may confront problems not encountered in the two-parent family:

- **Overinvolvement.** Because of the forced intensity of your relationship, one of the most likely pitfalls is too much mutual emotional dependency. This overinvestment of energy into the parent-child bond magnifies most of the problems involved with raising the child.

- **Noncustodial visitation.** When your child is temporarily not under your direct supervision, any physiological treatment program, whether medication, diet control, or toxinsulation, is at risk.

- **The child as a weapon.** During the last part of a visit, the noncustodial parent might allow an off-limits allergenic food, chemical exposure, or skipping of medication, causing symptoms to flare up. Your child then returns home in a very symptomatic state.

- **Undercutting treatment.** The noncustodial parent may wish to impress your child with how much fun can occur during visits. Or the noncustodial parent may simply challenge the diagnosis, the need for any treatment, or the specific treatment program you have chosen.

- **Limited time and energy.** Especially if you are an employed single parent, you may have little time and energy left. The extra services your child needs to improve social relationships, self-esteem, or school adjustment may seem like more than you can deliver.

- **Fears.** Common fears are that you can't live on your own and that your children can't possibly be normal in a one-parent household.

How to Meet These Challenges

The best solution for limited time and energy is arranging as balanced and well-rounded a life as possible. Make timesaving arrangements and plan how to streamline housekeeping chores, including meal preparation. Discover and develop your whole personhood beyond your role as parent. Make sure you get adequate sleep, nutrition, exercise, and mental relief from pressures at work.

If the noncustodial parent is allowing your child to deviate from the treatment program, find out why. If the matter is open to discussion, explain the need for maintaining the program by using pre-post contrasts. Converse in a businesslike and courteous manner. Harsh confrontation won't work and reinforces attempts to hurt you and cause more upset in your life.

Let the natural consequences of treatment deviations persuade the noncustodial parent. Though you and your child will suffer from the experience, some undeniable evidence of ADHD symptoms will flare up during the visits. Refer to that fact in your attempts to regain at least a minimal level of cooperation for supporting the treatment during visits. If that arrangement seems unattainable, drop the issue and resume the treatment only during the times when your child is under your supervision and care.

Develop the attitude that "no spouse" is better than "any spouse." Make it clear to anyone you date seriously that you and your children are a package deal. Any potential future spouse should enjoy the children as much as you do and should be supportive of whatever steps are needed to give each child a successful life.

Left unattended, the stress in a family with a child who has ADHD can harm the emotional stability of a marital relationship or a custodial parent. Identify potential trouble spots early and maintain open, complete emotional communication.

CHAPTER 13

Obtain the
Best Schooling

D ESPITE RECENT FEDERAL laws to protect services for students who have ADHD, school programs for these children range from elaborate special classes to no special help. The extent of awareness and cooperation among teachers and administrators is wide, with flexible individualized approaches at one extreme and outright denial of the disorder at the other.

This chapter examines learning disabilities and how to identify them, how to obtain help through special educational and legal processes, and how to enlist teacher cooperation as you work with your child and the school.

UNDERSTANDING LEARNING DISABILITIES

Just over a century ago, observers noted learning problems in children that resembled deficits shown by adults with known brain damage. By the turn of the century, it was proposed that some developmental quirk occurred in the brains of these children. Soon the term "congenital word blindness" was introduced.[1]

Starting from the introduction of congenital word blindness, the scientific study of learning disability (LD) has always been hindered by lack of a clear definition. By the early 1970s, researchers were able to inventory nearly 40 different terms used to describe this collection of difficulties, and additional terms have been proposed in subsequent decades.[2]

Learning disability is considered a legitimate concern among many disciplines and professions, including psychology, neurology, optometry, psychiatry, speech and language pathology, neuropsychology, developmental optometry, and education. Despite its popularity as an educational concept, LD is one of the least generally understood of the major handicapping conditions.

> Learning disability is one of the least understood of the major handicapping conditions.

The current psychiatric title for learning disabilities is learning disorders, which is subdivided into four diagnoses: reading disorders, mathematics disorders, disorders of written expression, and learning disorders not otherwise specified (NOS, the "wastebasket" diagnosis). The primary diagnostic criteria are that:

1. Achievement on tests of academic skills is substantially below what would normally be expected for a child of that age, schooling, and IQ.

2. The learning problems significantly interfere with academic achievement or daily living tasks requiring skill at reading, math, or writing.

Learning disabled high school students have a dropout rate that is about twice that of their nondisabled classmates.

About one-third of LD children are from families with at least one other LD member. Learning disabilities affect more boys than girls, and these children often have a history of complications during pregnancy or delivery, head injury, infection, or exposure to toxins. Over one-half of school-age children being provided special education services have LD, and of these, 80 to 90 percent manifest their difficulties in the areas of reading and language. Dyslexia is by far the most common form of recognized learning disability.

Modern research is uncovering an assortment of apparently inherited brain abnormalities among LD students, thus verifying the initial suspicions of the pioneers in this field from the 1890s. The distribution of abnormal brain developmental problems is unique in each case, though the vast majority of individuals in these studies have difficulties in reading.[3]

Most of these deviations in the growth and placement of brain nerve cells seem to take place between the fifth and eighth months of fetal development. Normal processes are disrupted, and too many cells are placed in certain areas of the brain during this same time period.[4]

These studies provide yet another reason for my strong admonition to expectant mothers to avoid consuming neurotoxins during pregnancy. Hunting for the cause of learning disabilities in the form of postnatal brain deterioration or damage appears to be a fruitless and nonvalid quest, as the seeds for later LD appear to be sown within the womb.[5]

The pervasive, spreading nature of LD-related difficulties is intimidating. The scientific studies universally indicate that LD is a gigantic negative force in terms of social development, self-esteem, and overall adjustment throughout childhood, adolescence, and adulthood. To say that a child or teen "has learning disabilities" can mean so many different aspects of impairment that such a statement is almost useless as a way to indicate malfunctioning.[6,7,8]

The research also shows generally that teens and children with LD are at risk for low levels of:

- Self-concept
- Perceived social competence
- Sense of influence on their own fate
- Motivation to stay on-task

- Autonomy and self-directed coping
- Social acceptance by peers.

Learning disabled children and adolescents generally have impaired social competence. They use socially unacceptable behaviors when interacting with others, are less able than their peers to solve social problems and predict the consequences of their behavior, are more likely to misinterpret body language, are less likely to adjust to their listeners when carrying on a conversation, and are less likely to take into account the thoughts and feelings of others.

Several surveys have shown that compared with their nonimpaired peers, learning disabled children are less well liked and more rejected; they show more anxiety, withdrawal, depression, and impaired self-esteem. Learning disabled adolescents participate less in extracurricular activities. Children and adolescents with ADHD and learning disabilities (ADHD-ld) generally have trouble with complex social skills such as persuading, negotiating, adjusting to criticism, giving uncriti-

---

Pills for Learning Disabilities?

New research has shown that nutritional supplementation can enhance the school performance of LD students. A team of scientists enrolled LD students in a three-year program in which all students received vitamin and mineral supplements for one year, then the supplements were discontinued for some subjects. By the third year, those who had discontinued supplements after the first year were showing significant declines in academic performance and behavior, while the supplemented LD students continued to show gains in those areas. The most helpful nutrients appeared to be magnesium, zinc, B vitamins, and vitamin C.[9]

cal feedback, and resisting peer pressure. They are likely to have high rates of suicide attempts, depression, and family conflict.[10,11]

LEARNING DISABILITIES THROUGH CHILDHOOD

In the early grades, indicators of LD are severe distractibility in a wide variety of settings, reversals of letters and numbers through second grade, sloppy work, difficulty following directions, poor handwriting, poor spelling, poor reading comprehension, poor math performance, poor language arts performance, difficulty understanding concepts, poor planning skills, and inaccurate copying from the board.

These children often seem disorganized and distracted. While their sense organs and intelligence seem intact, the messages somehow get confused during their processing within the brain. The child may have 20/20 vision but confuses up with down or right with left and writes her letters backward. Or she may have perfect hearing but when asked to stand to the left of her desk, she stands to the right.

Often these children have trouble negotiating in three-dimensional space, becoming lost or temporarily disoriented. Small, clearly defined spaces are an excellent tactic. Always having the same living room chair, seat in the car, or kitchen table chair means comfort, predictability, and security to LD children. They often have difficulty with body image, not being aware of how far their body extends into space. They may perform tasks too slowly or too fast, too impulsively, or too piecemeal.

The labels applied most frequently by school personnel to children with ADHD-ld are "unmotivated," "immature," "underachieving," "bright but not working to potential," and "won't settle down." Sometimes a well-meaning teacher will not recognize a child's ADHD or learning disabilities, even though there may be definite problems in the classroom. During a conference, for example, the teacher might say that your child would get along better if she would

Learning Disability—
The Most Misunderstood Handicap

In a large national survey conducted in 1995, 38 percent of the parents of then-enrolled LD students believed their children had received less than equal treatment at school. Between 60 and 90 percent of the teachers surveyed had serious misconceptions about the definition of LD, confusing it with blindness, mental retardation, and emotional problems. Two-thirds of the general public surveyed thought that having mild mental retardation and being a slow learner indicated the presence of LD.[12,13]

sit still longer, write more legibly, slow down and take her time, not talk so much, or not hit the other children.

THE ADHD-LD CONNECTION

The parallels between ADHD and learning disabilities suggest that they stem from similar biochemical imbalances within the brain. The intrinsic relationship between attention processes, cognitive functions, and behavior makes it difficult to disentangle the various overlapping symptoms in children with ADHD and LD. Research consistently demonstrates the presence of attentional and behavioral problems in children with LD. The classic ADHD triad of hyperactivity, impulsivity, and distractibility are consistently found in research on LD students.[14,15]

In a large survey of research on behavioral difficulties in school settings for LD students, four chief factors clearly overlapped with ADHD. They were:

1. Conduct disorders.

2. Excessive off-task time.

3. Distractibility.

4. Shy and withdrawn social response.

The first three also apply to the ADHD hyperactive-impulsive type, and the last three apply to the ADHD inattentive type.

Estimates of the percentage of LD children who also have ADHD inattentive type hover around 60 percent; those who have hyperactive-impulsive type, about 40 percent. Among children with speech and language impairments, about 20 percent have ADHD hyperactive-impulsive type. About one-third of children with ADHD seem to have LD, according to most research.

> *The parallels between ADHD and learning disabilities suggest that they stem from similar biochemical imbalances within the brain.*

Language disorders are found in both groups. The most frequent additional diagnosis awarded to children with language disorders is ADHD, and about 50 percent of children with ADHD have a language disorder. One study found 91 percent of a group of LD children to have language impairments. Some researchers are now proposing that language disorders and learning disabilities represent a continuum and are often distinguished only by the fact that language disorders occur at a younger age and underlie most of the other LD deficits.[16]

Some children with LD also have impaired executive functioning or strategic problem solving, which is a core ADHD symptom. A recent theory is that dysfunctional mental flexibility and planning skills needed for strategic problem solving are common in LD and ADHD, contributing to the academic and social impairments shown by both groups.[17]

One researcher who recently surveyed over three dozen scientific journal articles concluded that LD-related impairments can evolve into at least five clusters or subtypes. The researcher could just as well have drawn the same conclusion about the various clusters of academic difficulty shown by students with ADHD.[18]

ADHD Academic Difficulties

Educationally, children with ADHD have just as many difficulties as learning disabled children. They underachieve because they don't understand or follow instructions and because they have difficulty storing and retrieving information once they have learned it. Numerous surveys comparing students who have ADHD with their non-ADHD classmates have found higher retention rates, failing grades, and need for special placement.

Here are the 17 most common areas of academic difficulty for children with ADHD. They are even more likely if the child also has LD. Many of these areas represent communication disorders; common names for specific disorders are indicated in parentheses. If you suspect any of these difficulties, seek professional advice. A breakdown in any of these areas interferes with the learning process and may signal the presence of learning disabilities.

1. **Reading.** Comprehending and decoding of printed letters, letter combinations, and words; understanding words or numbers; reading words accurately (alexia and dyslexia); understanding written directions.

2. **Math.** Performing calculations with and without paper and pencil; solving thought problems with concepts such as size, volume, or number of objects; keeping rows and columns of numbers separate; correctly placing decimals; understanding abstract concepts like times, dividing into, square root, and negative numbers.

3. **Writing.** Performing the mechanics of cursive writing or printing (dysgraphia).

4. **Attention focusing.** Sustaining attention, blocking out distractions, persisting in tasks, avoiding daydreaming.

How Do Students with ADHD Act?

From preschool through high school, the observations of teachers about these children consistently indicate nine distinctive classroom characteristics. Children and adolescents with ADHD show more of these traits, and in greater severity, than non-ADHD students:

- Being out of seat too frequently
- Deviating from what the rest of the class is supposed to be doing
- Not following the teacher's instructions or orders
- Talking out of turn or calling out
- Being aggressive toward classmates
- Having too short an attention span and being too distractible
- Bothering classmates by talking to them or intruding on their work
- Being oblivious, spacey, and daydreaming
- Turning in assignments late, incomplete, or sloppy

5. Thought processing. Understanding, organizing, prioritizing, symbolizing, and remembering; restating thoughts and concepts in similar words.

6. Visual memory. Remembering what something looks like, especially letters and numbers; remembering sequences visually; remembering written symbols used to communicate information.

7. Organizing. Sequencing—composing sentences and paragraphs within a logical order (first to last, prior to later, cause to effect); selecting important information and discarding unnecessary data;

understanding the length of time necessary for an activity; understanding the concepts of past, present, and future; labeling, classifying, and sorting information; recognizing parts of a whole; recognizing a whole when most, but not all, of the parts are present; breaking down a whole into its parts; recognizing degrees of comparison such as big-bigger or smaller-smallest.

8. **Prioritizing.** Selecting the main idea in reading, listening, or writing; emphasizing what is important to include in written compositions; discarding unimportant ideas; drawing conclusions independently.

9. **Bridging.** Remembering more than two events or instructions at once, understanding similarities and differences, relating one fact or event to another.

10. **Encoding.** Selecting the correct words with which to express ideas, producing several concepts and statements when asked to describe or talk about something (expressive language dysfunction), using correct syntax.

11. **Decoding.** Comprehending what is read; semantics—pairing of words with their meanings; receptive vocabulary and receptive language skills—understanding words read or heard (aphasia); understanding comparisons, poetry, and other abstract concepts; connecting cause and effect; recognizing oneness of objects, symbols, and words with separate identities; understanding marks, sounds, or patterns representing an object or an idea, for example: a question mark.

12. **Neatness.** Having orderly handwriting, keeping arithmetic columns vertical, turning in papers without smudges or erasures.

13. **Recall.** Remembering isolated facts, names, or dates, especially in subjects like math, science, history, and foreign languages; remembering to bring materials and completed work to class.

14. **Spatial relationships.** Knowing left from right and understanding left-to-right progression; visual perception skills such as recogniz-

ing whether an object is facing left or right, up or down; understanding and giving meaning to figure-ground perception and size, shape, and color.

15. Sound perception. Listening; discriminating one sound from another; discriminating and perceiving auditory input; sound blending; remembering sounds in sequence, such as a melody or a long word like *Mississippi;* rhythm timing; grasping phonics principles.

16. Perceptual-motor coordination. Kinesthetic awareness of position of limbs and torso; fine-motor and gross-motor coordination; visual tracking; eye-hand coordination; motor performance skills, such as acrobatics; responding to stimuli on a computer screen; legible handwriting; maintaining place when reading.

17. Selective attention. Distinguishing important from unimportant facts and activities; outlining essays and lecture notes; studying from textbooks.

GETTING HELP FOR LEARNING DISABILITIES

An effective approach starts with a comprehensive psychoeducational evaluation to pinpoint the child's learning style and identify difficulties in any of the 17 areas listed above. The evaluation should include measures of intelligence quotient (IQ), achievement (knowledge level), and aptitude (potential for learning certain skills) as well as social and emotional adjustment, classroom behavior, and level of school survival skills.

The classroom teacher can submit rating scales or checklists summarizing your child's adjustment. Speech and language problems often occur in students with ADHD. A specialist in speech disorders can assess receptive (hearing) and expressive (speaking) language. Children with ADHD often have trouble with small or large muscle coordination, though seldom with both. An occupational therapist can evaluate your child's coordination and suggest specific exercises.

Does Your Child Have Dyslexia?

Dyslexia is a Greek word meaning "reading difficulty." Dyslexic individuals have trouble recognizing letters, understanding the meaning of letters and words, associating sounds (phonemes) with letters, visually perceiving letters and words correctly, or summarizing the meaning of reading material that most readers of the same age would be able to read without error.

At school, almost every other category of performance pivots off of reading skill. If children with dyslexia are not identified and given proper interventions by age 9, they are much more likely to remain dyslexic throughout their school years. Teacher-usable screening tests are available for administration to children as young as 5 years of age. Unfortunately, most LD children are not identified until they are 8 or 9 years old and have already demonstrated many of the incapacitating symptoms of LD in their school performance.

Explicit training in phoneme recognition, referred to as phonological awareness, is a must. The most common type of dyslexic difficulty is acquiring accurate and fluent word identification skills—taking advantage of letter-sound regularities in reading unfamiliar words.

Here are 23 indicators that a youngster may have a reading impairment sufficient to be considered a learning disability. The presence of even one of these calls for a psychoeducational evaluation and Irlen screening assessment.

1. Comprehends less than half of the words.

2. Can pronounce only 90 percent or less of the words.

3. Can't summarize what the material means.

4. Can't restate facts read a moment ago.

5. Frequently uses her finger as a pointer when reading.

6. Sighs, shows an unusual breathing pattern while reading.

7. Squirms, blinks, appears nervous while reading.

8. Refuses or tries to avoid reading.

9. Shows excess lip movement and whispering while reading.

10. Reads word by word without proper flow or rhythm.

11. Ignores punctuation, gives wrong inflections.

12. Stutters or stammers when reading.

13. Reads a few words at a time, repeats the last word in each group as the first in the next group.

14. Inserts incorrect new words into sentences.

15. Omits words from sentences.

16. Partially or completely reverses words.

17. Substitutes meaningless new words for words in a sentence.

18. Holds reading material closer than seven inches from her eyes.

19. Moves her entire head back and forth with each line of type that is read.

20. Complains of blurring, double vision.

21. Often loses her place when reading.

22. Skips to the wrong line when reading.

23. Prefers dim light, complains about fluorescent light.

Activity-oriented groups such as music, dance, art, or sports can help your child increase self-confidence and expand social skills, and their suitability should be included in the assessment.

Make sure the teacher has a copy of the psychoeducational report and follows its recommendations. Have a conference and include the examiner if necessary to guarantee clear, specific recommendations that fit your child and can be used by the teacher. Proper placement in school is crucial. Don't expect your child to sit still and focus in a class far above or far below his correct readiness level.

Some children with ADHD profit from a resource class because of difficulty with some of the demands of a regular class. The emphasis in the resource room should include training in problem-solving skills that can be applied to subjects taught in the mainstream classroom. The resource room should not simply imitate the mainstream inclusive classroom.

In concert with the popular de-emphasis on labeling and categorizing children, the inclusive classroom represents a significant turning point in public education. Its goal is to integrate each child's educational experience into a regular classroom setting to the maximum feasible extent. Being placed in the regular (inclusive) classroom will be sufficient to the extent that your child:

- Wants to be in the regular classroom for most or all of the day
- Has the minimum reading, writing, and note-taking skills to participate successfully in the regular classroom
- Is likely to be accepted by his classmates
- Is willing to take advantage of friendship opportunities and other positive social growth experiences

And if your child's teacher will:

- Follow the teaching approaches given in this book or similar guidelines from another reputable source

- Have a small enough class to allow the needed individual attention to your child

- Have the necessary energy and a positive attitude

- Have a support staff and specialists with whom to consult if problems occur

- Have a cooperative relationship with you and be willing to receive as well as give counsel

- Maintain good coordination with the resource teacher

Does Your Child Have a Speech Disorder?

Speech and language pathologists are an integral part of the treatment team for students with ADHD. Various speech disorders, for example, are commonly classified as variations of LD for the purposes of addressing the academic needs of students. About two-thirds of students with ADHD have one or more of these major difficulties:

- **Fluency disorder.** Repeating sounds or words, prolonging sounds, stuttering and stammering, avoiding words, or inappropriate inhaling or exhaling while reading

- **Voice disorder.** Mutism or abnormal speech in the form of unusual pitch, loudness, duration, nasality, or resonance

- **Articulation disorder.** Absence of developmentally appropriate speech sounds, or incorrect production, such as pronouncing *r* as if it were *w*

- **Language disorder.** Breakdown in communication caused by difficulty expressing needs, ideas, or information; sometimes with difficulty understanding words the child hears or reads

- Support whatever physiological treatment approaches you choose to employ

A Bright IDEA and a Magic Number: 504

One of the most tragic ironies of special education is that it is often withheld until the child is severely behind academically, almost to the point of no return. Finally, a discouraged, depressed, disheartened child with only the slightest remnant of self-confidence about academic ability is given special instruction in a too-little-too-late attempt to make up for years of being underserviced by the schools.

> *Ironically, special education is often withheld until the child is severely behind academically, almost to the point of no return.*

You might be able to avoid such a fate for your child and secure some extra help through the legal provisions of the Individuals with Disabilities Education Act (IDEA) and Section 504 of the 1973 Rehabilitation Act. Both are civil rights laws intended to help ensure that individuals with handicapping conditions get equal access to services. The Americans with Disabilities Act (ADA) is also useful in some cases.

Like much legislation, the intentions behind these laws are more impressive than the follow-through. Even districts that act in good faith are somewhat bound by restrictive definitions of learning disabilities; thus, many children with ADHD who have severe learning problems are denied protections. Ask to talk to the "504 coordinator" of your school district or the director of special education for more details.

Help During Transitions

Any switch in schools can be difficult. The greatest such challenge for children with ADHD is a transfer from a small elementary school to a large middle school or junior high school. Besides the many new faces, large secondary schools have complicated class rotation schedules, time pressure between classes, confusing lunch procedures, and significantly reduced individual attention to learning problems. Your child needs a transition plan. Make arrangements ahead of time with a counselor, homeroom teacher, or another supportive adult at the new school.

Never leave the matter of your child's educational needs entirely in the hands of the schools. Expect to spend some time during evenings and weekends helping him compensate for learning challenges. For the child with ADHD, there are no substitutes for early diagnosis of academic problems, carefully orchestrated classroom techniques, and alert guidance through the educational process by concerned parents.

> *Any switch in schools can be difficult. The greatest challenge for children with ADHD is transferring from a small elementary school to a large middle school.*

Winning the Teacher Over

Your child's classroom teacher is the key figure in determining school success. Everything you can do to develop a positive, trusting relationship is beneficial. Introduce yourself as a parent who is not overprotective, is concerned about the needs of the other students as well as your own child's, and believes in win-win solutions. Make clear your intentions to assist the teacher in every way possible. Then offer to provide audio, video, and written materials, including the resources in appendix A "For More Help."

Teachers are more likely to respect you and cooperate if you are polite, self-assured, and firm. If you approach them as potential allies, you will usually find them cooperative and willing to work for the benefit of your child.

If the teacher makes excuses to sidestep the obligation to deal appropriately with your child, talk with the school principal or counselor and arrange for a joint conference or request a classroom reassignment.

Maintaining Contact with the Teacher

The importance of maintaining close communication is illustrated by an experience related by the parent of a child with ADHD:

Does Your Child Have a Suitable IEP or 504 Plan?

Use this checklist to evaluate the usefulness and correctness of the Individualized Education Program (Individuals with Disabilities Education Act) or Educational Plan (Section 504 of the 1973 Rehabilitation Act).

Multi-Disciplinary Approach

❏ Did the student, the student's family, school personnel, and individuals from other agencies serving the child all contribute to the plan's development?

❏ Are the types and amounts of needed special services (speech therapy, counseling, etc.) clearly indicated?

❏ Is there clear indication of who is directly responsible for each part of the plan?

Parent Involvement

❏ Has the parent seen all of the child's school records prior to participating in developing the plan?

❏ Was the parent offered a copy of the child's school records?

❏ Has the parent been informed of the qualifications of each person working with the student?

❏ Does the parent understand the results of the tests used in evaluating the student?

Objectivity

❏ Is the focus clearly on the student's needs above all other considerations?

❏ Was more than one test used in evaluating the student?

❑ Has the student been observed objectively by qualified persons other than the teacher?

❑ Is progress to be measured by objective means, other than by the opinion of the teacher?

Proactive Emphasis

❑ Does the plan include a statement of the student's strengths and weaknesses and present skill levels?

❑ Are year-long and short-term goals and objectives clear and specific?

❑ Are "start" and "end" dates indicated for the student's learning objectives?

❑ If the student is 16 or older, have transition goals been included?

Least Restrictive Environment

❑ Does the plan indicate to what extent the student will participate in the regular education program?

❑ Are special services scheduled so that the student will miss the least possible time in the regular classroom?

❑ Are in-class modifications and accommodations (for the regular classroom) included?

At school, they don't seem to understand Ryan's problems. At first, they thought he was being abused in some way and called social services. They thought the only reason a boy would be so angry and obnoxious was that he was abused. I was so hurt when the principal did this.

I have observed that a history of difficulty with children who have ADHD has prepared teachers and parents to be somewhat on guard about the support each is willing to give to the other. Let your involvement and concern be your calling card and approach the teacher as a willing partner in a joint venture for the benefit of your child.

The formula for maintaining an effective partnership with the teacher is to observe the four Cs of good communication:

1. **Clear.** No possibility of misunderstanding.
2. **Cordial.** Polite, courteous, respectful.
3. **Continuous.** Frequent contact throughout the entire school year.
4. **Complete.** No gaps, no innuendoes, no assumptions.

Communication between you and the teacher will usually occur by five methods: school visits by you, home visits by the teacher, conferences, telephone calls, and notes. Each method has its strengths and weaknesses.

One of the best techniques for keeping the teacher alert to your child's needs is to volunteer as an aide in your child's classroom. The second-best method is to visit to observe your child.

Arranging Other Help for Your Child

Research has shown that ordinary stress reduction training (breathing, concentration, and movement exercises) given over the course of a school year can significantly reduce test anxiety among students with learning challenges.[19]

Research has recently verified the helpfulness to students with ADHD-ld of constructing visual cues such as signs and reminder notes, using word associations and "cheat sheets" to aid in memory, using tape recorders and computers with spell-checkers, asking for demonstrations to supplement verbal instructions, conducting extended practice and repetition of tasks, having others read to them about material to be learned, saving more difficult aspects until last, using calculators and other mechanical devices, and using concrete manipulatives such as small plastic blocks or dominos to understand math concepts.[20]

VISUAL TRAINING—THE "EYES" HAVE IT

Vision problems are both physiological and psychological—involving both body and mind. Eyesight has to do with the sharpness of the image on the retina. Vision is psychological and applies to everything that happens after the retina starts sending its coded messages back into the brain. Most children placed in special-needs categories at school don't have eyesight problems but do have vision problems.

Vision involves over 20 separate processes and employs more than two-thirds of the nerve pathways to the brain. Nearly 80 percent of what a child perceives, comprehends, and remembers depends in part on the visual system, which helps control attention and packages information for processing by the brain. Because vision helps direct thinking, organizing, and even listening, it greatly overlaps the processes that are at risk with ADHD.[21,22]

Several scientific studies over the last few decades have demonstrated that disorders of eye accommodation and convergence affect emotional, social, intellectual, and academic functioning of children.

In one study, researchers measured eye convergence in 753 primary school children with normal vision refraction (no need for glasses). Results indicated that the children with stable convergence read, on average, at six months' higher level than students without stable convergence ability.[23]

Are You Keeping the Right Records?

Maintain a file, bin, drawer, or set of notebooks of your child's academic history. It will help you keep track of progress, prepare for meetings, and obtain appropriate educational services. Review your child's school file and request one copy of everything in it. In addition, here's what to include:

- Professional reports and evaluations
- Medical history
- Applicable special education laws
- Names, addresses, contact information for relevant organizations
- Observations and notes about your child's academic strengths and weaknesses; report cards and progress reports
- Samples of schoolwork (strengths and difficulties)
- Academic problems encountered and attempted solutions

In another study, two-thirds of the dyslexic children were unable to make proper eye convergence movements when tracking small targets moving in simulated depth.[24]

Research involving children with LD indicates that 50 to 80 percent have major deficits in one or more of the aspects of vision treatable by visual training. This research points out the high involvement of abnormalities in the visual perceptual system of LD children.[25-28]

One of the persistent difficulties for students with ADHD in classrooms is incorrect copying of material such as homework assignments from the board. The repetitive alternating between far-point and near-point vision that such copying entails often becomes disabling for students with LD or ADHD. Researchers working with school-age and college students have now verified that this skill is

- Individualized Education Program (IEP)
- 504 Plan
- Notes and results of IEP meetings
- Questions asked and answers received at teacher conferences
- Notes of visits to special education programs
- Notes of all meetings and contacts with teachers
- Letters sent and received
- Calendar of the school year
- Photocopied articles or sections of books relevant to your child's situation
- Summary letters sent and received after school conferences
- Medication records and history
- Toxinsulation records and history
- Dietary treatment records and history
- Visual training, sensory integration, other services

trainable, can be improved with vision therapy, and, when improved, aids in correction of other visually related impairments.[29,30]

A variety of perceptual training programs have been developed to assist LD children with and without ADHD. One of the most effective, though still highly controversial, is visual training. The purpose is not to strengthen eye muscles but to improve the coordination, efficiency, and functioning of the visual system. Visual training consists of an individually tailored program of nonsurgical therapeutic procedures to cure or lessen difficulties with eye tracking, binocular visual clarity, certain types of perceptual and visual information processing, binocularity (eye teaming), visual form perception, visual memory, convergence (eye aiming or alignment), eye movement smoothness, fixation (locating and inspecting a series of objects one after another, as in reading), and accommodation (eye focusing). Most of these aspects of vision are relevant for children and teens with LD and ADHD.

It starts with analysis of the child's unique visual and perceptual needs by a developmental optometrist. The examination usually covers eye movement control, focusing near to far, sustaining clear focus over a period of time, eye teaming ability, depth perception, visual motor integration (eye-hand coordination), form perception, and visual memory. This examination differs from the 20/20 vision test for refraction, which is the standard eye exam and the most common reason for glasses and contact lenses.

The typical visual training program for a child with ADHD takes from six weeks to six months. The optometrist assigns visual tasks to be performed as homework or under controlled conditions. Often, they are repetitive and similar in spirit to an athletic workout but on a much smaller scale. The emphasis is always on coordinating the eye muscles, straightening the alignment of gaze, improving the smoothness and control of eye movement, sharpening the coordination of movement between the two eyes, and improving the ability to focus for near and far vision. Simple tools might be supplied as part of the treatment, such as special lenses to look through, eye patches, or small cards to block vision in one eye temporarily.

> *R*esearch has shown a high incidence of vision problems among juvenile delinquents and children who have ADHD and emotional disturbances.

Research has shown a high incidence of vision problems among juvenile delinquents and behavior-disordered ADHD children with emotional disturbances, and that these problems seem to be related directly to antisocial misbehavior. Treatment programs that have incorporated visual training have reported significant reductions in repeat offenses among delinquents.[31-34]

Irlen Syndrome—Reading by the Colors

One common type of vision impairment is Irlen syndrome, named in honor of the psychologist who first developed a simple, effective

Visual Training—Deceptively Simple

Though visual training is pleasant and noninvasive, it may seem confusing to a child who is not helped to understand its purpose. As one teen with LD explained:

> I complained constantly. I couldn't see the sense of being yanked from my school study hall to do seemingly senseless exercises—like drawing circles on chalk boards or writing down numbers flashed on a screen or putting pegs in proper holes.

> In this case, the optometrist was training this student's eyes to work as a team—a successful treatment for which this teen became very grateful later on. Maybe you have heard of her. She is Lucy Johnson Nugent, daughter of President Lyndon Johnson.

method of correcting many of the deficits that occur in this syndrome. The child experiences distortions of print and background that cause the letters to seem to fade away, move sideways, vibrate, blur, stack up on top of each other, twirl, have shadows and halos, or in other ways become unintelligible and illegible. These difficulties typically affect other aspects of the child's performance and behavior, including increases in fidgeting, headaches, and avoidance of reading situations. The syndrome seems to become worse under bright fluorescent light and bright sunlight. According to recent surveys, up to one-half of children with ADHD have the Irlen syndrome, formerly known as word blindness and scotopic sensitivity syndrome.

Working with LD college students in the mid-1980s, Helen Irlen discovered that colored spotlight lens filters overlaid on reading material enabled dyslexic students to perceive the letters much more clearly. The technique became known as the Irlen method. It is quite simple and user-friendly for the child.

First an assessment is made using over 400 different colors of overlays to discover which hues provide the greatest help in straightening out the distorted perceptions of printed material. Once the most corrective color is discovered, overlays using that color are provided for the child to use when reading. The various shades can also be incorporated into plastic lenses worn as glasses or added to the child's prescription lenses for use when reading.

As this method became more widely known, it attracted the attention of scientists who explored the use of various colors to aid reading impaired students and found that this practice did, indeed, bring about substantial improvements in reading performance almost effortlessly.[35,36,37]

Some recent research directly assessing brain nerve pathways has added strong scientific credibility to the method. The scientists discovered faulty visual pathway processes within the brains of LD children that respond to various wavelengths of color. They also offered a credible physiological explanation for exactly why altering the tint of the background can straighten out faulty visual perception of print on paper.[38-41]

Additional benefits reported by users of the Irlen method are improved night vision, depth perception, concentration, and attention focusing. Some of the negative symptoms associated with stressful attempts at reading, such as migraine headaches and eyestrain, also reduce or disappear. The method does not solve all the problems, but it alleviates many and can easily be combined with visual training, remedial instruction, and other approaches to improve the child's reading skills and academic efficiency.

To preserve the procedure intact, the Irlen Institute provides information about this method. It also oversees the training and certification of Irlen diagnosticians at centers where the evaluations using the 400-plus colored filters can be obtained.[42]

CHAPTER 14

Ensure the Best Teaching Efforts

NUMEROUS STUDIES HAVE revealed that teachers give more negative feedback, punishment, raised voice warnings, and commands to students with ADHD than to their classmates. The average student with ADHD occupies about 15 percent of the average teacher's time and energy. Effective, successful teachers of children and adolescents with ADHD generally pursue these six major goals:

1. Learn to know the child as an individual.
2. Assist with physiological treatment (medication, diet, and/or toxinsulation).
3. Guard the child's self-esteem.
4. Help the child improve relationships.
5. Use humane, preventive discipline.
6. Adjust academic tasks to fit the child.

In classrooms where teachers don't address these areas, children with ADHD usually show increased resistance, decreased interest in schoolwork, frequent conflicts with other children, and lower grades.

LEARNING TO KNOW YOUR CHILD

The teacher should regard ADHD symptoms as a challenge, an opportunity to expand teaching skills to reach a child with special needs. When your child does poorly, the teacher should ask: "What am I doing that might be slowing this student's progress? Was the material too demanding? Should it have been broken into smaller steps? Should I have checked more often on his progress? Did the activity offer too many choices? Was his perception fragmented because of distractibility?"

> *The teacher should regard ADHD symptoms as a challenge, an opportunity to expand teaching skills to reach a child with special needs.*

The effective teacher will want to obtain a brief history from you about what other teachers have found to be effective for disciplinary as well as instructional purposes. He'll want to learn your child's particular styles of dealing with potentially threatening or stressful tasks, so that he can find ways to stimulate wholehearted participation in the class.

If your child has developed a fear of failure, gives up quickly, or refuses to try tasks that look challenging, the teacher should be alert for comments like:

> I can't do this now. I already know how to do this. I haven't been able to do it before, so why try now? I'll do it at home . . . tomorrow . . . later . . . in a little bit . . . as soon as I finish this other thing.

ASSISTING WITH PHYSIOLOGICAL TREATMENT

Surveys consistently show that teachers feel underused and isolated from physicians and parents in helping to determine the best type and level of medication treatment. This lack of coordination among teachers, parents, and physicians is a consistent stumbling block to successful treatment.

Helping with diagnosis.   In the diagnostic phase, the teacher should submit the Taylor Hyperactivity Screening Checklist (see page 37) to provide helpful indications of ADHD symptoms at school. A narrative report summarizing the teacher's concerns will also be helpful.

Monitoring medication effects.   When medications are first prescribed, give the teacher a small supply of Taylor School Medication Effectiveness Report (TSMER) forms (see page 81) with dates for mailing them already filled in. She should send a TSMER to you or to the physician weekly for one month and less frequently thereafter. To monitor medication effects if your child has several teachers each day, have the school counselor distribute and collect the TSMER forms.

Reminding about medication.   If your child is having an unusually bad day, the teacher might suspect that medication was skipped. She should not mention the issue in front of the class or speak of it within hearing range of any student. If someone discovers the pill-taking routine and brings it up during class, the teacher should avoid the issue and should inform you about what happened. It is best if your child coordinates taking of noon medication with another activity, such as going by the office on the way to lunch or recess.

If your child still forgets to take the noon medication, such forgetting is a direct reflection of medication wear-off and has nothing to do with his attitude about cooperating with treatment. Even when they understand that the faulty memory for the noon medication is proof of the need for it, however, some school personnel might balk at the idea of being asked to remind your child. The most common statement parents receive in such instances is "We believe children as old as yours should have learned to take responsibility for their own actions, including their medication."

If such conflict starts to occur, ask the physician to switch to a timed-release form to eliminate the noon dosage. A second option is to appeal to the teacher to give your child a simple, unobtrusive signal, such as "Remember our secret." The third is to provide additional structure and reminders yourself, such as by giving your child a timer or reminder notes.

Supporting diet and toxinsulation treatment.   The teacher can use the first section of the TSMER form to report behavioral improvements. Because there are no toxic or side effects to be concerned about, the rest of the form will have little use, except for the "other changes" section. The parallel to reminding your child to take a pill at noon is helping him resist temptation to eat off-limits foods, trade food with other students, or partake of snacks brought to class by well-meaning parents. Have a safe food snack available at school for your child's use whenever treats are given to the students.

GUARDING YOUR CHILD'S SELF-ESTEEM

If instructions must be stated slowly for your child, the teacher should direct the instructions to the entire class to avoid singling out your child.

Placing colorful hand-drawn smiles, stars, or stickers on your child's papers can acknowledge special effort, or the teacher may send a personal letter of encouragement to him. Such a letter would be treasured.

> *If instructions must be stated slowly for your child, the teacher should direct them to the entire class to avoid singling out your child.*

Effective teachers know the best ways to teach responsibility are to expect it and to create situations in which it can be shown. They use all the principles of encouragement discussed in chapter 9, and they minimize competition. The teacher should not display the classroom work of only a handful of favored students. Instead, *all* students' work should be displayed around the room, including your child's work. The teacher should use your child's strengths as the foundation for his classroom participation. The most successful teaching approaches maximize these strengths to help compensate for weaknesses while simultaneously attempting to strengthen the weak areas. The multimodal approach, discussed later in this chapter, is excellent for accomplishing both objectives.

There are many additional ways for the teacher to use your child's interests and talents to increase his self-esteem. For example, the teacher can acknowledge your child's hobby by having him share with classmates the steps that were necessary to complete the project. Make sure the teacher knows about these special areas for bolstering your child's feelings of success. An excellent example of this support was given by a teacher of a boy in my practice who enjoyed making backyard items in his home workshop. The teacher thoughtfully invited him to make a presentation to the class on his bird feeders and birdhouses as part of a science unit. On another occasion, he spoke about their construction and demonstrated tool safety as part of a safety and health unit.

Having Student of the Week bulletin board displays is an excellent way for any teacher to provide a positive experience for students. Another idea is to arrange for every student to write a brief statement of appreciation about the Student of the Week, then summarize all the statements and give the student the final copy.

HELPING YOUR CHILD IMPROVE RELATIONSHIPS

The teacher should try to involve your child is a social awareness program, small group discussions, self-concept exploration, or similar experiences. She can develop a group spirit and a sense of cohesiveness among the students by minimizing competition and emphasizing projects involving cooperation.

By privately explaining your child's relevant symptoms to individual classmates who are temporarily frustrated or angry, the teacher can help them better accept him. Relationships can remain smooth with well-placed statements such as: "It is sometimes hard for Matthew to sit still and to avoid talking to you, even when he knows you are trying to concentrate."

There are many opportunities at school for pairing your child with suitable prospective new friends. The teacher should coordinate with you on this project.

Discharging Extra Energy in the Classroom

Holding and Manipulating Things

Slinky	Piece of cloth (velvet, felt, silk)
Bean bag	Balloon filled with sand, salt, or flour
Worry beads	Sponge-rubber squeezable ball
Paper clip chain	Isometric grip strengtheners
Sharpening pencils	18-inch piece of string or yarn
Modeling compound	Handkerchief
Rosary beads	Worry stone
Silly putty	Agates

Helping undo the wake effect is a further step in bolstering your child's social standing with classmates. The teacher can instruct the class in the destructiveness of ridicule, scapegoating, exclusion, name-calling, boasting, and similar tactics. She can teach these skills without isolating your child or using him as an example.

Many school counselors conduct groups for children who are having relationship difficulties. Such a group, if well administered, can be of great assistance.

USING HUMANE, PREVENTIVE DISCIPLINE

The teacher should anticipate and prevent problems, rather than merely react to them. The kind-but-firm combination is best, socially and academically, for children with ADHD. Effective classroom discipline must rest on a positive, happy atmosphere and a spirit of caring and cooperation between teacher and students. The teacher should have spare pencils, paper, and facial tissues handy for minor upsets in routine.

There should be a neutral time-out area where your child can go to calm down. The area might have games, art supplies, or other ma-

Chewing on Things

Sports bottle

Cough drops

Gum

Football mouthpiece

Surgical tubing necklace

Making Regular Movements with Hands and Arms

Thumb twiddling

Note pad for doodling

Petting a small animal

Popping plastic bubble
  packaging material

Combing and brushing of arms

Putting on hand lotion

Rubbing hands together in a
  circular motion

terials. It could be in a corner of the classroom or just outside on a small bench or chair. It is most effective when there is someone available to accompany your child and talk about the incident while it is fresh. The second best alternative would be a brief discussion after school, and the teacher should inform you about the incident.

There should be provisions for music or lights that the teacher can turn on and off as a behavior-control measure. The effective teacher will realize the importance of routine and will write a schedule on the board, for example, outlining each day's activities.

The teacher will emphasize cueing and reminding as ways to prevent problems from developing. He should touch your child's arm or shoulder while giving a softly spoken, direct message that specifically indicates what your child is to stop or start doing. A private signal system can be developed for the teacher's use in reminding your child to get back on task.

The thinking teacher will not overwhelm your child with the responsibility of making too many choices in a short period of time. Your child must always be permitted to finish speaking when she has started to say something, even if the teacher would like her to stop.

Providing periodic opportunity to discharge built-up energy is also a useful strategy. Perhaps your child can assist another teacher, run an errand, or jump on mats or jog at the gym. Try to arrange a silent signal between your child and the teacher to allow for emergency energy discharge, such as a colored card your child can wave. It is also very important that your child be allowed to participate in recess.

If your child is especially disorganized about coming to class prepared, turning papers in on time, or self-control of classroom behavior, consider using the Taylor Classroom Daily Report (see page 251).

ADJUSTING ACADEMIC TASKS TO FIT YOUR CHILD

The effective teacher always tries to meet each student where that student is in terms of readiness for each assignment. There are several aspects to fine-tuning academic expectations to fit the unique needs of a student with the many possible academic snags that children with ADHD have.

Multimodal learning.   Combinations of sight, hearing, touch, movement (kinesthesis), taste, and smell can be involved simultaneously to create an integrated experience.

To teach the sound of the letter *M*, for example, the teacher has the child say "mmm" after hearing the teacher say it, as the child traces a large "M" with a fingertip on a piece of sandpaper. Because students with ADHD are often kinesthetic and visual learners, supplementing lecture with hands-on teaching is a wise idea. By writing the assignment on the board, the teacher can reinforce verbal instructions.

Individualized instruction.   One-on-one teaching is often very effective with a child who has ADHD, but it usually has to be severely rationed in most school systems. Your child is likely to make more progress with 5 minutes of individual attention and help than with 25

THE TAYLOR CLASSROOM DAILY REPORT

STUDENT _____ DATE _____

	Yes	No	Comments
Behavior—Did my child:			
Arrive on time?			
Bring needed materials?			
Remain on task?			
Participate appropriately?			
Behave correctly?			
Schoolwork—Did my child:			
Complete seat work today?			
Turn in homework on time?			
Was homework neat?			
Was it complete?			
Did it have proper headings?			
Was it according to directions?			

Overdue or incomplete work still out:

Homework given today:

Additional comments:

I request a telephone call from you if initialed: _____

_____   _____
TEACHER   PARENT

What Is Your Child's Best Learning Channel?

VISUAL	
Clues	**Teaching Tips**
• Needs to see it to know it	• Use graphics to reinforce learning (films, slides, illustrations, videos)
• Strong sense of color	
• Might have artistic ability	• Color code to organize notebook and possessions
• Difficulty with spoken directions	• Give written directions
• Overreacts to sounds	• Use flow charts and diagrams
• Trouble following lectures	• Use images and stories to help student visualize (spelling words, facts for tests)
• Misinterprets words	

AUDITORY	
Clues	**Teaching Tips**
• Prefers to get information by listening	• Allow tapes for reading and for notetaking
• Needs to hear it to know it	• Allow the student to learn by participation in interviews and discussions
• Difficulty following written directions	
• Difficulty with reading	• Encourage choose-a-partner assignments
• Problems with writing	
• Trouble reading body language and facial expression	• Have test questions or directions read aloud or put on tape

SKIN & MUSCLE

Clues

- Prefers hands-on learning

- Can assemble parts without reading directions

- Difficulty sitting still

- Learns better when physical activity is involved

- Might be very well coordinated and have athletic ability

Teaching Tips

- Use experiential methods such as making models, lab work, and role playing

- Give frequent breaks

- Change activity twice per class period

- Have the student trace letters and words to learn spelling and remember facts

- Use a computer to involve sense of touch

- Encourage walking or exercising while the student memorizes

- Encourage dance, drama, gymnastics, martial arts, band or orchestra

minutes of lecture. Providing one-on-one instruction for your child will be much easier if aides are helping the teacher. Don't be afraid to volunteer for such a duty.

Providing individualized instruction does not always mean forcing your child to work alone. Assignments can be given so he is working in small groups with other students.

Individualized curriculum.   The effective teacher should try to teach at your child's approximate achievement level. Curriculum planning should provide opportunities to exercise abilities without becoming frustrated. It is important to dilute challenging material with enough other work so the total experience is not too stressful.

Individualized assignments.   The teacher should introduce material one step at a time and divide the assigned work into units, such as three 20-minute assignments rather than one 60-minute assignment.

After each new group of concepts is introduced, it should be reviewed. New knowledge should be presented, reviewed, absorbed, tested, and integrated step-by-step with previously learned material. The teacher should allow your child to complete one activity before starting another.

> *It is important to dilute challenging material with enough other work so the total experience is not too stressful.*

The course of progress should be from simple tasks to complex ones, from mastery to challenge, and be geared to your child's particular needs.

I dislike homework in general and overburdening homework loads in particular. A rough general guideline is a half-hour daily in fourth grade, expanding to $2^1/_2$ hours in high school. A heavier homework load is probably too severe for most children and adolescents with ADHD, and I don't support giving homework under the age of 10.

Physical education.   One part of your child's curriculum that merits special attention is physical education. He needs opportunities to release energy, and a physical education class is such an opportunity. In a truly effective and creative physical education program, he can experience release of energy, control of breathing, improvement of muscle coordination, sharpened sense of balance, and knowledge of exercise and nutrition principles. These results can be attained if the physical education curriculum includes such activities as dance, relaxation training, structured exercise programs, posture and body movement training, and individual sports such as swimming, bowling, tennis, skating, golf, racquetball, handball, and archery.

To prevent any one student's feeling hurt and rejected during round-robin selection of teams, the teacher should establish permanent, well-balanced teams and eliminate the selection process altogether. An alternative would be to allow each captain to choose two players, then assign all remaining students randomly.

CLASSROOM AND DESK ARRANGEMENTS

For students with ADHD, small classes or high adult-to-student ratios are more conducive to learning than crowded classrooms. Anything out of place can be distracting. Supplies should always be in the same place, and the board should be cleaned at the start of each day. The teacher should be calm and unhurried, avoiding quick or extreme movements of the hands, fingers, pointers, or pencils.

> Your child's desk should be in an area relatively free from distractions and where supervision is easy.

Your child's desk should be in an area relatively free from distractions and where supervision is easy, preferably in the front row corner away from the door. If the classroom has clustered seating, opt for a cluster on the perimeter with your child's desk facing a wall. If your child is chemically sensitive, avoid having his desk next to a heating duct or a source of offending chemical inhalants.

If the desk is in a corner, it can be conveniently insulated against distractions by a bookcase, a filing cabinet, a blanket draped over a rope, sides of a large shipping carton, or specially constructed opaque screens. Although a screened desk may seem at first to hinder any child's sense of belonging, the opposite is usually true if the arrangement is handled properly. Your child should be invited to use a pointer or hand-held cardboard border to aid in reading. Another useful tactic is to tape onto the desk a large piece of poster board cut to be a picture-frame rectangle that outlines the desk. Using a clipboard will also help your child focus on the work at hand.

The desk should be uncluttered. The only items on it should be those necessary to complete each assignment as it is given. At other times, the desk should be cleared of all objects, with the possible exception of a brightly colored contrast mat, which can help limit his visual field during desk work.

Helping a child with ADHD in the classroom is an exciting and fulfilling challenge that represents teaching at its finest. The next chapter details methods for ensuring success on seat work, homework, tests, and the other academic tasks that represent potential difficulty for students with ADHD.

CHAPTER 15

Encourage
Academic Success

❦

THIS CHAPTER DESCRIBES the study skills and homework monitoring methods parents have found most effective for children and adolescents with ADHD.

MAKE LEARNING MORE INTERESTING

The best learning is relevant, high energy, and fun. Encourage your child to undertake creative projects. Select materials and activities for play that have an educational component. Play educational games and extract the instructional elements out of board and card games. Read to your child and find other ways to show that learning is an exciting process.

Share your joy and excitement about what your child is learning. Discuss ideas at home, sharing opinions about social and political trends that affect your community and your family. Show an interest in books, seek out informative internet Web sites, read informational magazines, and use encyclopedias and other reference materials. Attend educational programs and use the library often.

START EACH DAY WELL

When asked what parental support they most want, teachers in elementary and middle schools consistently put providing a good breakfast at or near the top of the list. Research shows that children who miss breakfast perform poorly at school in the morning. Breakfast should supply about 40 percent of your child's daily nutritional needs. By breakfast time, your child has already been without food for about 12 hours. For children with ADHD, protein consumption is somewhat more crucial than for most other people.

> *Encourage your child to undertake creative projects. Select materials and activities for play that have an educational component.*

Breakfast doesn't have to consist of the so-called breakfast foods. There is nothing wrong with a bowl of whole-grain cereal, but try to accompany it with some cheese, an egg, or meat. Creamed tuna on whole-grain toast or a hamburger patty with melted cheese would be an excellent way for most children with ADHD to start the day. A fruit smoothie with cold-pressed freshwater blue-green algae should accompany the main course. The best breakfast beverage? You guessed it! Pure water, and a lot of it.

ARRANGE AN ORGANIZED NOTEBOOK

Basic to your child's ability to stay organized is a notebook. Discourage a collection of pocket portfolios; a standard three-ring notebook is a far better choice.

Children with ADHD are less able than other students to recall what they have heard. Even their immediate memory for simple two-part or three-part requests tends to be faulty. Don't assume that your child can rely on memory without the advantage of writing down important parts of what is being taught at school. Efficient note taking improves memory and is absolutely essential if your child is to survive

Is Your Child's Notebook Organized for Success?

I recommend these features to build an effective notebook for students who have ADHD:

- Three-ring binder
- Clip inside front cover (banker's clip)
- Commercially available "notebook organizer"
- 3-hole punch to allow hand-outs to be placed in notebook
- Weekly reviewing of the notebook to keep it organized
- Sturdy weekly assignment sheet in rotating colors, under the clip
- Homework pocket or sheet protector taped to back cover
- Color coded dividers without pockets on them
- Fresh paper in every section of the notebook
- Laminated study aids, 3-hole punched
- Zipper pouch with objects to assist students: tissues, erasers, sharpener, extra pens and pencils, ruler, notes from home, school-approved snack, lunch tickets

academically. It is even more complicated than listening skills, because note taking starts where listening leaves off and involves several additional skills.

Have your child study from and take notes on 4-inch by 6-inch note cards. For written material, your child should transfer onto cards anything that could become a list, one proposed test question from each paragraph, whatever the teacher designates as likely to be emphasized on an upcoming test, and anything printed in distinctive type.

WIN THE HOMEWORK WAR

Establish a quiet, protected place for study. The chair should be straight-backed with just a little padding. Purchase or make a special study desk or table. You may want to glue a small corkboard border on the edge of the desk to keep your child's attention on the desktop and block out noises and visual interference. Provide supplies: paper, pencils, pens, erasers, ruler, clock, assignment book, 4-inch by 6-inch cards, stapler, paper clips, folders, and items for specific classes such as a compass and protractor for geometry. Store all of these study materials in one place, such as a small box or plastic bin.

Arrange nonfluorescent lighting that is not too bright. Have a special place for the finished work where it will not be forgotten the next morning, such as in a homework pocket glued to the inside back cover of the notebook.

Some parents purchase extra copies of textbooks to keep at home. Up-to-date reference books should be available, including grammar aids like a thesaurus and a dictionary. A computer and printer, of course, are helpful also.

What Will Be on the Test?

Students with ADHD should take notes on "whatever will be on the next test." The best way to tell is by the word *broil.* Your student should write it down on the next 4-inch by 6-inch card if the teacher:

- Writes it on the **board**
- Says it, then **repeats** it
- Says it will be **on the test**
- Acts as if it is **important**
- Presents it as a **list** (two or more items)

At each study session, make sure your child is neither hungry nor tired. The study desk should be free of all items except those needed that evening. Allow taped music but protect your child from all other interference and distraction, including phone calls, television, radio, and visits from friends. Consider a "do not disturb" sign. The best time to start homework is immediately after an after-school break involving exercise and a petrochemical-free protein-rich mini-meal or large snack. The second-best time is immediately after the evening meal. Refer to the clock: "It is 4:00 now; homework time!"

To avoid missing any assignments, ask the teacher to send a schedule of assignments for each week home with your child every Friday. Be available to assist but don't stand over your child's

> *At each study session, make sure your child is neither hungry nor tired.*

shoulder. Some children with ADHD require more structure and profit from the parent's actually remaining in the same room during study time. Observe the rule of 25/5: a 5-minute break after every 25 minutes of studying.

Give suggestions and support but don't do the entire task. Do the first problem or part of the assignment as a model, then stand by as your child tackles the second item or part. If a homework assignment seems particularly troublesome, assist by breaking it down into smaller segments. Or alter the sequence of steps for approaching the task by recommending doing a certain part of the work before proceeding to other parts.

If your child has a history of school difficulties, think seriously of purchasing or borrowing a computer. Numerous computer programs ensure successful learning and thereby bolster sagging self-confidence. The computer embodies many of the characteristics of a skilled special educator. It gives your child undivided attention, individualizes instruction to any readiness or skill level, responds with positive and encouraging feedback, accommodates any working pace, teaches skills in small steps, provides incentives for learning, repeats a task or question until

Links in the Homework Chain

There are 13 breakdown points between a teacher's assigning homework and a student's turning it in on time and with satisfactory quality. Find out which links in your child's "homework chain" are weak, and repair them:

1. Realize an assignment is being given

2. Understand the assignment

3. Record the assignment accurately

4. Understand how to perform the assignment

5. Check to bring correct books home

6. Arrive home with materials and homework assignment

7. Begin homework on time

8. Complete all homework

9. Check that it is complete, accurate, and neat

10. Set completed homework in a special place

11. Take completed homework to school

12. Arrive at class with completed homework

13. Turn completed homework in on time

the principle involved is learned, informs continuously and immediately about progress being made, is fun and entertaining, minimizes failure and frustration, and measures areas of relative strength and difficulty.

OVERCOME DISTRACTIBILITY

Their distractibility causes some children and adolescents to fritter away homework time. Here are nine methods many parents of students with ADHD have found helpful:

1. **The stopwatch.** Tell your child to produce a certain number of minutes of *on-task* study during the study period. Wasting time simply extends the period he has to remain studying.

2. **Irregular check-in.** Every so often, check on what your child is doing during the designated study period.

3. **Self-monitoring.** Suggest a useful self-reminder, such as "I need to get back on task."

4. **Segmented tasks.** Keep the tasks as short as possible and arrange a pause for reviewing each segment.

5. **Work before play.** No other activity is permitted until the study time has met the criteria you have set. The best time for homework is after school, before dinner and any other activities.

6. **Staggered tasks.** Vary the tasks by alternating hard and easy or liked and disliked subjects.

7. **Distraction control.** Remove sources of distraction, such as television.

8. **Sequenced tasks.** Save hard items until last. "If you can't get it in two minutes, drop it and try again later."

9. **Increased meaning.** Magnify the meaning and relevance of the assignment by explaining its usefulness and direct applicability to your child's life.

REINFORCING READING SKILLS

The best remedial reading program for most children with ADHD is multifaceted; it emphasizes phonics and ensures mastery at one level before proceeding to the next level.

Poor readers have difficulty understanding what they read by how it sounds. Skilled readers, on the other hand, depend on how the written material looks as well as how it sounds. Children with ADHD who have difficulty reading usually profit from training in phonics and breaking words into syllables and common letter combinations. Although becoming familiar with configuration—how words look— might help a little, the major victory in learning to read is knowing how the letters and words sound. Your child needs to know the sounds of the individual letters, the sounds of common letter combinations, and the rules for piecing together the parts of words.

Individualized instruction in phonics is usually superior to small group instruction. If your child is having trouble, placement in the slow reading circle might not be sufficient remedial reading. Follow your child's progress and ask for more help from the school if there is little improvement. At the same time, I recommend providing supplemental phonics instruction at home. The best methods are to play with phonics flash cards for 10 minutes each evening and to have your child read to you. Whenever your child makes a reading error, tactfully explain the phonics principles or letter sounds involved. Give your child a sense of having learned something important and having conquered a new word. Maintain a "my new words" list to help your child celebrate these successes.

HELP YOUR CHILD PREPARE FOR TESTS

In reviewing for tests, typed notes are easier to study than handwritten lecture notes. Typing the notes forces your child to rethink the material and aids understanding. Reading aloud is a more efficient way to remember the information than silently reading the notes.

Several short review periods provide better preparation for a test than one long cramming session. A good plan is to devote at least 15 minutes of study each day, starting on the day the test is first announced.

Active review and rehearsal provide the best memory strengthening. Encourage your child to go beyond simply memorizing unconnected facts or lists. Help her examine the underlying issues,

Teach Phonics the Easy, Fun Way

Understanding the sounds of letters and letter combinations (phonological awareness) is crucial. Teach these word analysis skills:

- **Matching.** Do <u>dog</u> and <u>dig</u> begin with the same sound?

- **Deleting a phoneme.** What word happens when you take the /<u>m</u>/ sound away from <u>mat</u>?

- **Breaking into segments.** What sounds can you hear in the word <u>goat</u>?

- **Blending.** What word consists of /c/, /u/, /p/?

- **Initial bookending.** What is the *first* sound in <u>nice</u>?

- **Extracting.** What is the *middle* sound in <u>nice</u>?

- **Final bookending.** What is the *last* sound in <u>nice</u>?

- **Phoneme counting.** How many sounds are in the word <u>think</u>?

- **Phoneme deleting.** What sound in <u>think</u> is missing in <u>ink</u>?

- **Initial bookend discrimination.** What word starts with a different sound: <u>cup</u>, <u>can</u>, <u>dine</u>, <u>carve</u>?

- **Extracted sound discrimination.** What word has a different sound in the middle: <u>bun</u>, <u>tan</u>, <u>run</u>, <u>fun</u>?

- **Final bookend discrimination.** What word ends with a different sound: <u>fun</u>, <u>sub</u>, <u>tub</u>, <u>cub</u>?

- **Sound matching.** Is the /n/ sound in the word <u>tuna</u>?

concepts, and relationships. For lists, self-quizzing is a useful technique, facilitated by a cassette recorder, commercially prepared or homemade flashcards, and the 4 by 6 cards from notes in class.

When using a cassette, your child records vocabulary words and their definitions, spelling words and their spellings, states and their capitals, historical events and their dates, or any similar facts. There should be a brief pause between each entry and its matching answer; for example, "Vitamin A . . . carrots." Then your child can self-quiz by listening to the first item of each pair, answering out loud during the pause, and comparing her response with the correct answer.

> *Even when they are receiving medication, sleep and nutritional factors are the two most common sources of day-to-day variation in the mental functioning of children with ADHD.*

Pacing the floor, riding a stationary bike, or lifting weights while someone provides a mock quiz is an excellent way for a student with ADHD to practice for a test. Those 4 by 6 cards are the mainstay for the studying.

Have your child get to sleep early the night before a test and arise early to review. Even when they are receiving medication, sleep and nutritional factors are the two most common sources of day-to-day variation in the mental functioning of children with ADHD. That nutritious, additive-free, protein-rich breakfast will also make a big contribution to your child's test-taking success.

HELP YOUR CHILD WITH INDIVIDUAL SUBJECTS

Handwriting.   If difficulties with handwriting hamper your child's school performance, four basic adjustments are possible. One method is to negotiate with the teacher regarding the form of the work. Perhaps assignments could be presented orally, through tape recordings, by transcription expressed in your handwriting, using printed letters rather than cursive writing, or with a word processor. Another method is to arrange for fewer assignments requiring handwriting.

The third method involves tutoring and practicing handwriting skills, letter by letter, at home. Have your child write extra-large letters, approximately five inches by eight inches. Pay careful attention to the sequence of strokes or letter parts and follow the sequence being taught at school. Gradually reduce the size of the letters until they are the correct size for normal handwriting. Drill for about five minutes each evening until the handwriting improves. The last method, which asks the least of the teacher, is to allow increased time for completing written assignments.

Better handwriting is the most frequently cited academic change reported by teachers of children with ADHD who start the Feingold program or prescribed medication. Therefore, adjusting the physiological treatment is often an integral part of helping a child with ADHD improve his handwriting.

Spelling. Help your child learn the meaning of the spelling words by explaining how each word can be used. For an especially difficult or unusual word, look up its root (often Latin, Greek, or Old English) that helps explain its spelling.

Devise simple humorous statements to help recall a letter sequence. If your child is having trouble remembering the *a* comes before the *u* in *gauge*, give an example such as:

> Two people are riding in a car. One thinks they might run out of gas.
> The other says, "*Aw, you [a, u]* are wrong   look at the *gauge!*"

Incorporate the sounds of the words into the studying by helping your child learn to pronounce each word correctly. If a word obeys common phonics principles, refer to them: the *e* at the end of a word is usually silent, every syllable requires a vowel, *i* before *e* except after *c*, and so forth.

Combine several channels of learning by using the multimodal approach discussed in chapter 14. Have your child trace the letters (sense of touch and muscle control), see the tracing (visual), say the letters out loud (vocal), and hear the word and letters spoken (auditory).

Touch and Spell

The sense of touch is a powerful channel on which to teach most children with ADHD. Successful teachers are using textures and techniques such as these to teach spelling:

- Materials placed on student's desk (burlap, corduroy, carpet sample, window screen, sprinkled-on salt, sandpaper)
- Sandpaper with the word already printed on it with a marker
- Student writes on own arms, hands, legs
- Student writes on other student's back (guessing game)
- "Magic slate": an upside-down shoe box lid with cornmeal or oatmeal in it
- Pudding-like mixtures (peanut butter mixed with honey, cornstarch mixed with water)
- Squishy or jelly-like substances in a reclosable plastic food storage bag

Another method is to play the "spelling teacher game." Let your child teach you the words on the list by pronouncing them and then spelling them out loud. You can even have a mock oral or written test, in which you purposely make some errors for your child to catch. The manual alphabet used by the hard of hearing is another excellent way to teach spelling, because it involves skin and muscle senses. Your child pronounces the letters while giving the manual version at the same time.

Math.   If your child has trouble with word problems, part of the difficulty could relate to reading comprehension. Explore that possibility before you conclude the fault lies in difficulty with mathematics concepts.

Perceptual problems can pose a special challenge. Poor figure-ground perception would cause your child to have trouble deciphering which parts of the math problem have been included as a distraction and which parts are important for obtaining the answer.

Other perceptual problems include lining the numbers straight down the paper, keeping the decimals in the correct position, subtracting downward rather than upward, progressing from right to left when multiplying, and so forth. The best solution to these problems is to arrange with the teacher to have your child use graph paper or regular lined paper turned sideways. To prevent orientation errors (up-down, left-right), teach your child some simple self-reminders: "Make sure things add *up*." "*Sub*tract means go *down* like a sub(marine)."

Memory problems also plague mathematics efforts. Often children with ADHD have not memorized the necessary addition, subtraction, multiplication, and division facts or the decimal equivalents of fractions. One of the best ways to strengthen this area is to play a game of rhythmic chanting to the sound of a drum or hand clap: "3 times 2 is 6; 3 times 3 is 9; 3 times 4 is 12," and so forth. Because money is based on the decimal system, coins and dollars provide convenient and effective examples of fractions and percentages. A quarter, for example, is 25 percent of a dollar as well as one fourth of a dollar.

The abstract concepts that abound in mathematics sometimes represent formidable stumbling blocks to the student who has ADHD. Ideas such as square root, infinity, negative numbers, ratios, and logical proofs can confuse any child who tends to think in concrete and literal terms. The best approach is to find a factual example of the abstract concept. Have a box with many small parts in it, such as miniature plastic building blocks, pennies, checkers, marbles, or buttons.

HELP YOUR CHILD PREPARE LONG-TERM ASSIGNMENTS

Long-term assignments are especially troublesome. If the teacher will not agree to letting your child turn in segments of the work, make sure she works at least 15 minutes nightly on them and builds steadily toward completion of the task. The master chart (described in chapter 16) will help greatly. Check regularly to see that your child has entered all long-term assignments and upcoming tests on it.

For book reports, your child should write the major event or idea from each page of the book on a 4-inch by 6-inch card. The cards can then be sorted by topic, forming the basis of the outline for the report.

USE A STUDY BUDDY

An increasingly popular method among teachers of students with ADHD in mainstream and self-contained classrooms is peer monitoring. A reliable classmate functions as a teacher's aide to help your child. You pay a reasonable fee (a pizza per month, for example) to the study buddy for this service.

Selecting a private school is an option preferred by many parents of children with ADHD. A comprehensive psychoeducational evaluation is a helpful first step. Obtain a directory of private schools from a library and carefully investigate each prospective school. Be frank and assertive when inquiring about any school's ability to meet your child's educational needs. Make lists of these needs and then compare what each school offers with your criteria. On-site visits are much better than catalog shopping for private schools.

Home schooling is another option that is catapulting to great popularity. Currently, about 3 percent of school-age children in the United States are educated in their own homes. If you have the necessary time, patience, and ability, and if the public and private schools seem less likely to meet your child's needs, home schooling may be a viable option. Home-schooled children consistently outscore class-room-educated children on achievement tests.

Concerns about limiting your child's social experiences, frequently given as an objection, shouldn't prevent you from considering it. Many home-schooled children experience gains—not losses—in social contacts, both in the quality of supervised contact and the number of new friends. The best way to ensure success is to purchase texts and workbooks specifically published for home schooling or obtain copies of the materials used in the public schools in your community. You will need to register with your local school district or the office that keeps records of home-schooled children.

KEEP YOUR PRIORITIES STRAIGHT

Although academic achievement is a prominent issue and certainly merits your concern, don't sacrifice the bonds of family love to enforce academic goals. Even if your child continues to have difficulties with arithmetic and handwriting, the long-term results are not extremely damaging. Personal computers are suitable substitutes for penmanship, and hand-held calculators can overcome many arithmetic deficiencies.

> *Don't sacrifice the bonds of family love to enforce academic goals.*

By teaching good study habits, monitoring homework, providing support for long-term assignments and tests, starting each day with a nutritious breakfast, and investigating alternative education, you can help your child gain increased academic skill and confidence. With consistent effort, you can make education much more fulfilling and exciting for your child.

CHAPTER 16

Prevent and Counteract Misbehavior

P ARENTS OF ADHD children often exhaust their supply of disciplinary techniques in a desperate attempt to stop the relentlessly continuing misbehavior. They try everything from talking quietly to spanking severely, but nothing works for long. Rewarding, ignoring, explaining, time-outs, pleading, punishing, depriving of privileges, and every other tactic seem to have the same fate—ineffectiveness. The bottom line is that nothing works until the physiological cause of the ADHD is stopped or muted through medication, dietary changes, toxinsulation against chemical irritants, or nature's method of hormonal changes during adolescence.

Your discipline attempts have little to do with your child's continuing misbehavior. To be realistic about discipline, stop overdoing it. Harshness and severity do very little except make things worse.

If I were to summarize in one sentence what my experience has taught me over the past three decades of assisting parents of children who have ADHD with discipline, it would be: "Get the emphasis off after-the-fact discipline and put it into prevention and supervision."

PREVENT MISBEHAVIOR WITH THE FOUR S'S

Refocus your disciplinary efforts away from the retroactive "gotcha" mentality to proactively motivating your child toward desired behavior. Four key principles, all beginning with S, can help save your sanity as you learn how to cope with ADHD misbehavior.

> *Misbehavior reflects unmet needs. If you keep your child's needs met, misbehavior disappears.*

1. Schedule need-meeting activities. All misbehavior reflects unmet needs. If you keep your child's needs met, misbehavior disappears.

2. Structure. Carefully place and arrange objects ahead of time and follow orderly processes and routines to prevent problems from occurring.

3. Supervise. During any activity, check periodically to make sure your child is proceeding correctly; deal with problems while they are still manageable.

4. Support. To ensure continued success, provide instruction on any changes needed next time and offer encouragement.

Schedule Need-Meeting Activities

External order compensates for the internal chaos children with ADHD experience. Establish routines at every potential high-stress event—arising, mealtimes, doing chores, after-school hours, and preparing for bed in the evening. Maintain the routines as much as possible. Explain why significant temporary changes in routine are necessary.

Inadequate sleep is probably the most common reason why children with ADHD have bad days. It is also one of the most controllable factors for preventing bad days. Although children vary in their need for sleep, most toddlers require 10 to 12 hours nightly. By the time they enter first grade, they should be sleeping 10 or 11 hours nightly. Elementary-school students should get about 10 hours of sleep, and the ideal duration for teens is 9 hours.

Use Structure Wisely

Preventing discipline problems requires the thoughtful placement of objects. Examples: Don't leave money on the dresser in an unlocked bedroom while you are away. Don't have food available that is apt to trigger an S-R state in your child. Set out clothing needed for the next day. Have schoolbooks in a special place so they won't be forgotten in the morning.

Charts provide constant reminders and are silent and efficient substitutes for your memory and your tongue. Put the steps your child is supposed to follow onto charts, using pictures if she is too young to read. I have found the four charts listed here especially useful for families with children who have ADHD.

1. Fun Idea List

This list of fun things to do can be extremely useful for preventing discipline problems. For children with ADHD, boredom is one of the major contributors to misbehavior. At the first feeling of boredom, your child can consult the fun idea list for something to do. Invite her to use the special phrase "I'm bored" whenever boredom sets in. I have found the "I'm bored" phrase very helpful in preventing arguments and misbehavior. The few moments spent helping your child find something constructive to do pay off richly.

The fun idea list should be mounted low enough to be easily seen and should include various categories of activities: indoor and outdoor, quiet and active, alone and with other children. In just a few minutes, you can come up with dozens of ideas, and you can supplement your list with additional ideas from time to time. Detailed suggestions for the fun idea list and a fun idea drawer can be found in appendix F.

2. Chore Chart

Simple chore charts let each family member know instantly who is supposed to do what chore each day or each week. Review chores at family meetings and post them on charts. You may need to compensate for the common sensory integration problem among children with ADHD of not sensing the internal cues for the passage of time. Simple chores can be completed in short periods of time, and a small timer may help give your child a sense of the passage of a few minutes. An instruction such as "You have 10 minutes to pick up the toys" or "You have 5 minutes to finish watching TV" can be reinforced with the timer.

3. The Master Chart

Make a master chart for each quarter and mount it on a wall in your child's room to remind him of deadlines and appointments. Have all waking hours in large blocks of paper and include school-related tasks; long-term assignments; test dates; appointments; extracurricular programs, meetings, events, and activities; visits during the evenings and weekends; and similar information. Have your child pencil in his class hours, mealtimes, travel times, work hours, and regular activities.

4. The Daily Activities Chart

Start with the skeleton of each day, divided into half-hour segments. Write down the proposed daily schedule on a large chart and mount it on the child's bedroom wall or closet door. Fill in the spaces with the activities for the day. Consider including coming home from school as well as household chores, after-school snacks, homework, extracurricular activities, recreation, personal time, entertainment, socializing, mealtimes, and church or scout activities.

Here is a sample of the afternoon and evening portion of the daily activity chart.

3:00–3:30	Arrive home, snack, and rest
3:30–4:00	Homework
4:00–4:20	Break
4:20–4:50	Homework
4:50–5:15	Practice piano
5:15–6:00	Play outside

6:00–6:40	Dinner and cleanup
6:40–7:20	Homework and flashcards
7:20–7:30	Tidy room
7:30–8:30	Free time
8:30–8:45	Protein snack
8:45–9:00	Prepare for bed
9:00	In bed, tuck-in, and tapes

Supplement the structure of charts by thoughtfully arranging your child's day to prevent flare-ups of misbehavior. Remember that ADHD symptoms operate on several overlapping cycles and that a daily cycle is one of them. When you schedule an activity, consider your child's readiness at different times of day.

Have alternative plans available when weather or transportation problems occur.

For a very distractible child, keep the stimulation level low by allowing visits from only one friend at a time or permitting only one toy at a time. If your child is working at a table, clear it of all objects except those needed for the activity. Turn off chaotic background TV and radio noise. Designate a room or part of a room for arts and crafts work, reading, imaginative play, or brief computer games.

When the events at home are scheduled and predictable and your home is orderly, with things in their proper places, your child will be less likely to become overstimulated or confused.

Make changes slowly and gradually whenever possible. Deviations in routines or furniture arrangements should be announced ahead of time. It is better to say "Five more turns" to bring a game to a close than to announce suddenly that the game is over.

How to Make Requests

Approach and touch your child rather than giving only verbal direction from a distance. Avoid showering with commands. If you want toys to be picked up, for example, stand next to your child, pick up one toy, put it into the proper bin, then say, "Please pick up the rest of the toys now; I'll be back in five minutes." Make a definite statement rather than asking a question. Avoid an apologetic "Okay?" at the end of your statement. Don't haggle or negotiate. Take a firm position, state clearly and concisely what you want, and stick by it. Word your requests in positive terms. In a theater, say "Whisper" rather than "Shhh, don't talk so loud." Say "Please carry your coat" rather than "Don't drag your coat."

If your child has trouble understanding more than one request at a time, state your request in simple, clear, one-concept statements. Have him repeat the request to you if necessary. Speaking slowly is also helpful, as is writing the request. Be willing to show your child what to do, in addition to telling him.

Schedule Personal Private Interviews

Have a special interview with your child in a private place such as the bedroom. Schedule it weekly at first. Your role is similar to that of a newspaper reporter. You want to discuss how your child is doing in the major areas of day-to-day living. Review her academic performance and needs, social life, material needs, medical needs, and her roles within the family, including chores and responsibilities.

In preparation, each of you should have a "concerns notebook." An attractive, clever picture of a worried person, a cartoon figure, or a funny animal and a title such as "These Are My Concerns" will give the notebook special appeal.

> *Regular private interviews with your child can keep problems small and manageable.*

Parents of children with ADHD who have used this method marvel at its simplicity and effectiveness at keeping all of their children's problems small and manageable. Issues never fester unnoticed but instead are dealt with in an open and direct atmosphere of mutual respect and frankness. Children and adolescents with ADHD who can bring their concerns to their parents with confidence that they will be listened to and respected do not need to resort to misbehavior or tantrums.

Are You Keeping Your Child's SOCs On?

Summers can be especially difficult for school-age children. Arrange activities to minimize the likelihood of misbehavior during summertime by keeping your SOCs on. Choose:

- **Structured activities,** rather than unstructured time
- **Outdoor activities,** rather than indoor ones
- **Companion activities,** rather than leaving the child to play alone

Respond to the expressed concerns with decisive action toward a change for the better, so that your child experiences direct benefits from the personal private interview (PPI). You want the entire procedure to teach assertion and negotiation. There is no need to give final answers to requests during the interview. Simply arrange a date by which you will have a response ready. The PPI is not a blank check; it is an assurance that you will address the expressed issues.

An additional advantage of this system is that it can assist when you must have instant obedience. Introduce this procedure for obeying ahead of time:

1. Your child complies with your request now.

2. She writes down her frustrations about the event in her concerns notebook.

3. She shares the concern at the next PPI.

So when you simply must have instant obedience and there is no time to deal with the issue, say, "Write it down in your concerns notebook and I'll talk with you about it. But right now do as I ask." Then keep your word and deal with the issue at the next PPI, including making amends if your child has a legitimate complaint about how things occurred during the crisis.

Supervise to Prevent Misbehavior

Children with ADHD tend to lie, omit information if not asked directly for it, selectively perceive and remember facts and sequences of events, and use questionable judgment and limited observational skills about themselves and others. The net result is lowered trustworthiness. My experience has been that parents often simply cannot afford to believe what their child tells them, even though they wish they could. They sense their intimacy with the child is disrupted as a result.

Use close supervision and don't rely simply on the honor system. Outline what you expect, then check for compliance. Clearly state behavior guidelines. Decide in advance how you and the child will both know when a rule is being observed or when it has been broken.

Suppose the rule is that homework must be completed, checked, and corrected before the TV is turned on. The method for enforcing the rule is to have your child bring the checked and corrected homework to you; after you have examined it, you allow the television to be turned on.

You can influence your child's decision making through your example, reasonable rules, calm discussion, and personal private interviews. Don't expect, however, to be able to control all of your child's decisions even with the best supervisory techniques.

Provide Emotional Support

Confronting your child should be a two-sided instructive process. He should learn about better behavior choices, and you should learn more about his needs. I developed the I CARE sequence to assist parents of children with ADHD, and I have found it to be a highly effective method of confronting any misbehaving child. The first letter of each segment is the key to giving support and encouragement:

Are Your Rules Reasonable?

Here are general guidelines for making and enforcing rules that are reasonable and that work well for children with ADHD. Try to provide:

- **Positively-worded rules.** Be sure to include specific actions you want your child to take. Instead of, "Don't be mean to your sister," say, "Show her how to dress her doll."

- **Segmented assignments.** Break complicated tasks into smaller units.

- **Written rules.** Write specific instructions and post them.

- **Illustrated guidelines.** Post a photo of the straightened bedroom or tucked-in bedcovers as a visual standard for room cleaning, for example.

- **Child-specific rules.** Keep rules reasonably in tune with your child's age, judgment, memory, and activity level.

- **Important rules.** Confine rules to issues that really matter when health, safety, social learning, personal development, or key family processes are at stake.

- **Realistic rules.** Make enforceable requests, such as "Be sure to ask before borrowing your brother's sweater," rather than, "Don't do anything that your brother doesn't like."

- Interrupt.

- Cool off.

- Affirm.

- Redirect.

- Educate.

Let's suppose that your son, Matt, is bothering his little sister, Melissa, again:

Interrupt

Move people or objects. When you send the children off in different directions, they must face a new set of issues having to do with your presence and your involvement.

Use the code word *huddle* as you call your child aside for a quick talk. Be calm in your approach and agree with him ahead of time that either of you can call a huddle whenever there is something amiss.

> Matt [you go up to Matt and gently pull him away from Melissa], this is the third time you have made her cry in the last hour. I can tell Melissa's bugging you and you're bugging her.

Cool Off

Send your child to a time-out place such as his bedroom for a few minutes before discussing the event. Refer to the time-out place as your child's quiet place, relaxing place, or calming-down place and the period of time as a quiet time, relaxing time, or calming-down time. If your child bites, scratches, lashes out, and refuses to go, gently nudge or carry him. Tell him you will be back shortly. Urge your child to write down his concerns or to lie on the bed to calm down.

At the same time, take advantage of the moment to gather your composure and do your own cooling off. When you are ready, enter the room and sit next to your child. This procedure differs markedly from ordinary time-out in that the main emphasis is that you have calmed down, whether or not your child is calm.

Affirm

Start with empathy for your child's feelings and convey your concern. Empathy includes these six actions:

1. Listening ("Tell me more about how you feel.")

2. Understanding ("I understand how you feel.")

3. Accepting ("I accept your feeling as real and valid from your point of view.")

4. Identifying ("I would feel that way too.")

5. Caring ("I wish you happiness and don't want you to have this painful feeling.")

6. Desire to help ("How can I help you so you'll feel better?")

The universal empathy statement to make to your child when you can't think of what else to say is: "This is a hard time for you, isn't it?"

Include as much affectionate touching or holding as he will allow during this step. If touching or holding seems unacceptable, proceed with the conversation while simply sitting nearby.

> This is a hard time for you, isn't it, Matt! Are you mad at Melissa about something? [Matt answers yes.] Well, I want you to feel happy about being home with her today, not feel bugged by her. What's going on? [Matt explains.] I know you can be so kind to her when you want to! You often help her color the pictures in her coloring book, and she likes it when you read to her. Your daddy and I love you a lot, Matt, and we want you to be a happy boy.

Redirect

Steer your child in a new direction, perhaps toward re-entering the situation with a new mind-set. This is an especially prudent moment to use the fun idea list for instant access to entertaining activities. Often it is better to save this step until after you have proceeded through step E: Educate.

Since you seem to be having a hard time enjoying being with Melissa today, let's take a look at the fun idea list and get you started on something interesting.

Educate

Explain clearly in simple terms the exact domino effects of the misbehavior, along with the natural consequences likely to develop as others react.

Now Melissa doesn't want to be with you because she feels hurt that you threw her toys and insisted that she play your game. She will probably want to play with you in a little bit, but she's not going to want to continue playing with you if she can't have a more pleasant time with you.

> *Find legitimate channels for meeting whatever needs seem to be reflected by the misbehavior.*

The events that occurred in the few minutes preceding the incident provide important clues to the reasons for the misbehavior. Find legitimate channels for meeting whatever needs seem to be reflected by the misbehavior. Ask what can be learned from the event and what can be changed so that next time can be better. Label the misbehavior as a mistake and clearly give better alternatives for next time.

What could you say next time when she asks you to play but you don't want to play what she suggests?

If your child answers, "You should make Melissa act differently," respond with "Yes, but what can *you* do to help make things turn out better?" Use the think-of-another-way approach: "What is another way you could handle this situation next time that would work out better for you as well as for your sister?"

This step is the hallmark of the I CARE method. It is a much more effective confrontation than the usual harsh, angry dialogue that ends up creating more problems than it solves. It is best to have all of your disciplinary interventions be instructive. It is easy to develop the habit of exaggerating and overemphasizing the point you want to make in an effort to "reach" the child. The E, however, stands for Educate; it is not an L for Lecture.

In discussing better choices of behavior for next time, stimulate strong moral values for these choices. Clear, polarized options help children with ADHD order their thinking about moral choices. Left to their own devices, many children are too suggestible, impulsive, and deficient in pondering future consequences to process complicated moral decisions. Be firm and blunt, simplifying the moral choices so that they are between good and bad, smart and dumb, or kind and mean behavior. The older your child, the less polarized these labels should be. It is much easier to loosen overly high standards as children mature and gain life experience than to tighten standards that have been too lax. Of course, avoid labeling the children themselves as bad, dumb, or mean.

> *It is much easier to loosen overly high standards as children mature than to tighten standards that have been too lax.*

Sometimes, you will not have the opportunity to use the entire I CARE method. Under those circumstances, provide temporary emotional support through empathy and touch, and maintain a thread of communication to prevent total withdrawal. Be an impartial referee between your child and the circumstances or other children.

DEFUSING OPPOSITIONAL DEFIANCE

Oppositional defiant disorder is the most common comorbid psychiatric condition among children and teens with ADHD. To minimize conflict at a tense moment, make clear, concise, directive statements. Approach your child so you can talk in a normal volume from a courteous distance. Stand within an arm's length. Try not to steer or direct your child with words from far away. In general, keep the amount of verbal directives low. Stoop, kneel down, or sit facing a young child.

Are You Correcting or Criticizing?

Here is how to confront your child about misbehavior or poor decisions in a way that doesn't devastate self-esteem. Are you correcting or just criticizing?

Effective confronting	Ineffective confronting
(Correcting)	(Criticizing)
Child's opinion is sought	Child is told what to think
Two-way communication	One-way communication
Parent listens, child talks	Child listens, parent talks
Child has choices, options	Child is told what to do
Child's logic is discovered	Child's logic is ignored
Ask leading questions	Preach

Wait until he is quiet, obtain eye contact, then give your instructions
in simple terms. Don't assume he will understand and remember your
message; ask him to repeat it, if such a request does not cause conflict.

For a very contrary child who simply won't listen, I have found
that making a special "deal" sometimes bridges the gap. I call it the
ticket-to-talk method. Introduce it as a way for your child to feel less
nagged at by you. The deal is that you agree to give no more than
three sentences of instruction or correction. In exchange for being re-
lieved of "lectures," she agrees to "really listen" and take to heart
what you are saying. Although it is not the best parent-child communication, it is useful to prevent a deadlock and keep some communication flowing. Severe communication problems require the assistance
of a skilled counselor.

If your child is completely out of control in a dangerous situation,
you will have to restrain him physically. Approach him from behind,
so that your stomach is pressing against his back. Stand behind him,
cross his arms across his chest, and envelop him from behind with

Respect the child	Accuse, belittle
Problem solve	Demand obedience
Promotes harmony	Destroys harmony
Request the child to consider the adult's point of view	Demand that the child accept the adult's point of view
Child's opinion is accepted as a valid option	Child's opinion is rejected as not valid
Resolves underlying issues	Underlying issues are not resolved
Parent doesn't give repeated messages	Parent is wordy, nags the child
Parent models values being taught—kindness, courtesy	Parent models how to dominate[1]

your arms. Maintain your grip until he has calmed down and speak softly to him to subdue his frenzied state. Another method that some parents have found helpful in an emergency for stopping out-of-control behavior is sending the child into a cool (not cold) shower.

USE CONSCIENCE-BUILDING DISCIPLINE CONSEQUENCES

Logical and natural consequences are especially helpful because they provide the needed firmness to teach children the direct, specific, domino effects of their behavior. You can then stand by as a helpful ally without adding insult to your child's already fragile self-esteem.

Allow Natural Consequences

My definition of natural consequences involves only four words: *whatever will happen anyway*. The consequences are not manufactured by

parents; instead, they are simply allowed to occur. The natural consequence of your child's grabbing a small dog's fur is being nipped by the
dog; of running on an icy sidewalk, a skinned knee; of experimental
puffing on a cigar, coughing and choking; of grabbing playmates' toys,
being rejected by the playmates. Natural consequences are spontaneous ways of learning about life and can be powerful teachers.

When you want a natural consequence to become a corrective influence on your child, do not intervene. Temporarily divorce yourself
from the situation and be patient and quiet. Be your child's ally and
avoid giving I-told-you-so speeches afterward. If she brings up the
event for discussion, express hope that she will change her actions in
some way next time so that things work out more pleasantly for all
concerned. Treat the experience as you would any mistake—an opportunity to learn and improve.

In many instances, however, a natural consequence would not be
the most efficient learning method. It might take too long to materi-
alize, or it might jeopardize your child's health or safety.

Use Logical Consequences

When it seems inappropriate to permit a natural consequence, you
can intervene in a humane, sensitive, and loving way. The consequence of the misbehavior can be your *emotionally honest response* to it,
thus logically related to it. Logical consequences are known ahead of
time by all concerned. You guide them, and your child experiences
them as logical in nature. If the conflict involves your child's tracking
in mud, your emotionally honest response would be to not allow any
more tracked-in mud. Inform him that he is to leave his muddy shoes
on a mat near the door from now on or he will have to mop up the
kitchen if mud is tracked in.

Explain to your child the new actions you will take in response to
his misbehavior. Tell your child what you will do and let him decide
what he will do. After your initial explanation, there is no need for

nagging about your new policies. Simply take whatever action would be an emotionally honest response to enforce your intention.

When your child starts to misbehave, put the emphasis on controlling yourself rather than on controlling him. Stop cooperating with him. Don't do him any favors relevant to the misbehavior. Control what you will give to, do for, or permit for your child. Set a time limit for your child's combined work and play. The longer he takes to do the dishes, the less time there will be for you to read a story, because both must be accomplished by bedtime. Work must come before play. "As soon as you show me your homework, you may watch television."

Withdraw a privilege he abuses and give him a chance to regain it later when he shows he can handle it responsibly. Let the consequence do the teaching. For example, temporarily deny him the use of his bicycle if he rides it carelessly or forbid his use of the computer temporarily if he has not used it properly.

> *When your child starts to misbehave, put the emphasis on controlling yourself rather than on controlling him.*

Provide logical consequences firmly, dramatically, quickly, and calmly. Don't allow a second chance or an opportunity for your child to manipulate his way out of facing the consequence. The consequence should be fair, humane, and justified, not delivered with vengeance. "Next time, you'll have another chance" is sufficient in response to any plea he may make for a second chance.

Although logical consequences will not make you the helpful ally that you could be when you allow natural consequences, you will at least not be the adversary that you become when authoritarian punishments are used. Your proper attitude should be one of mild regret that your child has chosen to act in a way that has led to these consequences.

Logical consequences are a form of natural consequences in that they reflect your honest emotional reactions. Never refer to logical consequences with I-told-you-this-would-happen speeches. Try to replace nagging with one directive message; then combine the message with an enforcing action. Actions are the salad and words the dressing of effective parenting of children with ADHD.

When responding to a request, try to use "yes, with conditions" or "no with possibilities" as your answer. "Yes, you may go to Derek's house, as long as you call and ask his mother's permission and are home by 8:00," "No, you may not go to Derek's house tonight, but we will see about inviting Derek over this weekend."

The repayment logical consequence is an important social skill. Far more relevant and effective as a disciplinary maneuver than ordinary punishments, this approach allows your child to have a meaningful part in setting things right after a judgment error. It is an integral part of the eight A's of apology (see page 180). If there is a monetary value to damage done through misbehavior, your child helps replace the loss directly by paying for it or indirectly by performing labor services to you or to the offended person.

PREVENT COMMON FAMILY CONFLICTS

Here are methods for preventing conflict at some of the most consistent moments of high stress for families with children or teens who have ADHD. Notice the emphasis is on *prevention* of future conflict and maintenance of calm order as much as possible.

Household Chores

Household chores provide opportunities for learning self-discipline, promptness, neatness, reliability, and the importance of being helpful. Organization and supervision of chores are doubly important when your child has ADHD. Give instructions for each chore and be sure to do some chores along with your child. If household chores are natural and expected parts of the daily routine, conflicts diminish.

A regular family chore time works the best. The set time can be daily, weekly, or both. Try a brief tidy-up period before bedtime each day and on Saturday morning.

Develop a system to distribute chores among family members, a method of supervision and inspection, and the motivation or incentives you want to use. The goal of these arrangements is to get all family members, including the child with ADHD, involved in keeping everything clean, usable, and in its place.

Present a list of chores for your children to choose from or simply assign tasks. Rotating chores daily, weekly, or monthly is usually helpful. Post the chore assignments on a chart to avoid complaints. An effective chart informs everyone of who is supposed to do what, when, and for how many days.

> *H*ousehold chores provide opportunities for learning self-discipline, promptness, neatness, reliability, and the importance of being helpful.

Don't let your child get by with "I didn't do it, so I shouldn't have to clean it up." Explain how chores help the family and why they are a shared part of family living—this home is *our* home, this family is *our* family, and these dishes are *our* dishes. The person doing dishes did not eat off all the dinnerware, use all of the utensils, or drink from all the cups.

Stay as outwardly uninvolved as possible; avoid nagging and reminding. Supervise from a distance and randomly check on performance unless more stringent monitoring is needed. If you use too much pressure, a contrary child will not feel a personal sense of ownership of the chore, including the pride of accomplishment. The issue might then become a power struggle over your right to assign the chore. Use the I CARE method if grumbling occurs as chore time approaches. Repeated balking and grumbling about chores by a child with ADHD usually indicates that the physiological treatments are not yet fully effective. Also check to see whether it would be helpful to divide the chore into smaller units.

Clear, sincere appreciation for chores completed goes a long way toward training children to be helpful. Comment on the large amount of effort shown. Nobody likes to try hard only to have others dismiss the effort by not seeming to notice or value it.

Does Your Child Wet the Bed?

Food allergies sometimes contribute to bed-wetting. The chief offenders are milk, orange juice, tomatoes, tomato juice, chocolate, pineapple, and peaches. Recently, an interesting study was done on children with ADHD who were bed wetters. The researchers took them off offending foods and food additives, and two-thirds stopped entirely or significantly decreased the incidence of wetting the bed. The researchers were then able to challenge those who improved by giving them offending foods, causing bed-wetting to reappear in over half of the children. The moral of the story is clear: Start by checking for food allergies and toxinsulate against petrochemicals.[2]

Bowel and Bladder Control

If daytime wetting or soiling occurs, review the activities preceding the elimination control problem, checking for any other motive or mechanism aside from insufficient awareness of internal body signals that is one of the sensory integration dysfunctions common among children with ADHD.

These children are at risk for bed-wetting as well as for daytime wetting and pants soiling (encopresis). The national incidence rate is 15 percent for bed-wetting after age 5, but the rate for children with ADHD is somewhat higher. The brain is muting messages from the bladder that it should be paying more attention to. The key is to find a way to make the brain more alert to bladder messages during sleep. Usually, the solution is to keep your child in a state of normal depth of sleep and prevent too-deep sleep. Prescribed antidepressants at bedtime are sometimes used for this purpose.

I recommend proteins at bedtime and no depriving of water for the sake of trying to prevent bed-wetting. Disallowing liquids before bed is an unnecessary and usually profitless restriction. Your child will manufacture urine out of whatever food has been ingested, whether or not accompanied by liquid before bedtime. A small sip of liquid will not affect the bed-wetting but might help contribute to a smoother tuck-in and a more contented child at bedtime. Milk allergy, particularly in children with ADHD-sa, can aggravate bed-wetting. A medical examination and consultation is appropriate, though problems with the physical structure of the bladder and related body parts seem to account for less than 5 percent of instances of bed-wetting.

Urinary alarm systems using a moisture-sensitive pad are available from major retailers. When the pad is moistened with urine, the alarm buzzes. There are two types: one mounted under the sheet and the other in specially designed underpants that can be worn underneath pajamas. The underpants are more comfortable and convenient than the under-the-sheet type.

Bowel and bladder control generally improve with successful physiological treatment. I have found the antidepressants to be somewhat more consistent than stimulants in enhancing children's bowel and bladder control. A nasal spray developed in the late 1980s also helps prevent bed-wetting in children with ADHD.

Grocery Shopping

As in most situations, the key is prevention. Provide something that occupies your child during the shopping excursion. If tantrums occur, sit with her in the car briefly and use the I CARE sequence.

Try giving her a large fruit, such as a banana from the produce section. Your child remains silent and occupied, and you retain your composure. Another method is to involve her in the shopping process, such as by having her fetch the items you specify, stack them in the cart, or help read labels. Label reading is not only an exciting adventure but quite educational, and your child knows she is helping find the foods that will prevent many of her ADHD symptoms.

Consider playing "food bingo." It is one of the many useful suggestions from the fun idea list. Have your child make food bingo cards by cutting out pictures of food items from magazines. This game holds the interest of most young children quite well and also keeps siblings from squabbling if they play it simultaneously.

Untidy Bedroom

Most children and adolescents with ADHD prefer to decorate their rooms in an "Early Tornado" theme. Closing the door so others don't have to experience the room by sight, sound, or smell is probably the simplest solution, though it doesn't teach much in the way of self-care.

To encourage a cleaner, tidier bedroom, use structure to advantage by devising a place for everything. Use dishpans as bins and provide plenty of shelves and drawers as well as small sturdy cardboard storage boxes (available from business supply stores). Color-code the bins and boxes for different purposes—building blocks in the red bin, clean underwear in the white drawer, doll clothes in the pink box, for example.

Have a minimum of furniture. The fewer items of furniture, the more easily your child will locate toys and other items within the room. If only one child is using the room, a bunk bed provides an excellent storage area that quickly transforms into a bed for overnight guests. A hamper (cover and decorate it with your child), a wastebasket, and adequate shelving are essential structural aids. Consider converting half the closet into shelves. If your child has chemical sensitivities and allergies, be sure to follow the recommendations in chapter 6 for making his bedroom a safe haven.

Lying

Lying is one of the most difficult misbehaviors to correct, in part because it prevents a frank discussion of what really happened. It also gives your child a great amount of illegitimate power because you can't *make* him tell the truth, and the lying can provide a cover-up for almost any kind of misdeed. Many children with ADHD become so skilled at lying that they lose their awareness of what is real and what is fantasy. If your child lies to evade consequences or avoid a responsibility or chore, try these steps:

- **Discuss.** Discussing the lie helps put your child in a more objective, emotionally removed position. Explain that all lies are of two basic types—claiming to be more than you are or claiming to be less than you are:

  > Some lies say you are more than you are, like bragging about something you have or something you did. And other lies say you are less than you are, like saying you didn't do something wrong or didn't take something that belonged to someone else. Which type of lie was this, the first or the second?

  Explore your child's thoughts that led to the lie. Get him to state his motives and intentions behind the lie—what he was trying to accomplish or avoid.

- **Empathize.** Make it safe emotionally for your child to convey these feelings to you by showing empathy for his underlying need, such as to gain favor or to avoid being criticized.

- **Explain the negative impact.** Having shown empathy for your child's logic and motives, label them as mistakes. If the lying occurred as a cover-up for a misdeed, two mistakes have occurred—the misbehavior itself and the cover-up attempt:

  > You made two mistakes here. The first was thinking the best way to make the other boys like you was to tell them your teacher intends to give you the prize. The second was to think you needed to lie and deny what you had said when the teacher asked you about it.

  Gently explain the undesirable domino effects of each mistake—the natural consequences most likely to occur if the mistake is repeated. For example:

  > Now it will be harder for the boys to like you, rather than easier. You tell me why. [Child answers.] And it will also be harder for the teacher to trust you. Why?

- **Explain the negative natural consequences.** Outline the natural consequences of developing a reputation as an untrustworthy person—people will learn not to trust him, a reputation as a liar will be hard to change, people will stop telling him their secrets, and so forth. Keep this and the preceding explanation in simple, concrete terms with a clear cause-and-effect sequence.

- **Explore the positive natural consequences of truthfulness.** Discuss the likely favorable results of becoming honest about this matter. Focus on the impact on other people and their feelings—they will be more likely to bring him into their confidence, treat him with greater respect, and so forth.

- **Encourage apology.** Review the eight A's of apology to clear up any damaged feelings or relationships over the incident.

- **Get a commitment for change.** Help your child think of what to change so he can make wiser choices next time. Children often lie to avoid being punished. Arrange that in return for an agreement not to lie about future incidents, only logical consequences will apply; that is, simple compensation or repayment.

Stealing

One of the best preventatives for stealing is physiological treatment. If your child attempts to explain away the actions as merely taking, taking without returning, borrowing, borrowing without returning, or taking and not asking, label the actions as stealing.

Stealing can reflect a variety of motives and indicate a variety of psychological issues. Uncover the needs your child is trying to meet by stealing. In a calm discussion, explore these possibilities:

- **Inadequate understanding of property rights.** Have other children been allowed to appropriate your child's toys? Have adults confiscated his belongings or allowed too much access to their property?

- **Denial and minimizing by adults.** Have adults assumed your child is too young to understand what stealing is? Have adults wanted to avoid the hassle of confronting your child about stealing?

- **Too much temptation.** Have powerful temptations been placed before your child? Is your child under the age of 6?

- **Feeling unnoticed.** Is he stealing to gain a sense of connection? Is he trying to be "one of the gang" or "get something" from someone?

- **Feeling powerless.** Is he stealing to feel influence and power? Does he want to be the boss about the stolen object?

- **Feeling hurt.** Is he stealing to get revenge? Does he want to hurt someone or teach someone a lesson?

- **Wanting to be different.** Is he stealing to be excused from having to conform? Is he trying to show contempt for adult standards of behavior?

- **Boredom.** Is he stealing to create excitement? Is he bored, hunting for adventure, wanting the thrill of finding out whether he will be caught?

- **Inappropriate response from adults.** Have adults overreacted to prior incidents?

This exploration can be quite enlightening for you as well as your child. To prevent further stealing, follow these steps:

- **Determine the specific need your child is trying to meet.** For full discussion of the process, see my book *Understanding Misbehavior: Using Misbehavior as a Guide to Children's and Adolescents' Needs*.

- **See that stealing fails as a method of meeting that need.** Deny any benefit to your child from the stolen object. Give it back, give it away, or destroy it.

- **Seek out an acceptable means of need-meeting for your child.** Find legitimate, socially appropriate avenues for meeting whatever needs your child was trying to meet by stealing.

- **Use the logical consequence principle of undoing.** Have your child apologize and return or pay for the item. Use additional logical consequences from my booklet *Creative Answers to Misbehavior*.

- **Interpret the natural consequences that have occurred.** Make sure your child understands the negative aftereffects on other people as well as on their reaction to your child. Explain how stealing leads to lose-lose results that end up hurting the thief as well as the victim.

- **Stay calm and treat the incident as an opportunity for learning.** Avoid treating it as an emotional issue.

- **Express confidence about future improvement.** Use the encouragement principle of always building toward the future. Indicate that you are sure your child can find better ways of obtaining things and meeting his needs.

Just as a carpenter must have a variety of tools available to accomplish the goals of the trade, you must also have many tools for the important stewardship and privilege you have of raising your child. No good carpenter would use a screwdriver in a situation that calls for a hacksaw. In the same way, you should carefully select the approach that best fits your child and the situation. If you emphasize the four S's of scheduling need-meeting activities, structure, supervision, and support, you will become calmer, more confident, and more effective as your child's leader. Good discipline is not harsh, nor does it involve a long string of deprivations. By implementing the four S's to prevent misbehavior, using natural and logical consequences, and overcoming common disciplinary problems, you can train your child in a positive way that maintains an atmosphere of mutual respect.

CHAPTER 17

Provide Positive Play Experiences

Recreation, Sports, Holidays, Summer Vacation, and Summer Camp

PLAY, WHICH OCCUPIES much of most children's days, teaches them about their social relationships, various academic skills, and numerous other talents that are useful throughout life. Play is, in some ways, children's work. It has an important role in developing their innate capabilities into effective life skills. Don't put your child in the difficult position of having to use several consecutive hours of playtime in random, haphazard actions merely to stave off boredom.

ENCOURAGE GROUP PLAY

Group settings are generally more stimulating than solitary play. Often, a child with ADHD will do well for a limited period of time in group play but will gradually become overstimulated and bothersome to her playmates. Try to ease her into play groups for short periods at first. By careful observation, you can determine how long your child can play with friends. End the play sessions before they deteriorate because of your child's increased excitability.

Occasionally, observe the situation from a distance to determine how your child is getting along with other children. Listening only to her explanation of what went wrong will give a one-sided picture. If she says, for example, "They won't let me play, and they hit me and told me to get out," the statement may be true; however, she may not have reported what she was doing to aggravate her playmates.

> *Such basic courtesies as waiting a turn, sharing, and talking politely may be hard at first. Under your supervision, however, your child can develop good play habits.*

Cooperative group play can work better if all of the children understand basic principles of courtesy. At the beginning, explain that whoever is using a toy keeps it until finished with it. Throwing heavy or sharp-edged toys, taking toys apart, and any other acts of destruction are not allowed. Pushing or hurting each other is forbidden. The children should be asked to share.

Acknowledge even small gains and improvements and be very specific in describing them. "It was very nice of you to let Billy take a turn right after you," emphasizes improvement, while, "I see you still can't shoot baskets very well," stresses defeat. The actions that constitute being a good sport are sometimes difficult for children with ADHD.

ESTABLISH THE BEST PLAY SETTING

Arrange the setting ahead of time. Laying out the necessary materials and saying something like "Here are some papers for you to cut out and put together" is better than asking an open-ended question like "What would you like to do now?" Provide an apron and some cleanup rags as part of the preparation if the activity involves the possibility of spilling things.

Young hyperactive children with ADHD are by far more challenging to supervise during play than their inattentive ADHD counterparts. Hyperactive children generally need a lot of space to move around, tumble, explore, run, and discharge their large amounts of energy. In addition to providing a large outdoor play area, many parents have found that a high fence or other protective partition helps assure them of the child's whereabouts and safety. The hyperactive child's unbridled curiosity and poorly developed sense of danger make a physical barrier surrounding the play area even more necessary.

At home, every hyperactive child needs a safe place for being very active. The best location would be a playroom with inexpensive and sturdy furniture. It should be arranged for quiet as well as active play. For bouncing and tumbling, place one mattress on top of another in a corner. The corner of a basement, attached garage, porch, or other defined area will serve equally well. Despite intentions to the contrary, most parents of hyperactive children find that the bedroom ends up being a playroom, too.

Furnish the room with pieces that can stand heavy wear and tear, and expect some physically rough treatment of the room and its contents through the years. The walls should be drab; avoid bright colors, stripes, and mirrors. Encourage your child to display his artistic creations. Arrange a place on a wall or shelf. Store playthings in color-coded, labeled bins about the size of dishpans. If your child is very sensitive to phenols, use cardboard or metal bins rather than plastic bins and hang two spider plants (or other air-purifying plants) in a corner.

PLAY FOR THE YOUNG CHILD

Preschool children's work is their play. Play provides the main medium through which they learn many important skills and lessons about life. By reciprocating with a play partner, they learn to build basic trust in the world and in other people. They must learn to negotiate with others to settle differences and make decisions within their play experiences. They learn to resolve conflicts without force or violence.

As they talk and move about, they learn to express themselves through language and body movement. They gain increased mastery over their own bodies, developing speed, strength, coordination, and self-confidence.

Play often with your child; offer to become a playmate in some sort of activity daily. Convey that you think play is a good thing to do, not an unimportant or frivolous activity. Provide sufficient props and materials for rich, imaginative, vigorous play experiences, regardless of weather or the availability of playmates. In addition to providing entertainment, many activities can be instructional and can help build basic learning skills.

Develop Auditory Skills

With her eyes closed, have your child try to identify objects you're holding by the sounds they make (toothbrush against cardboard, small electric motor, pencil on paper). Have her try to find an object with her eyes closed, locating it by the sound that it makes (bell, whistle). Wear a tinkling bell while your blindfolded child tries to catch you. A tape recorder, used under your supervision, can provide hours of entertainment and be an aid in self-expression.

Letter sounds can be used for many interesting activities. "Riddle chaining" is done by having your child make up a riddle whose answer starts with the last sound of the preceding answer. For example, "I say meow; what am I?" (cat—ends with *t*); "I am tall and have leaves; what am I?" (tree—begins with *t*, ends with *e*); "I am a very thin fish; what am I?" (eel—begins with *e*). Tell a story and leave out a word, pausing so your child can fill in the correct and obvious word. ("'Twas the night before Christmas and all through the . . .")

Compose rhyming answers to "Wouldn't it be funny if . . .": "Wouldn't it be funny if bees had fleas? . . . if sharks stayed in parks? . . . if flowers counted the hours?" Say several words beginning with the same sound. Occasionally, include a different beginning sound and have your child clap her hands when she hears the different sound. Your child can tap out variations in rhythm and loudness that you first beat or tap out

Develop Visual Skills

Have your child look carefully at a picture or drawing with a number of details in it. Then have her draw it from memory, practicing until she can remember everything in the picture. Place several objects on a table; ask your child to turn away while you remove two of the objects. Then have her try to guess what is missing. Draw a picture but leave out one part; let your child fill it in.

Using pictures of familiar objects, cut out one or two pieces from each and have your child identify what is missing and replace the missing parts.

Have your child join dots to form patterns of increasing difficulty, then have her also draw letters, numbers, and objects outlined in dots. Using two checkerboards, make a pattern with four checkers on your board and have your child duplicate it on hers, gradually increasing the number of checkers. Eventually, ask her to try to duplicate the pattern from memory after she looks briefly at yours.

Have your child arrange a collection of miscellaneous small objects by size, then by shape, color, or composition. Change the order in which pictures or objects are arranged and have her put them back in correct sequence.

Cover a word with a card, then move the card slowly to the right so that the letters your child will read appear in proper sequence. Do the same for sentences, sliding the card so that words appear from left to right at a comfortable pace. Make the sentences fun to read by including loving messages or humor in them.

Develop Coordination

Construct a balance board by placing a board about two feet long on a horizontal cylinder and have your child balance herself by placing her feet near each end of the board. Play family follow the leader and include skipping, jumping, crawling, and use of right and left feet and hands. Have your child walk while balancing a beanbag on her head or while pressing it between her knees. Then have her hop, sit, lie down, or run with the beanbag in those positions. Play family charades and act out sentences, ideas, or activities (going fishing, opening a jar). Play Simon says as a family or play it with your child in front of a full-length mirror.

Do rhythms and dances as a family, such as stamping your feet, slapping your sides, or doing the hokey pokey or farmer in the dell. Have your child walk and skip backward with you. Have your child close her eyes and write in large letters on an extra-large sheet of paper or a small blackboard. (Avoid whiteboards because of phenols from the markers.) Cutting with scissors is an excellent activity. Start with large simple shapes and gradually have her cut out more complicated and smaller shapes. Ball and jacks is another good activity, as are large sewing cards.

Develop Concept Formation

Start a scrapbook, organized into categories of your child's favorite things, and collect pictures and news clippings about animals, sports, or other interests. At a simpler level, have her categorize a collection of pictures of various objects (cut out of magazines) into appropriate subgroups, such as animals, plants, or buildings.

Memory games are also useful. "Going on a picnic or trip, I will take . . ." is an entertaining activity for the entire family. Each person repeats all previously named items plus one more. Have your child memorize a short poem or nursery rhyme. Write it down and cut out the phrases, then scramble them and have her replace them in order. Guessing games also allow the development of concept formation ability. Have her try to guess what object you are thinking of, providing only slight clues such as color or approximate size. Having your child feel objects in a bag to guess what they are will also improve concept formation ability. Play 20 questions, in which your child is allowed 20 yes-no guesses at an animal, sports implement, or food item you are thinking of.

Select Toys Thoughtfully

Your child will most enjoy toys that she can feel, move around, and make sounds with and that exercise her imagination. She should be able to control the toy. Avoid complicated gadgets that perform by themselves while the child sits and watches.

Hyperactive children are usually attracted to activities involving self-expression rather than those requiring focused or restricted movement. Finger paint, modeling compound, guns that shoot foam balls or darts, slimy semifluid, and wheeled miniature cars may be more attractive than restrictive items such as coloring books, small building pieces, table games, plastic target shooting machines, and plastic models. Practicing focused attention is probably more beneficial in the long run because it is a skill that is useful at school and in adult life.

> Your child will most enjoy toys that she can control and that exercise her imagination. Avoid complicated gadgets that perform by themselves while she just watches.

Toys for hyperactive children should be simple, durable, and safe. In many instances, it is better to provide a genuine item rather than a toy imitation. The added durability and realism of a genuine pocket radio, for example, make it preferable to a toy radio. A small glider that really flies makes more sense than a heavy airplane that can only roll along the floor.

These guidelines are very general, and allowance must be made for your child's own uniqueness and readiness for certain activities as well as for the play environment. Coordinate your fun idea list and fun idea drawer with toy selection. If your child is phenol sensitive and an S-R state occurs during play, track down the source. It will probably be an inhaled (such as fumes from glue or paint) or a skin-contact (such as from colorings in modeling dough) source of chemical exposure.

Provide for Active Play

Appropriate toys for punching and pounding include sturdy punching bags, inner tubes nailed to outdoor walls, and pillows. I have found the large duffel bag–size punching bag far superior to the small basketball-size version. You can make a homemade version with a large pillowcase or duffel bag filled with several pieces of cloth, such as discarded bedding. Some commercially available inflatable punching toys are not sufficiently sturdy.

Climbing, tunneling, and tumbling enhance coordination. Start with a large plastic trash can with large holes cut in the sides. A simple tent made with bedspreads, sheets, or blankets draped over a card table or other piece of furniture can keep your small child happy. Large cardboard shipping cartons can become pretend caves, but make sure there are air holes. Hopscotch markings chalked on cement and a basketball hoop placed low stimulate play that further helps develop coordination.

Riding and moving toys may be useful. Plastic balls, plastic flying discs, and similar items can be used in safe and enjoyable lawn games. With appropriate structure and supervision, water play can be an enjoyable experience for your child. Running through a sprinkler or playing with the hose on hot days can be fun. All children enjoy water fights with squirt guns and cups, using buckets of water as "ammunition." The goal is to douse the other person without getting doused in return. A helpful rule is that neither team may destroy the other's water supply.

A very vigorous, high-energy, fun activity is mock fencing with safe homemade imitation swords. You can obtain some plastic piping and stiff plastic foam insulation at any plumbing supply store. For each sword, simply insert pipe that has been cut into 30-inch lengths into the foam insulation, then wrap thoroughly with duct tape. Make a crosspiece by cutting a hole in an 8-inch piece of insulation and impaling it upon the larger piece. Slide it down a few inches, then wrap thoroughly with duct tape.

Consider Martial Arts

The central focus of well-taught martial arts is self-control, the hallmark of goals for helping a child or teen who has ADHD. Other primary emphases include learning to concentrate on a specific goal, showing respect for the teacher and for others in general, learning to follow a precise system that involves planning ahead, and waiting until the proper moment to make a move. The students must care for their uniforms and go through a ritual showing respect for their clothing. They must learn how to breathe with proper timing. Students progress at their own pace, with almost no competition with each other. In fact, they are required to provide caring assistance to other students who are working on a lower ranking belt.

> *The central focus of well-taught martial arts is self-control, the hallmark of goals for helping a child or teen who has ADHD.*

Suzann Wancket has designed an outstanding and very popular karate program in Saint Paul, Minnesota. Her classes typically have long waiting lists, composed primarily of hyperactive boys and girls. Hers is a model for others to follow. She explains:

> Self-discipline and self-control are essential in karate. If students want to learn karate, they must learn self-discipline, self-control, and concentration along with it. It provides them with a system. You don't do anything in karate without thinking it out first.

Many parents have discovered, much to their delight, that these basic aspects of martial arts lessons carry over into other aspects of their children's lives. They find their children have greater self-discipline, improved self-esteem, decreased disruptive behavior, enhanced ease and social grace, and even increased participation at school.

Like bowling and bicycling, martial arts does not have the built-in limitations of some other athletics. There are almost no height, weight, body build, or age requirements. Athletic ability is not a prerequisite. The entire body is involved in the exercising. Coordination and balance are enhanced and emphasized. The more dancelike, the better, with tai chi being the most dancelike form. Kata is a choreographed expression of karate that is performed accompanied by music.

Unfortunately, not all karate classes are as useful as Ms. Wancket's. The effectiveness of her classes for helping hyperactive children is magnified by consistent involvement of the parents who attend to watch their children participate. Unlike many competition-oriented karate studios that tend to rush students through early ranks and focus prematurely on sparring and aggressive moves, this *sensei* takes the time to develop each student at a comfortable pace suited to his readiness and interest.

The father of one of Ms. Wancket's students who has ADHD expressed the outcome of his son's experience with this karate program:

> Where in the past Jason has often struggled with classroom learning and the reaction his classmates had to his performance, this year has been increasingly marked by academic successes. The classroom environment hasn't changed. The distractions of too many students and stuff are still there; the small indecencies of childhood persist; materials and methods designed for mainline students are still the main menu; the self-defeating standardized tests and testing methods still exist. What changed this year was Jason's growing ability to focus, to respond to constructive discipline, to experience cumulative successes, and most importantly, to believe in himself.

These same outcomes can happen in virtually any well-taught athletic endeavor, whether or not it's competitive in nature. In general, however, the less competitive and the more individualized the instruction, the less threatening it will be to the fragile self-esteem of participants with ADHD.

Provide for Quiet Play

Toys for quiet play for a child with ADHD are often artistic in nature. She will enjoy making art paper designs using blunt scissors, tape, or paste. In general, chalk and pencil are probably preferable to paint, ink, wax crayons, and felt markers. Although chalk creates dust, it is only a temporary nuisance and can easily be washed from clothes and walls. Paint-with-water books avoid the hazards of real paint while giving your child the experience of painting.

Art projects should allow for quick success and easy completion. For example, choose snap-together rather than glue-together plastic models. Display finished and decorated pieces on a wall or shelf. With greater experience, your child can successfully enjoy more complicated and time-consuming projects.

Liquid non-oil-based paints such as watercolor and tempera are preferable to paint powders, which can be accidentally inhaled by

---

Does Your Child Like Play Dough?

Commercial play doughs often contain petroleum-based dyes. You can make your own, without any worry about a reaction in your small child, from this recipe.

1 cup white flour
¼ cup salt
1 tablespoon cream of tartar
1 cup water
1 tablespoon vegetable oil
(optional) natural coloring agents

Mix the flour, salt, and cream of tartar in a medium saucepan. Gradually stir in the water, oil, and coloring (if using). Cook over medium heat, stirring constantly, for 3 to 5 minutes. Keep stirring even after the mixture becomes stiff, until it comes cleanly away from the sides of the pan. Remove from heat and let it cool. Knead the dough on a floured surface and store in a plastic bag or airtight container.

your child. Aerosol spray paints are particularly liable to be inhaled and get on your child's skin. Consider spatter painting with a toothbrush, popsicle stick, or pipe cleaner.

Puzzle pieces are too easy to lose. When the puzzle is assembled for the first time, place it facedown on newspaper and paint the back of the puzzle with a distinctive color. Use a different color for each puzzle.

Modeling clay and modeling dough can be meaningful forms of expressive play. You can use cookie cutters, rolling pins, and other utensils to help your child make things from these materials.

Pay careful attention to structuring the play environment and selecting activities that match your child's readiness, energy level, and interests. Use play to enhance social skills and family relationships as well as to strengthen academic abilities and compensate for learning problems. Coordinate toy selection with your fun idea list and fun idea drawer so you are always ready to suggest wholesome activities. By following these suggestions, you can artfully integrate play into your total plan for helping your child.

RECREATION FOR THE ADOLESCENT

Individual outdoor sports are generally a safer bet for maintaining self-esteem than outdoor team sports. I recommend running, swimming, hula hooping, roller-skating, snowboarding, juggling, bicycling, supervised rock climbing, hiking, weight lifting, bodybuilding, jogging, and skiing. There are no teammates to disappoint or seek approval from, and there are no opponents to become angry at or feel inferior to. Your teen competes against his own past record and thus improves his self-confidence and his skill level.

> *Individual outdoor sports are generally a safer bet for maintaining self-esteem than outdoor team sports.*

Vigorous sports and athletics allow discharge of energy, often don't require high coordination, and provide opportunity for socialization and success in a different arena from the scholastic pressures of school. If dexterity is a problem, select a sport not requiring complex coordination, such as cycling. One parent of an adolescent boy with ADHD happily reported that her son had finally found a sport he could succeed in:

> All his life, Erik was awkward and too poorly coordinated to participate in sports. Finally, we found an answer. He got a new 10-speed and has joined a bicycling club. He's doing great! Take his feet off the ground and he's all right!

Suitable indoor recreation depends more on personal preferences. Teens with ADHD tend to enjoy table games if they are not too complicated and if there is not too much emphasis on competition. Table tennis, Foosball, and billiards also seem to be attractive to them.

SAFETY FIRST WHEN BICYCLING

In a collision with any car or truck, the bicycle always loses. Over half of fatal collisions with vehicles occur when a child rides out into the street from a sidewalk or driveway. Hyperactive children are at risk because of their inherent exuberance, impulsivity, and carelessness. The second most dangerous bicycle maneuver is attempting to ride rather than walk a bike across an intersection without a crosswalk. Both of these dangers can be reduced with a simple rule—always walk the bike out into the street when beginning the ride. When crossing an intersection, either walk the bike or look carefully both ways as if there were a stop sign. Obeying regular traffic laws for bicycles, including honoring all stop signs, should also be part of the rules of the road for the young bicyclist.

> *This simple rule can reduce children's bicycle accidents: "Always walk the bike out into the street when beginning the ride."*

The largest death risk in bicycle accidents comes from head injuries, which are involved in about three-fourths of all serious bicycle-related

Get Your Teen's Act Together: Theater and Drama

Getting involved in theater and drama is an ideal pastime for many teens with ADHD because it involves:

- Strengthening memory (lines and body expression)
- Developing reading skills by reading script
- Strengthening social skills
- Hyperfocusing on the role
- A legitimate arena for getting positive attention
- Patience, timing, and waiting for the right moment
- Achieving a shared goal with the entire cast
- Achieving a personal goal of performing the role
- Being part of a team working toward a common production
- Having a responsible, productive relationship with adults
- Creativity (costume, lighting, makeup, set design)
- Movement (dance, music, choreography, facial expressions)

accidents. Helmets are the obvious first line of protection, and they prevent 80 to 90 percent of brain and head injuries occurring in bicycle traffic accidents.

HOW TO SELECT A SUMMER CAMP

Sending your child away to camp for a week or two is a tempting solution to a lot of summertime problems. Make the experience pleasant for everyone by following these recommendations that I have gathered from parents who have sent their children with ADHD to group camps.

Select Early

Plan ahead and think small. Some summer camps fill all their available slots in winter. Send a form letter to several prospective camp directors, specifying your concerns. Have your child's first extended camp experience be one that lasts one week or less, in a camp with only a small or moderate attendance. Games should include, or better yet emphasize, noncompetitive activities and situations where group cooperation is necessary. Try to find a camp with a ratio of one counselor or teen leader to each six to ten campers.

Watch Out for Chemical Exposures

In addition to the usual factors of facilities, location, cost, and leadership, you should probably check on chemical exposures. Even with a cooperative staff, your child needs to understand which foods and chemicals to avoid. So don't expect anything but ADHD symptoms if your child goes to a camp that's unable or unwilling to do the necessary screening against allergenic food and phenolic toxins. If your child is chemically sensitive (as are the majority of children who have ADHD), interview the camp director beforehand, either by phone or in person.

Ask about arrangements to toxinsulate your child during the camp. A nature-oriented camp may be more flexible in this regard. Add that you can supply some petrochemical-free food to compensate for any menu alterations on your child's behalf. Try to find out about arts and crafts, where the most likely exposures for a chemically sensitive child would be tie-dyeing, finger paints, aromatic or oil-based paints, wood-finishing chemicals such as varnish, and aerosol sprays used indoors.

> *When choosing a camp, you should check on chemical exposures in addition to the usual factors of facilities, location, cost, and leadership.*

A chemically sensitive child should try to avoid harsh repellents, petrochemical insect sprays, and lotions. Have your child take 100 milligrams of thiamine three hours before planned exposure to mosquitoes or three capsules of Kyolic garlic extract 45 minutes before exposure. Older teens and young adults can take more of each. For sunburn and itchy rashes, aloe vera, vitamin E oil and baking soda paste won't cause S-R states in chemically sensitive children. Jewelweed and goldenseal juice can also be directly applied to itchy skin and create a soothing, drying effect.

Arrange for Food at Camp

Believe it or not, some of the most important factors determining your child's enjoyment of the camp center on food, in terms of both nutrition and food-related toxic exposure. I strongly recommend that you arrange for a section of the camp freezer to be devoted to your child's food supplies.

The easiest method of all is to interest the camp director in providing petrochemical-free food to all campers. If you are not so fortunate as to have a camp director willing to make such an arrangement, the next best maneuver is to obtain the camp menu a week or two in advance, so your child can plan around what the other campers will be eating during each meal. If pizza is on the menu, for example, your child can arrange to have suitable toppings that day.

> *I strongly recommend that you arrange for a section of the camp freezer to be devoted to your child's food supplies.*

Relying heavily on canned and frozen food and a supply of nut butter and bread seems to work well for most campers who need to toxinsulate their food. I recommend walnut or other nut butters over peanut butter for children with ADHD. The nut-butter-and-bread sandwich is your child's emergency backup system for unacceptable meals served at camp.

Put the nonperishables (cans, jars, lock-top plastic pouches of cereal, nut butter, and bread) for each meal in its own lunch sack, marked for the date and meal type. Your child would prepare for a one-week camp involving 21 meals, for example, with 21 lunch sacks, each dated and filled with the nonperishables for that meal. At each meal, your child simply adds the perishable component—perhaps some frozen food heated at camp—to the materials and food in the sack. Be sure to plan for three between-meal protein-rich snacks per day also.

Barbecued foods can cause an S-R state in children sensitive to the heavy phenol content of smoke. An electric fire starter is of course much preferred over petroleum-based charcoal lighter fluid.

Cold cereal is the breakfast mainstay for many camps. You can send acceptable brands with your child. Make sure the eggs your child has at breakfast are fresh, real eggs, not those in liquid or powdered form and not so-called egg substitutes. Require that your child be served eggs cooked only in water or butter, never in margarine.

During lunch, your child will probably have another margarine-exposure risk, especially if hundreds of sandwiches are prepared ahead of time for the campers. Again, insist on butter. Camp beverages are too risky for most children with ADHD, so have your child bring along acceptable fruit-based beverages along with plenty of filtered water.

Deep-fried foods at camps are usually prepared in oil containing BHT and similar petrochemicals, so have acceptable substitute food available for your child. Consider canned salmon as an option or insist that your child be served food panfried in butter rather than deep-fried in petrochemical-laced oil.

Part of having fun is fun food, and desserts form a significant part of camp food fare. Puddings and gelatin from boxed mixes are laced with petrochemicals, so have your child bring suitable desserts. Cakes, cookies, carameled pop corn, and brownies brought from home can last several days into the camp. Cold desserts and desserts to be consumed beyond the third day can be stored in the camp freezer in a sack identifying them as belonging to your child. Ice cream that is free of petrochemicals is easy to find, and soy and rice-based frozen desserts are suitable for the child who is milk-allergic.

HOW TO ENJOY VACATION TRAVEL

Nothing beats advance planning to make any trip go better. Plan your travel, and travel your plan. Don't expect children to sit quietly and "enjoy the scenery" en route. That plan never works. If you plan to travel to a place unfamiliar to your child, don't simply have the trip be a surprise. That plan never works either.

Make Careful Arrangements

Let the whole family help plan vacation trips, making a list of possible things to do or see. Plan a variety of activities and alternate them for a change of pace. Let each child arrange to take clothing and items for self-entertainment. Consider seating arrangements thoughtfully. Plan for someone to supervise the least self-controlled child and rotate that duty among the travelers. Try to avoid having two volatile or hard-to-entertain young children next to each other. Consider the length of time your child tolerates being in the same position. If she customarily becomes fidgety and unruly after an hour in a car, don't expect greater tolerance on a lengthy trip.

> *Don't overschedule your child when on vacation. Settle right into your overnight lodgings rather than cramming in sightseeing after a day of travel.*

Be careful not to overschedule your child. Consider the time of day for best travel; nap time and bedtime are ideal for taking a two-hour trip. Pack favorite playthings along but save the best for last. Include a new toy or activity, and perhaps put it in a sack marked for a specific time to be opened. When you arrive at the destination, settle into your overnight lodgings rather than trying to cram in busy sightseeing activities after a day of travel.

Control for Chemical Exposure

If your child is chemically sensitive, decide ahead of time how you are going to toxinsulate her. To avoid needless chemical exposures in restaurants, order à la carte. A baked potato with butter or sour cream from your cooler can complement a protein item. Use the restaurant's salad bar but don't trust any dressings; take along your own or use lemon juice. Ask that meat dishes be prepared without marinade, seasonings, sauces, or spices. To assure more cooperation from the restaurant staff, use the old trick of claiming that your child has allergies. Don't forget supermarket deli counters as useful options, complete with specialty breads and varieties of meats, cheeses, and salads.

A safer bet is to bring acceptable food along, packed especially for your child. A sturdy cooler and insulated lunch box are invaluable, especially if you are including fresh meat or produce. Take along a box for nonperishables like utensils, unbreakable dinnerware, paper towels, washcloths, soap, condiments, and related items. Consider small sizes of perishables like mayonnaise or dressings, so that you have minimal half-used food to take back home after the trip.

Is Your License Plate Hungry?

One way to keep young travelers occupied is the "hungry license plate game." Take turns announcing food dishes beginning with the letters in the license plate of oncoming or passing cars. If the next car's license plate includes the letters NPT, the person whose turn it is says "noodles, peppers, and turnips."

Advanced players can limit their choices, for example:

- Holiday food ("nog, pumpkin pie, and turkey")
- Yukky food ("nematodes, puppy tails, and tortoise feet")
- Crunchy food ("nuts, popcorn, and tea biscuits")
- Desserts ("Neapolitan ice cream, peach cobbler, and tarts")

Cereals last well and are convenient to haul and store. If electricity will be available, you'll find many uses for one or two electric skillets.

Snacks like crackers, nuts, dried fruit, pretzels, and individual containers of juice keep for a long time. Sandwiches made from nut bread spread with cream cheese are filling and easy to pack. Cartons of yogurt are portable also. Practical snacks include tuna salad sandwiches, baked chicken or turkey, and cheeses.

Arrange for Peace and Harmony

Keeping a child with ADHD occupied and stimulated is the key to successful long-distance car travel. Plan a 10-minute stop after each two hours of travel. The stop should include a restroom visit, exercise for everyone, and washing of hands and faces, if needed. Have some special activities planned ahead of time, such as jumping rope, blowing bubbles, playing tag, or tossing a ball.

Keep your child's mouth full, mind occupied, and hands busy. Use snacks advantageously. A mouth chewing on a fruit strip or a banana

---

Is Your Child Nice and Busy?

To enjoy extended travel with your child, provide something for her:

- Mouth (appropriate snacks)

- Mind (games, reading material, entertainment)

- Hands (toys, art supplies)

Also, try to leave in plenty of time for extra stops and breaks along the way.

has a hard time whining. Periodically provide nuts, cheese, chewable algae wafers, algae chewy bars, or other suitable snack food.

Play word games, counting games, and quiz games. Use an almanac or atlas to generate fun quiz questions. Games like 20 questions and hangman are ideal.

Bring along a supply of items to keep little hands busy during long hours of travel: new crayons, handicraft supplies, magnetic board, clipboard, folding lap trays, paper plates to color, sticker books, peg games, playing cards, adhesive strip bandages, telescope or binoculars, tape recorder, maps of the trip route, reading materials, pads and pencils, "magic" slates. These should not, however, be expected to take the place of periodic rest and exercise stops.

HOW TO SURVIVE SUMMER VACATION

Summer vacation is a bad idea. It poses several major challenges for you. Inventory those that apply to your family and make plans to compensate for and meet these challenges.

At the beginning of summer vacation, sit down as a family and make lists of suitable activities for good weather outdoors, with and without playmates, as well as for inclement weather. Use your fun idea list as a starting point (see appendix F). Let the children take turns organizing a family outing and being in charge of cooking the family dinner on various days; put these arrangements on the family calendar and discuss them at the family council meetings.

Disruption of routines.   One challenge is to maintain routine and order within your family processes. Continue to have the regular meetings I recommend. Give daily and weekly events structure by putting them on charts and calendars and by discussing them during family council. (See chapter 12.)

Pressure for constant entertainment.   Another challenge summer vacation suddenly thrusts upon you is to keep your child entertained and out of mischief for extended periods day after day. Don't overdo passive entertainments; keep your child active and absorbed in high-quality, routinized, supervised experiences. Take advantage of the good weather by frequently playing with her. Don't interrupt ongoing contented play, but if a playmate seems needed, consider offering yourself, at least for a few minutes.

Make sure there are adequate materials for a wide variety of enjoyable play experiences. Use common household objects as much as possible. There is no need to resort to elaborate expenditures of money in order to keep a child entertained. Follow the recommendations in this chapter for outdoor play and use the fun idea list you've drawn up.

Forced sibling contact.   Another challenge is the suddenly forced intensity and extended contact with siblings. Given the cutthroat level of sibling rivalry that can occur in your family, this magnification of potential conflicts represents an annually renewed threat to your family's stability. Hunt for ways to get your children involved in separate friendships and differing activities. Maintain your family council and private interviews with your child to defuse any potential sibling conflicts.

Worsening of dehydration.   Because of their essential fatty acid derivative problem, most children with ADHD are partially dehydrated. Encourage your child to drink plenty of fluids during hot summer months, with pure water being the ultimate preference. Second choices would be diluted lemonade or fruit juice, boxed juices, frozen natural fruit pops, fresh melons, watermelon frozen pops, and teas.

Risk of chemical exposure.   The mother of a child with ADHD made sure her child discharged a lot of his built-up energy by a weekly one-hour swimming spree in an indoor pool. She asked me why he would invariably seem more hyperactive and irritable, rather than less so, after the swim. The answer was simple: because of the concentrated chlorine compounds he breathed and absorbed through his skin. If this problem is likely for your child, choose outdoor pools rather than indoor pools and limit swimming in heavily chlorinated water to brief periods. Better yet, limit swimming to lakes and streams. Follow the toxinsulation recommendations for insect bites and related exposures that I've provided in the section on summer camps.

HELP YOUR CHILD ARRANGE FOR A PET

Some hyperactive children are simply too rough and careless to trust with a pet. Most children with ADHD, however, can successfully discharge the duties of a pet guardian. Everyone needs to be touched and to touch. Well-trained and gentle pets can provide unconditional touch and a quality of reciprocal affection that is second to none. Animals don't have any prejudice—they are blind to any child's physical deformities, handicaps, shortcomings, and social class. Spending quality time with a pet gives your child a chance to be quiet and have peaceful time alone.

Animal care encourages pro-social skills in the act of caring for another being. Learning how to express affection to the pet gives your child practice in honoring boundaries, approaching others courteously, being gentle toward others, and related skills. By stepping outside his or her own needs to care for the pet, your child learns valuable lessons and experiences a higher sense of giving.

> *Spending quality time with a pet gives a child the chance to be quiet and have peaceful time alone.*

Animals provide an opportunity to learn about life and death, and as such, they provide an excellent method of helping any child work through a grieving process. Caring for an animal helps increase curiosity about learning, and it allows your child to be in control in a safe, productive way.

YOUR CHILD CAN HOST A PARTY

Involve your child in the planning as much as possible, so that very little comes as a surprise. Keep the number of invited guests small enough to manage and to avoid creating an overstimulating experience for your child. Don't expect much expansion of friendships from parties. Remember that having one guest over at a time for a visit is the best way to increase your child's friendships. Colorful decorations and nonfood party favors such as balloons and small toys can help produce a festive atmosphere without risking petrochemical exposure for your child.

> *Having one guest over at a time for a visit is the best way to increase your child's friendships.*

Planning for parties should include consideration of chemical sensitivities or food allergies your child has. Fun food does not have to mean petrochemical-containing food, and you can include fewer sweets and more protein-containing foods than there are at a typical party. Consider making a pizza as part of the party activities or serving chicken drumsticks, make-your-own tacos, beans with burgers, fresh hearty salads, or other nutritious foods.

Cake is always a favorite at any type of party, but most supermarket boxed brands are laden with petrochemicals, as are the canned frostings. Try a homemade cake baked from scratch (or from an all-natural boxed mix) with whipped cream or brown sugar meringue frosting. Or consider baking a carob or carrot cake with white or naturally colored frosting. Green Magma, made from dehydrated barley sprouts and available at health stores, makes a bright neon-green coloring for cake and cookie decorations. Or place a paper doily on an unfrosted cake and sift powdered sugar over it, creating an attractive design on the cake. Use small plastic toys or ornaments to dress up any frosting.

All-natural ice cream is almost always a pleasing companion to cake. Or try making homemade ice cream as part of the party activities. All-natural fruit punch is easily made from three parts juice to one part sparkling mineral water, and pure lemonade is always an acceptable option.

ASSIST WHEN YOUR CHILD IS INVITED TO A PARTY

If your child is invited elsewhere for a party, it is harder to prevent an S-R state from food or chemical reactions. Don't expect others to understand what it means to have a petroleum-free dessert. Explain that your child has food or chemical sensitivities and offer to provide key food items for the entire party or have your child take along food you provide. Suggest to the host a convenient brand switch, such as to an all-natural brand of ice cream.

> *If your child is invited to a party, explain that she has food sensitivities and offer to provide key food items for the entire party.*

If all else fails, ask your child to save the party food and bring it back home, where you will buy it from him. Maintain a batch of all-natural cupcakes or cookies in your freezer at all times for your child's last-minute invitations to get together with friends.

ENJOY HOLIDAYS WITH YOUR CHILD

Many holidays have little meaning for children other than an excuse to get out of school and pig out on holiday food. All food-centered holidays represent a special challenge for parents of children with ADHD.

Keep the petroleum out of food and confined to the plastic trinkets and decorations during parties for holidays associated with specific theme colors, such as Saint Patrick's Day, Halloween, or Valentine's Day. Theme-color doilies, napkins, straws, party plates and cups, balloons, and crepe paper are enough to provide the festive atmosphere. There is no need to provide petroleum-based green, red, or orange food. Instead of serving petrochemical-containing cookies on a white dish, bake all-natural cookies, dust them with powdered sugar, and serve on a colored dish. Use colored plastic trinkets to decorate white-frosted all-natural cake. For Halloween, cook and mash carrots, then force them through a sieve and decorate the frosting with them. To make a white frosting orange, use carrot juice; for red, use beet juice. If your child is sensitive to phenols from scented candles or phosphorus from any candles, simply avoid candles.

Easter

As with any shower-the-child-with-candy holiday, the best way to deal with the issues of petrochemical additives and piles of candy is to avoid both. Some parents of children with ADHD have successfully altered the theme of the day by substituting sand pails for Easter baskets. The pails contain trinkets, a shovel, inflatable plastic toys, playing cards, sunblock, tanning lotion, sunglasses, or other items indicative of beach play.

> *Consider substituting sand pails full of fun trinkets for traditional candy-laden Easter baskets.*

There is no limit to the number of noncandy themes you can create to dress up the Easter baskets into something actually uplifting and beneficial for your child. One mother who carefully watches her children's exposure to food additives reports:

> My kids' Easter baskets are the envy of all the children in the neighborhood. Just use your imagination and think about what your child would really like.

Her advice is sound. Include a few all-natural sweet treats but emphasize nonfood items such as a ring, ball, book, action figure, costume jewelry, kite, sports trading card, puzzle, coloring or activity book, stationery, coin bank, coupon for privileges, pair of barrettes, audiotape, Matchbox car, video, collection of stickers, fancy pencil set, earring set, joke or riddle book, comic book, finger puppet, seasonal cookie cutter, or homemade modeling compound. Wrap some of the items just as you would a birthday gift and include some in plastic eggs.

Easter basket food gifts that are petrochemical-free and low in salicylates and that parents of children with ADHD have successfully given include nuts, baby carrots, hard candies, popcorn balls, string cheese, dates, figs, miniature muffins in a sandwich bag, caramel corn, pumpkin and sunflower seeds, blue-green algae chewy bars, a ripe pear or banana, and dried fruit. Remember that an exorbitant amount of sweets consumed on an empty stomach in the morning spells disaster for some children with ADHD and their parents. Also bear in mind that proteins will prevent sugar-based behavior deterioration in most children who have ADHD. The best compromise is to allow consumption of the treats occasionally throughout the day, always accompanied by a protein-rich food. See chapter 6 for a thorough discussion of this topic.

Try an indoor egg hunt using hollow plastic eggs filled with nonfood items, anything from a few pennies to a piece of jewelry. They can be refilled with walnuts and used by your child to entertain neighboring children with an outdoor egg hunt.

An indoor or outdoor treasure hunt with rhyming clues leading to each progressive step on the hunt is a favorite activity. Follow the same procedure as the Halloween treasure hunt (see page 328).

How about those Easter eggs? While eggs are one of the best foods a child with ADHD can consume, Easter eggs should be eaten soon after being boiled, as long as the shells are intact and they have not been colored. Once they are colored or decorated, they are merely decorative items not fit for human consumption.

Blowing out raw eggs is an interesting activity. Use a pin to break a small hole in each end of a raw egg, making one hole slightly larger than the other. Stick a toothpick through the larger hole and break the yolk. Remove the toothpick and blow into the smaller hole until the egg's contents come out through the larger hole. The evacuated contents are edible for a short period if kept sanitary and cool. Decorate the shell as you would a hard-boiled egg.

Decoration of Easter eggs can provide meaningful and enjoyable family activity. Use all-purpose white glue to attach construction

Do You Know the Easter Bunny's Big Secret?

The Easter bunny wants you to have a Taylor-ific Easter and doesn't want your child exposed to nasty petrochemicals from commercial egg dyes. Try using what the Easter bunny uses—all-natural dyes.

The Easter bunny's secret method: Wash and chop the coloring material (see below) into small pieces. Boil it in one to two cups of water mixed with a small amount of vinegar for eight minutes in an enamel or porcelain saucepan. Strain through a colander lined with cheesecloth or a clean rag, then cool.

Hard-boil the eggs in a porcelain or glass saucepan with a little vinegar. Set the eggs in the natural color solution for at least five minutes. Afterward, make them shine by rubbing them with a few drops of vegetable oil on a soft cloth.

paper bits, spices, lace, ribbon, raisins, string, buttons, cotton balls, other small objects, or dried noodles, beans, or corn.

To avoid those commercial petrochemical-containing dyes, use the Easter bunny's all-natural colors.

Halloween

Halloween trick-or-treating is a special challenge. The best way to meet that challenge is to eliminate it. Organize a party as a substitute for trick-or-treating. Avoid petrochemical-laden treats and commercial face paints.

> The best way to meet the challenge of Halloween trick-or-treating is to organize a party as a substitute.

Try having a pumpkin decorating contest, keeping the shell of the pumpkin intact. There is no worry about accidents with sharp knives when your child isn't carving the pumpkin. Colored paint pens are available from craft stores. For "baby pumpkins," use oranges. Pumpkin is a low-salicylate vegetable, so treats made from it, including pumpkin pie, are acceptable for most children with ADHD (see appendix E for

Here's what to use for vibrant colors.

- For *yellow:* turmeric, saffron, crocuses, daffodils, skins of yellow onions
- For *orange:* skins of yellow onions
- For *green:* young grass, broccoli, spinach, moss, rhubarb, birch leaves
- For *blue:* blueberries, red cabbage, grape skins, grape juice
- For *brown:* plums, coffee, tea, walnut shells
- For *red:* beets
- For *purple:* crush a frozen blackberry with your fingers and rub it over the hot, dry egg

information on salicylates). Use the decorated pumpkins as sources of fun food over the subsequent couple of weeks.

Don't forget those precious pumpkin seeds. Remember, they are one of the best snacks for your child because of their rich content of essential fatty acids and protein. Wash some and lightly roast them at 400°F for about five minutes, just long enough to provide a slight crispness. Use a dash of sea salt to bring out the flavor of the roasted seeds.

For party prizes, use stickers, plastic toys, spider rings, badges, stick-ons, stuffed animals, pencils, patches, puzzles, posters, balls, novelty jewelry, certificates for favors and privileges, and similar trinkets. Have your child dress up in a costume and serve trick-or-treaters during part of the evening.

Have the children make ghosts from clean empty plastic milk containers. They can cut out ghost shapes and string them up outside or inside as a party decoration using fishing line. Lean an ironing board against the wall, covered with a white sheet. Have the children join in creating a ghost-monster with various art materials.

Have a jack-o'-lantern carving contest. Start by cutting a large hole in the bottom so that the entire pumpkin can be conveniently lifted off the base where the candle is placed. Place a chunk of dry ice in a glass of hot water on the base of each pumpkin and watch the reaction from the children at the party when the pumpkins start to emit their spooky fog.

Avoid high-salicylate and petrochemical-containing foods. Tart apples are very high in salicylate and may present a problem for some children who have ADHD. Pears and yellow (Golden Delicious) apples are better alternatives. Try bobbing for pears and serving hot pear juice as a substitute for cider. Have a "Halloween egg hunt" with walnuts or almonds, make popcorn balls, play pin the broom on the witch, or make frozen banana-dipped-in-carob sticks. Make pumpkin-face pizzas with cheese for hair, carrot rounds for eyes, and pineapple chunks for teeth and nose. Try pumpkin-face cheese sandwiches on dark rye bread. Cut out the jack-o'-lantern face on the top slice of each sandwich.

A perennial favorite is a spooky treasure hunt with rhyming clues. Prepare the clues ahead of time and insert each into an envelope. During the party, someone hides the envelopes in various places, careful to put each envelope in its assigned place. The last envelope contains the prize or instructions as to the location of the prize. The prize could be a video for everyone to watch at the party. Mark each envelope with the location that it is to be placed in, for example "under rock by back door." The clue in the preceding envelope might say, for example, "When you read the next clue, your knees will knock, because it is under a certain big rock."

> *A*llow a thin layer of cold cream to dry on your child's face prior to putting on commercial face paints. Or make your own face paint.

To have more "treat" than "trick" and to avoid being haunted by a very hyperactive ghoul, keep petrochemicals and other phenols off your child's skin and out of your child's mouth. If he insists on some trick-or-treating, arrange for him to serve as a collector for a charity, so that less time is spent ob-

Is Your Child Going Trick-or-Treating?

Give your child the thrill of fantastic face decoration without the chemical exposure that makes commercial face paint so likely to produce more trick than treat among children with ADHD. (To remove the greasepaint later, use cold cream or baby oil.)

- **For white greasepaint.** Using a rubber spatula, mix 2 teaspoons white shortening, 5 teaspoons cornstarch, 1 teaspoon white flour, and 4 drops glycerin (from a drugstore; the glycerin makes it creamy).

- **For fake blood.** Mix 1 tablespoon beet juice into the white greasepaint.

- **For brown greasepaint.** Mix 1 teaspoon white shortening and 1 tablespoon cocoa powder.

- **For eye blackening.** Use any of these methods: a burnt cork, a piece of charcoal, or beet juice mixed with petroleum jelly.

- **For red rouge.** Mix beet juice, petroleum jelly, and flour.

- **For "witchy warts."** Mix peanut butter and shredded coconut.

taining all those chemical-laced sugary treats. Allow a thin layer of cold cream to dry on your child's face prior to putting on commercial face paints. Regular commercial eyeliners and eye shadows are generally free of the types of chemicals that will create S-R states, but check the labels for BHA, BHT, or TBHQ.

Deal with the issues of unacceptable food additives and mountains of candy by arranging some trade-offs. Divide treats obtained from neighbors into two piles: "safe" and "unsafe." The unsafe pile can be donated to someone else, traded for a gift or privilege of equal worth, or traded for all-natural treats of equal worth to be consumed gradually over the next several weeks. Remember that, in general, proteins will prevent S-R states caused by too much sugar, and essential fatty acids will prevent S-R states caused by food additives. Have some EFA-rich and protein-rich food available for your child to consume along with all those Halloween treats. If you are hunting for safe alternatives to give to neighbor children, consider nonfood items such as balloons, pennies, stick-ons, erasers, or unscented stickers.

Thanksgiving

A plain fresh or frozen locally grown whole, unbasted, unstuffed turkey with one ingredient—turkey—is a fine food for your child. Avoid turkeys labeled with the words "butter" or "hydrolyzed protein" because they usually don't contain butter but do contain numerous petrochemicals in the form of artificial flavorings, colorings, preservatives, and flavor enhancers.

For many reasons, this fantastic fowl is one of the best foods your child can eat. Its chief claim to fame among families with a hyperactive child is its ability to cause sleepiness shortly after consuming it, and thus it is an ideal bedtime snack. Of more consequence to the general public, it is rich in B vitamins, minerals, calcium, phosphorus, lysine, potassium, and iron.

> *Turkey is one of the best foods your child can eat. And because most hyperactive children become sleepy shortly after consuming it, it's an ideal bedtime snack.*

To avoid endless leftovers, consider cooking half of the turkey and put the other half in the freezer for another meal. Cook it in a large nonaluminum roasting pan, cut side down. Prepare stuffing in a separate nonaluminum container. For an excellent side dish, bake sweet potatoes, then peel and mash them. Add crushed pineapple plus its natural juice and bake in a greased nonaluminum baking dish until heated through.

To preserve the greatest amount of B vitamins and other nutrients, I recommend this slow-cooking method. Coat the outside of the turkey with olive oil. Place the turkey breast down in the roasting pan and bake at 350°F for one hour to kill surface bacteria. Then turn the oven to 190°F and cook one hour for each pound of turkey. The result will be a flavorful, tender, juicy turkey loaded with nutrients that would have been destroyed by the ordinary high temperature baking method.

Homemade fruitcake is delicious. There is no need to include those artificially colored cherries, and you can keep salicylates low by using dried papaya, pineapple, dates, and figs plus walnuts, pecans, and Brazil nuts.

Christmas and Hannukah

The end-of-year holiday season can become very stressful for parents of a child with ADHD. Not only does the school vacation cause wholesale disruption in routines, but just about everyone is involved in chaotic high-energy activities and errands. Surprises are fine when gifts are presented, but the other aspects of the holiday season should involve minimal disruption of daily routines for your child. Try to keep everything low-key and keep your child informed ahead of time.

Plan ahead for additive-free treats and have them available in the freezer. Take some along on trips with your child to avoid those "you can't have a cookie until after you get home" conflicts. Regular vigorous physical exercise is one of the most reliable ways to keep any child or teen with ADHD in a state of heightened mental control. Don't let the disruptions of the holiday season erase this important component of your child's scheduled activities. In fact, maintain regular schedules of meals, sleep, and exercise for all family members. It is important to plan events carefully and coordinate personal schedules alertly. Use the family council for these purposes. Devote part of each day to a soothing and recentering activity with your child, such as reading together. Put a speed governor on the total number of exciting activities planned per day. I suggest a limit of three "projects" per day.

> *Regular vigorous physical exercise is one of the most reliable ways to keep any child or teen with ADHD in a state of heightened mental control.*

Don't overlook the central meaning from which our custom of gift giving derived. Give the holiday season a bigger dimension than merely a time for your child to take a break from school and receive presents. Involve him in some sort of benevolent activity—anything from baking cookies for the local homeless shelter to doing anonymous favors for a neighbor.

Turn greeting card giving from a chore into a delight by involving your child in making cards to send to friends and relatives. Use common arts and crafts supplies such as stickers and construction paper. Have your child compose the greeting statements and draw the pictures, incorporating decorations and stickers into the finished products. This activity has numerous advantages for your child and provides an excellent avenue for him to receive many encouraging and positive responses from the recipients. The resulting uplift in his self-esteem is hard to beat.

Your child will probably have many temptations to eat food that is especially deficient in nutrients and laden with petrochemical additives. Be watchful about such exposures and take action to prevent them. Maintain the pattern of toxinsulation and nutritional support recommended in chapters 6 and 7, especially consuming protein- and EFA-rich food regularly throughout each day.

Some children with ADHD are chemically sensitive to seasonal irritants, not the least of which is the heavily phenolic scent given off by pine trees. Airborne phenols are particularly common, from scented candles, gift perfumes and soaps, new clothing (freshly unwrapped but not yet washed), and fireplace smoke. Be aware of the extra load of potential toxins and make sure your child's bedroom remains a safe haven from environmental toxic overload. The spider plant that you've placed there will have extra duty during the holidays, soaking up all those additional airborne phenol molecules.

MEET THE CHALLENGE OF VIDEO GAMES AND TV

Video games were introduced in the 1970s and, within a decade, became the most popular childhood leisure activity in the United States.

There are prosocial and therapeutic uses of video games within the fields of physical rehabilitation and oncology. Video games provide a high-interest way to introduce children to computers and require continuous practice at important skills such as visual tracking, eye-hand coordination, and attention to detail.

The themes most preferred by teens are fantasy violence and sports. Fewer than 2 percent of children and teens prefer games with educational content. There has been a steady general increase in violent themes. Research is now tending to show a connection between the escalating violence in video games and the amount of aggressive and violent misbehavior shown by teen players of the games.[1,2]

There are, however, some redeeming factors. Most of the popular games feature an autonomous individual working alone or with modest assistance against an evil force. Current games allow for random joint participation to form teams with other players through Internet connection. The constant scanning, planning, and coordination of eye-hand actions keep the brain's beta wave activity going much stronger than when children are merely watching television. For this reason, most players stay more mentally alert during and after video games than during and after television viewing. The games can become a useful ingredient in the child's social acceptance among peers and can perform the functions of an emergency electronic sitter to give harried parents a few moments of relief.

The research is still scanty on the total impact of video games with respect to ADHD issues. Like most other aspects of family life, video games should be integrated with caution and supervised with care.

Television Viewing

America's favorite pastime is a powerful force, one that ends up occupying more total time of a typical child's life than school attendance and time spent with parents. The parallel silence of TV watching doesn't bring unity. Instead, it brings division into your family. Nearly 40 percent of family time is now absorbed by television watching, which far outweighs the other typical free-time activities. The 25 to 28

Are You Meeting the Challenge of TV?

The best solution is to not have a television in your home. The second-best solution is to integrate TV into your child's and your family's life while minimizing its negative effects, using these guidelines:

- Limit viewing to two hours or less per day.
- Choose programs wisely and have clear rules about forbidden programs.
- Discuss controversial or upsetting programs immediately with your child.
- Limit your own viewing to set an example and to keep your priorities straight.
- Watch with your child rather than leaving her unattended to watch for extended periods.
- Analyze with your child or teen the unrealness or valuelessness of the violence, promiscuity, or other undesirable elements of the program.
- Make TV viewing a deliberate choice rather than a habit.
- Ask yourself if entertainment is the most important and greatest need for your child at this time.
- Require a half-hour break between any two programs.

hours weekly the average U.S. child spends watching TV drastically cuts down on more helpful and more important activities. It constitutes more than six times the amount of time spent on homework.

The average U.S. family watches TV for more than twice as much time as is spent on socializing and more than six times the amount spent in outdoor recreation. The average graduating high school student has watched over 22,000 hours of endorsed impulsivity, oversexualized and exploitative relationships, gaudy special

- Encourage your child to follow up desirable TV content by looking something up in a dictionary or encyclopedia.
- Mark acceptable programs for the week on a schedule posted on the refrigerator.
- Have the children take turns determining which of two competing programs will be viewed.
- Have only one TV and keep it in the living room.
- At your family council meetings, determine who will watch which programs during the week.
- Require an "equal time" trade-off of reading and family activity.
- Discuss at the family council ways to upgrade the quality of your family activities other than TV watching.
- Discuss and refute ads pressuring your child to buy unimportant things.
- Turn the TV off when an important family activity, such as sharing a meal, is occurring.
- Don't let the TV dilute important interactions; turn it off if you want to talk with your child.
- Save it for its best purpose—to provide information or pleasant entertainment when those are the most important needs.

effects, profane and abusive language, and massive amounts of profound violence.

The fact that the *average* daily TV viewing period is between three and four hours indicates that there are many children who spend *much more* time in front of the TV set. Recent research has focused on these children. One group of scientists at Case Western Reserve University recently looked at the TV viewing habits of about 2,000 children. They found that those who watched the greatest amount of TV were more likely to feel depressed, anxious, or angry. Thus excessive TV watching was very attractive to children with profound inner turmoil who are desperate for solace, distraction, and pleasant stimulation. In other words, well-adjusted children have no need for such excessive and imbalanced use of their time.

On prime-time evening TV, there are an average of about 10 violent acts per hour on any one channel. There are 25 violent acts per hour on cartoon shows. The average U.S. child witnesses around 50 acts of violence on TV daily, most involving handguns. By his sixteenth birthday, the average U.S. child has witnessed over 200,000 acts of TV violence, including 33,000 attempted or completed murders. If aggressiveness is a problem, be doubly diligent in censoring the television messages coming into your home. Numerous research studies have demonstrated that children become more accepting of aggression and more physically aggressive themselves after watching violence on television, whether cartoon or human.

> *In a study of 2,000 children, those who watched the greatest amount of TV were more likely to feel depressed, anxious, or angry.*

A concern among parents is the many distortions presented on TV programs about how life works. The warped view of sexuality portrayed on TV, with its glorification of promiscuous, shallow, exploitative relationships and its neglect of frank portrayal of the terrible consequences of such activity is a case in point. A study by the Parents Television Council found, for example, that in the decade from 1989 to 1999, sexual activity on an hourly basis on television more than tripled. In a 1995 study, the American Academy of Pediatrics found that 62 percent of children age 10 to 16 felt that TV and motion pictures influenced them to have sexual relations when they were too young.

Twisted values can be taught through repetition. Teens and children with ADHD tend to have more early sexual experiences than their non-ADHD peers, and teen girls with ADHD are at risk for unwed pregnancy. The effect of an essentially valueless mass media influence on a child or teen who already has numerous difficulties with friendships, social judgment, and intimacy can be dangerous.

One of the most disastrous effects, and one of the least frequently mentioned, is that all this TV watching displaces the act of reading as a leisure activity. The ability to process language at a level needed for superior academic achievement is unlikely to develop in the absence of extensive reading and participating in active, rather than passive, interaction with others. Yet children watch TV for more than six times the total amount of time they spend reading.

> *One of the most disastrous effects is that all this TV watching displaces the act of reading as a leisure activity.*

Control the television set so that it doesn't control your family. Put a reasonable time limit on the total hours your child watches, as well as the time of day or night during which the watching takes place. The best arrangement, according to many parents, is to post a list of each week's approved programs. If conflicts arise over which program to watch at a specific time, arrange a simple rotation schedule so each child gets a turn at determining what to watch. Put the schedule on your family's daily activities chart.

Because most of your child's or teen's waking hours will be spent in recreational activity, the guidelines in this chapter are doubly important for sustaining your family's harmony. By attending to the various facets of recreation and play arrangements described in this chapter, you can help your child maximize the benefits of healthy entertainment and personal renewal. The next chapter shows you how to combine efforts with other parents to reduce the difficulties and challenges of parenting a child with ADHD.

CHAPTER 18

Join or Start a
Support Group

A SUPPORT GROUP can be an important source of help. United with other parents, you can sidestep bureaucratic bungling to bring about changes in community resources, health care, educational programs, and other related support systems. If existing support groups don't meet your needs or if none exist in your community, consider organizing one. Professionals may offer informational presentations, or parents may offer practical caregiving suggestions. Parents are the primary conductors of the type of support group discussed here. The oldest support organization for parents of ADHD children is the Feingold Association of the United States, and the most extensive support organization is Ch.A.D.D.

ORGANIZING A SUPPORT GROUP

Five steps are essential to organizing an effective support group:

1. Determine goals and services.

2. Arrange start-up meetings.

3. Recruit skilled leaders.

4. Expand the membership.

5. Take decisive action.

Determine Goals and Services

The creativity and involvement of the leaders and members constantly expand the group's horizons. Here are some examples of the types of services I've known successful support groups to provide.

Interaction.   Members learn from other families' experiences and receive and share emotional support. Knowing that they are not alone provides tremendous relief, particularly for single parents. Discussion groups that allow participants to express concerns, ask questions, find answers, and share successful home and school arrangements offer empathy and support.

Instruction.   The group can arrange for qualified persons to present programs on topics relevant to ADHD and related conditions. Common topics include just about everything covered in this book, from sensory integration therapy to surviving holidays. Educational group meetings have the additional advantage of providing a forum for controversial information to be discussed from differing points of view.

Standard parent education topics like encouragement, discipline, anger control, friendship skills, stress reduction, and study habits seem to be popular topics.

Research.   ADHD affects about 6 percent of U.S. schoolchildren but has received little research support compared with much rarer pediatric disorders. For every child with autism, for example, there are about 70 children with ADHD. Because a large number of parents and children with a specific disorder and cluster of behavioral difficulties are available for study, an ADHD support group can assist in research.

Community awareness.   As the group makes the community more aware of the needs and characteristics of children with ADHD, the families of recently diagnosed children can experience much greater understanding and help.

Special services. Camping programs for children with special needs, including ADHD and related conditions, are sponsored by various organizations throughout North America. The group can conduct a survey of nearby camping programs and develop a special one if none of the local camps seem suitable. The group can also organize special programs for the children who would not have easy access to other suitable activities. It can identify individual or family needs of member families and appropriate community resources to meet those needs.

Encourage your local school district to provide in-service training to familiarize teachers and administrators with the special characteristics of children and adolescents with ADHD. If necessary, have the support group sponsor or provide this training of school personnel. At a minimum, send a representative from your group to every school board meeting and open forum.

Advocacy. Supplying advocates and advice givers to individual families is another important function of a support group. Basic advocacy involves finding out what the family needs, outlining the options, assessing the family's chances of reaching the goals, and advising on courses of action.

The group should inform parents of their rights and provide as much information as possible to help obtain effective services. It should train parents to be their own advocates, and it should intervene only if the parent is personally unable to obtain legitimate services.

It can help parents prepare documentation to support requests for services on behalf of their children and can identify the correct appeals processes. The group can investigate grievances about current services and can make certain the grievances are heard and complied with. The group can also assist parents in going to court if other avenues fail.

Information gathering.   Support groups share information among members and other support groups. For example, the group can arrange visits to out-of-district school programs and treatment facilities to observe any especially successful or creative services. It can organize a resource network with a newsletter, a telephone hotline, or a catalog of helpful local agencies and services. I've often assisted in developing lending libraries, which turn out to be one of the most helpful of these types of services.

Networking.   The group can organize within the school district boundaries, then link with similar organizations within neighboring districts. It can also provide networking for services such as exchanging temporary child care among members. Another very helpful service is that of mentoring new members and members of nearby support groups.

A parent experienced at insulating a child from petrochemicals, for example, can obtain helpful materials from the Feingold Association, including a grocery shopping guide listing by brand name the foods sold in local markets that are additive free. That person can then serve as a resource for parents who are just starting out learning to read the fine print on food labels and learning to identify airborne phenols that are triggering their child's ADHD symptoms.

Arrange Start-Up Meetings

Launching a new support group takes effort but can be accomplished by anyone with enough determination. If possible, obtain the assistance at first from an umbrella organization, such as a church, public agency, private foundation, or local government group. A list of concerned parents, educators, mental health professionals, and physicians is a good basis for starting a group.

The Coordinating Council for Handicapped Children recommends three meetings for launching a support group: the organizational meeting, the public meeting, and the working meeting. Although a series of three specialized meetings is not suitable for every community, it provides an excellent starting point for understanding what these meetings should accomplish.

Get the word out for interested parents to contact you at a specified time and place. At this meeting, make plans for a large, more public meeting that will attract a large percentage of the parents of children with ADHD in your community.

An interesting featured speaker and a selection of brief workshops is the most popular and successful type of program to offer. Get the names and addresses of all who attend. At the next meeting, elect officers, develop a statement of goals, establish a Web site, and start the relevant legal processes, such as obtaining a bulk mailing permit and incorporation.

Recruit Skilled Leaders

Leaders should be dedicated to the group's goals, good at motivating others to contribute their efforts, energizing to be around, positive and friendly, and willing to share monthly reports and to communicate with the membership. They should be open to suggestions and supportive of democratic decision making.

Leadership responsibilities include recruiting new members, building team spirit, developing other leaders, supporting fund-raising projects, carefully matching the skills of volunteers with their assignments, encouraging a well-maintained Web site, and following projects through to completion.

Leaders need to pace the group's activities to avoid burnout or boredom of the membership and themselves. They should avoid giving too many duties to one or two faithful volunteers while others withdraw because they have too little to do. Skilled leaders will maintain frequent contact with volunteers, listen to their suggestions, and reward them with appropriate acknowledgments and tokens of their service.

Expand the Membership

There is no substitute for a strong membership committee that encourages individual memberships as well as group memberships of civic and community agencies. Dues should be low. Develop a small leaflet describing the group. A newsletter is one of the most potent tools for ensuring the survival and growth of a support group; pay special attention to developing a readable newsletter and constantly expanding Web site that keeps members active and generates continual interest. Try to obtain membership of some professionals from each of the relevant disciplines but avoid letting the group get too top heavy. Use the newsletter as a tool to keep the group prominent among the agencies and professionals in the community by asking a different administrator or helping professional to write an editorial or small informative article for each edition.

Take Decisive Action

One of the keys to a group's growth is making membership exciting by having real impact on the community as well as on the lives of member families. Complaints should become springboards for action. Leaders should ask for members' participation when a particular situation or problem is shared by several member families. Keep the focus on goals and avoid draining away resources on excessive parties, picnics, potlucks, or trips.

GENERATING AND MAINTAINING ADEQUATE RESOURCES

Most support groups don't run an office but operate instead as a core group of volunteers with minimal facilities. They often obtain supplies, funds, and services from local philanthropic and service organizations and nonprofit groups. Many groups obtain the needed financial base by selling seasonal items. Among the most successful printed materials to sell are cookbooks and community calendars, which can be placed on sale by most merchants within the community. This type of fund-raising provides not only financial support but also public exposure.

These guidelines represent the combined experiences of leaders and members of support groups that vary greatly in funding, membership size, and focus. A strong, vital support group can flourish in your community, and you can play an important part in that growth.

Epilogue: A Final Word of Encouragement

This book summarizes the guidance and suggestions I typically offer when working with the families of children with ADHD. Many of them are my own inventions, such as the I CARE discipline sequence, the concerns notebook and PPI method, the Taylor-Latta Diet Diary, the A through H effects of physiological treatment, the word *toxinsulation*, the documenting of six organ systems involved in ADHD, the fun idea list, the fun idea drawer, the eight A's of apology, the homework chain, and the charts and checklists. In these pages, I have attempted to provide you with the information and tools for preventing or solving the types of problems you are most likely to confront as the parent of a child or adolescent with ADHD or a related condition.

I don't want, however, to overwhelm or intimidate you with lists of potential difficulties. Although this book is devoted to correcting problems, that emphasis does not mean things never go right. There are many positive aspects to raising a child with ADHD. The vast majority lead successful lives, and those fortunate enough to have parents like you, who are willing to read and follow guidelines such as the ones in this book, function well.

Please select those suggestions most relevant to your particular situation. Have confidence that improvement will come and never let the negatives outweigh your awareness of the positives. Your gifts of time, resourcefulness, and commitment are priceless in helping your child achieve the best possible adjustment and success. Both of you are going to emerge as real winners!

Appendix A: For More Help

Chapter 1

John Taylor, *ADD/ADHD in Childhood: An Overview*, an "Answers to A.D.D." audiotape; Salem, Oregon: A.D.D. Plus, 1998.

John Taylor, *Answers to A.D.D.: A Practical Guide for Parents*; Warminster, Pennsylvania: Mar-Co Products, 1997.

John Taylor, *Hiperactividad y Deficiencia de Atencion la Ninez: Resumen en General*, an "Answers to A.D.D." Spanish language audiotape; Salem, Oregon: Sun Media, 1993.

The ADHD Challenge, P.O. Box 3225, West Peabody, MA 01960 (national newsletter).

Chapter 2

T. Atwood, *Asperger's Syndrome: A Guide for Parents and Professionals*; London: Jessica Kinsley, 1998.

D. Cohen and F. Volkmar, *Handbook of Autism and Pervasive Developmental Disorders*; New York: Wiley, 1997.

Elizabeth Gerlach, *Autism Treatment Guide*; Eugene, Oregon: Four Leaf Press, 1993.

Lisa Lewis, *Special Diets for Special Kids: Understanding and Implementing Special Diets to Aid in the Treatment of Autism and Related Developmental Disorders*; Arlington, Texas: Future Horizons, 1998.

M. Powers, *Children with Autism: A Parent's Guide*; Bethesda, Maryland: Woodbine House, 2000.

A. Wetherby and B. Brizant, *Autism Spectrum Disorders: A Transactional Developmental Perspective*; Baltimore: Paul H. Brookes, 2000.

Organizations

Autism Network for Dietary Intervention, P.O. Box 17711, Rochester, NY 14617-0711 (www. AutismNDL.com).

Autism Research Institute, 4182 Adams Avenue, San Diego, CA 92116.

Developmental Delay Registry, 6701 Fairfax Road, Chevy Chase, MD 20815.

Chapter 3

John Taylor, *Positive Prescriptions for Negative Parenting: The Counselor's Guide to Diagnosing and Assisting Troubled Parents and Children* (revised edition); Warminster, Pennsylvania: Mar-Co Products, 1995.

Chapter 4

John Taylor, *Los Medicamentos y el Desorden de Deficiencia de Atencion e Hiperactividad*, an "Answers to A.D.D." Spanish-language audiotape; Salem, Oregon: Sun Media, 1993.

John Taylor, *Pills and Skills: Using Medication Treatment Effectively*, an "Answers to A.D.D." audiotape; Salem, Oregon: A.D.D. Plus, 1998.

Chapter 5

John Taylor, *Los Medicamentos y el Desorden de Deficiencia de Atencion e Hiperactividad*, an "Answers to A.D.D." Spanish-language audiotape; Salem, Oregon: Sun Media, 1993.

John Taylor, *Pills and Skills: Using Medication Treatment Effectively*, an "Answers to A.D.D." audiotape; Salem, Oregon: A.D.D. Plus, 1998.

Chapter 6

Karl Abrams, *Algae to the Rescue! Everything You Need to Know About Nutritional Blue-Green Algae*; Studio City, California: Logan House, 1996.

Karl Abrams, *Attention Deficit Hyperactivity Disorder: A Nutritional Approach*; Westlake Village, California: Timeless Books, 1998.

William Crook and Laura Stevens, *Solving the Puzzle of Your Hard-to-Raise Child*; New York: Random House, 1987.

Joanne Gittelman, *Blue-green Algae: Super Nutrition for Your Child* (revised edition); Honolulu: Brian Associates, 1998.

Sandra Hills and Pat Wyman, *What's Food Got to Do with It? 101 Natural Remedies for Learning Disabilities*; Windsor, California: Center for New Discoveries in Learning, 1997.

Lisa Lewis, *Special Diets for Special Kids: Understanding and Implementing Special Diets to Aid in the Treatment of Autism and Related Developmental Disorders*; Arlington, Texas: Future Horizons, 1998.

John Taylor, *Assisting Brain Biochemistry: Dietary and Nutritional Treatment*, an "Answers to A.D.D." audiotape; Salem, Oregon: A.D.D. Plus, 1998.

John Taylor, *Nutrition and Neurochemistry: The ADD Link*, a VHS videotape; Salem, Oregon: A.D.D. Plus, 1999.

John Taylor and Sharon Latta, *Why Can't I Eat That: Helping Kids Obey Medical Diets*; Salem, Oregon: A.D.D. Plus, 1996.

Laura Thompson, *Our Children Are What Our Children Eat: Nutritional Solutions for Improving Behavior, Health, and School Performance*; Cardiff, California: Laura Thompson, 2000.

Skye Weintraub, *Natural Treatments for ADD and Hyperactivity*; Pleasant Grove, Utah: Woodland Publishing, 1997.

Organizations

Allergy Resources, P.O. Box 888, Palmer Lake, CO 80133 (800-USE-FLAX).

Autism Network for Dietary Intervention, P.O. Box 17711, Rochester, NY 14617 (www. AutismNDL.com).

Autism Research Institute, 4182 Adams Avenue, San Diego, CA 92116.

Developmental Delay Registry, 6701 Fairfax Road, Chevy Chase, MD 20815

Chapter 7

Russell Blaylock, *Excitotoxins: The Taste That Kills*; Santa Fe: Health Press, 1994.

Annie Costa, *The Feel Good Handbook*; San Mateo, California: LightHouse Press, 1998.

Cynthia Fincher, *Healthy Living in a Toxic World*; Colorado Springs: Pinon Press, 1996.

Jane Hersey, *Why Can't My Child Behave? Why Can't She Cope? Why Can't He Learn?* (second edition); Alexandria, Virginia: Pear Tree Press, 1999.

David Steinman and Samuel Epstein, *The Safe Shopper's Bible: A Consumer's Guide to Nontoxic Household Products, Cosmetics, and Food*; New York: Macmillan, 1995.

John Taylor and Sharon Latta, *Why Can't I Eat That: Helping Kids Obey Medical Diets*; Salem, Oregon: A.D.D. Plus, 1996.

Laura Thompson, *Our Children Are What Our Children Eat: Nutritional Solutions for Improving Behavior, Health, and School Performance*; Cardiff, California: Laura Thompson, 2000.

Skye Weintraub, *Natural Treatments for ADD and Hyperactivity*; Pleasant Grove, Utah: Woodland Publishing, 1997.

B. Wolverton, *How to Grow Fresh Air: 50 Houseplants That Purify Your Home or Office*; New York: Penguin, 1997.

Organizations

Autism Network for Dietary Intervention, P.O. Box 17711, Rochester, NY 14617 (www. AutismNDL.com).

Center for Science in the Public Interest, 1501 16th Street, Northwest, Washington, DC 20036.

Feingold Association of the United States, P.O. Box 6550, Alexandria, VA 22306 (800-768-3287, www.feingold.org).

U.S. Public Interest Research Group, 215 Pennsylvania Avenue, Washington, DC 20003.

Chapter 8

A. Jean Ayres, *Sensory Integration and the Child*; Los Angeles: Western Psychological Services, 1979.

Anne Fisher, Elizabeth Murray, and Anita Bundy, *Sensory Integration: Theory and Practice*; Philadelphia: F. A. Davis, 1991.

Carol Kranowitz, *The Out-of-Sync Child: Recognizing and Coping with Sensory Integration Dysfunction*; New York: Penguin-Putnam, 1998.

Organizations

American Occupational Therapy Association, P.O. Box 1725, Rockville, MD 20849.

Sensory Integration International, 1402 Cravens Avenue, Torrance, CA 90501.

Chapter 9

Eugene Anderson, George Redman, and Charlotte Rogers, *Self-Esteem for Tots to Teens: How You Can Help Your Children Feel More Confident and Lovable* (revised edition); Wayzata, Minnesota: Parenting and Teaching Publications, 1991.

Carrie Ivery-Cone, *Speak Out! Just for Teens, Get Some Attention*, a VHS videotape; Nevada City, California: Ivery-Cone Productions, 1994.

Gershen Kaufman, Lev Raphael, and Pamela Espeland, *Stick Up for Yourself! Every Kid's Guide to Personal Power and Positive Self-Esteem* (revised edition); Minneapolis: Free Spirit Publishing, 1999.

Susanna Palomares, Sandy Schuster, and Cheryl Watkins, *The Sharing Circle Handbook: Topics for Teaching Self-Awareness, Communication, and Social Skills*; Torrance, California: Innerchoice, 1992.

Jolene Roehlkepartain and Nancy Leffert, *What Young Children Need to Succeed: Working Together to Build Assets from Birth to Age 11*; Minneapolis: Free Spirit, 2000.

John Taylor, *Anger Control Training for Children and Teens: The Adult's Guidebook for Teaching Healthy Handling of Anger* (revised edition); Warminster, Pennsylvania: Mar-Co Products, 1995.

John Taylor, *Correcting Without Criticizing: The Encouraging Way to Talk to Children About Their Misbehavior* (revised edition); Warminster, Pennsylvania: Mar-Co Products, 1995.

John Taylor, *Encouraging the Discouraged Child: Boosting Your Child's Self-Confidence* (revised edition); Warminster, Pennsylvania: Mar-Co Products, 1995.

John Taylor, *Listening for Feelings: Helping Children Express Emotions in a Healthy Way* (revised edition); Warminster, Pennsylvania: Mar-Co Products, 1995.

John Taylor, *Person to Person: Awareness Techniques for Counselors, Group Leaders, and Parent Educators*; Salem, Oregon: A.D.D. Plus, 1984.

John Taylor, *Se Acabaron las Rabietas: Forma Efectiva de Controlar el Enojo*, an "Answers to A.D.D." Spanish-language audiotape; Salem, Oregon: Sun Media, 1993.

John Taylor, *Social Skills Solutions: Strategies for Teaching Children and Teens*, a VHS videotape; Salem, Oregon: A.D.D. Plus, 1995.

Barbara Valdez, *I Take Responsibility for Me and It Shows: Strategies for Enhancing Self-Esteem*; Torrance, California: Fearon, 1993.

Chapter 10

Terry Beck, *Building Healthy Friendships: Teaching Friendship Skills to Young People*; Saratoga, California: R and E Publishers, 1994.

Karen Burnett, *Simon's Hook: A Story About Teases and Put-Downs*; Roseville, California: GR Publishing, 1999.

Leah Davies, *Kelly Bear, Feelings*; New York: Bureau for At-Risk Youth, 1989.

Leah Davies, *Kelly Bear, Behavior*; New York: Bureau for At-Risk Youth, 1988.

Dorothea Lachner, *Andrew's Angry Words*; Zurich: North-South Books, 1995.

Barbara Lewis, *Being Your Best: Character Building for Kids 7–10*; Minneapolis: Free Spirit Publishing, 2000.

Stephen Nowicki and Marshall Duke, *Helping the Child Who Doesn't Fit In*; Atlanta: Peachtree Publishers, 1992.

Betty Osman and Henriette Blinder, *No One to Play With: Social Problems of LD and ADD Children* (revised edition); Novato, California: Academic Therapy, 1995.

Trevor Romain, *Cliques, Phonies, and Other Baloney*; Minneapolis: Free Spirit Publishing, 1998.

Dianne Schilling (editor), *Fifty Activities for Teaching Emotional Intelligence* (series of three: elementary, intermediate, and high school); Carson, California: Jalmar Press, 1996.

John Taylor, *Anger Control Training for Children and Teens: The Adult's Guidebook for Teaching Healthy Handling of Anger* (revised edition); Warminster, Pennsylvania: Mar-Co Products, 1995.

John Taylor, *Forma Efectiva de Resolver Conflictos: Como Mejorar la Sociabilidad*, an "Answers to A.D.D." Spanish-language audiotape; Salem, Oregon: Sun Media, 1993.

John Taylor, *Living in Harmony: Improving Sibling Relationships*, an "Answers to A.D.D." audiotape; Salem, Oregon: A.D.D. Plus, 1998.

John Taylor, *No More Sibling Rivalry: Increasing Harmony by Helping Your Children Become Better Friends* (revised edition); Warminster, Pennsylvania: Mar-Co Products, 1995.

John Taylor, *No More Tantrums: Anger Control Training*, an "Answers to A.D.D." audiotape; Salem, Oregon: A.D.D. Plus, 1998.

John Taylor, *Se Acabaron las Rabietas: Forma Efectiva de Controlar el Enojo*, an "Answers to A.D.D." Spanish-language audiotape; Salem, Oregon: Sun Media, 1993.

John Taylor, *Social Skills Solutions: Strategies for Teaching Children and Teens*, a VHS videotape; Salem, Oregon: A.D.D. Plus, 1995.

John Taylor, *Training in Peacemaking: Improving Social Skills*, an "Answers to A.D.D." audiotape; Salem, Oregon: A.D.D. Plus, 1998.

Winnifred Taylor, *Anger Answers: High Impact Interventions for Anger Management and Violence Prevention*, an audiotape set; Salem Oregon: A.D.D. Plus, 1996.

Winnifred Taylor, *Anger Answers: Strategies for Anger Management and Violence Prevention;* Salem Oregon: A.D.D. Plus, 1995.

Chapter 11

John Taylor, *Especially for Helping Professionals: Understanding Parents' Feelings and Emotional Stresses*, an "Answers to A.D.D." audiotape; Salem, Oregon: A.D.D. Plus, 1998.

John Taylor, *Intimate Encounter: A Self-Guiding Couples Retreat and Turning Point for Your Relationship;* Holmes Beach, Florida: Learning Publications, 1991.

John Taylor, *Positive Prescriptions for Negative Parenting: The Counselor's Guide to Diagnosing and Assisting Troubled Parents and Children* (revised edition); Warminster, Pennsylvania: Mar-Co Products, 1995.

Chapter 12

John Taylor, *Helping Hands and Smiling Faces: Getting Cooperation on Household Chores* (revised edition); Warminster, Pennsylvania: Mar-Co Products, 1995.

John Taylor, *Intimate Encounter: A Self-Guiding Couples Retreat and Turning Point for Your Relationship;* Holmes Beach, Florida: Learning Publications, 1991.

John Taylor, *Listening for Feelings: Helping Children Express Emotions in a Healthy Way* (revised edition); Warminster, Pennsylvania: Mar-Co Products, 1995.

John Taylor, *Living in Harmony: Improving Sibling Relationships*, an "Answers to A.D.D." audiotape; Salem, Oregon: A.D.D. Plus, 1998.

John Taylor, *No More Sibling Rivalry: Increasing Harmony by Helping Your Children Become Better Friends* (revised edition); Warminster, Pennsylvania: Mar-Co Products, 1995.

Chapter 13

David Cook, *When Your Child Struggles: The Myths of 20/20 Vision, What Every Parent Needs to Know;* Atlanta: Invision Press, 1992.

Pamela Gillet, *Auditory Processes* (revised edition); Novato, California: Academic Therapy, 1993.

Marnel Hayes, *The Tuned-in, Turned-on Book About Learning Problems* (revised edition); Novato, California: Academic Therapy, 1994.

Helen Irlen, *Reading by the Colors;* New York: Penguin-Putnam, 1991.

Linwood Laughy, *Getting the Best Bite of the Apple;* Kooskia, Idaho: Mountain Meadow Press, 1993.

Michael Rosenberg and Irene Edmond-Rosenberg, *The Special Education Sourcebook: A Teacher's Guide to Programs, Materials, and Information Sources;* Minneapolis: Woodbine House, 1994.

Lawrence Siegel, *The IEP Guide: How to Advocate for Your Special Ed Child;* Berkeley: Nolo.com, 1999.

Corinne Smith and Lisa Strick, *Learning Disabilities A to Z: A Parent's Complete Guide to Learning Disabilities from Preschool to Adulthood;* New York: Free Press, 1997.

John Taylor, *Answers to A.D.D.: The School Success Tool Kit*, a VHS videotape; Salem, Oregon: A.D.D. Plus, 1992.

John Taylor, *Ayudando a los Ninos Hiperactivos con Deficiencia de Atencion (DDA)* a VHS videotape; Salem, Oregon: A.D.D. Plus, 1994.

John Taylor, *Especially for Teachers: Understanding the ADD/ADHD Student*, an "Answers to A.D.D." audiotape; Salem, Oregon: A.D.D. Plus, 1998.

John Taylor, *The Attention Deficit/Hyperactive Student at School* (revised edition); Warminster, Pennsylvania: Mar-Co Products, 1995.

Susan Winebrenner, *Teaching Kids with Learning Difficulties in the Regular Classroom;* Minneapolis: Free Spirit Publishing, 1996.

Organizations

Beach Center on Families and Disability, 3111 Haworth, University of Kansas, Lawrence, KS 66045.

Irlen Institute, 5380 Village Road, Long Beach, CA 90808 (www.Irlen.com).

Learning Disabilities Association, 4156 Library Road, Pittsburgh, PA 15234.

National Center for Learning Disabilities, 99 Park Avenue, New York, NY 10016.

Optometric Extension Program Foundation, Inc., 2912 South Daimler Street, Santa Ana, CA 92705.

Parents Active for Vision Education, 7331 Hamlet Avenue, San Diego, CA 92120.

U.S. Dept. of Justice–Americans with Disabilities Act (ADA) Information Line (800-514-0301; www.usdoj.gov/crt/ada/).

Chapter 14

Janine Batzle, *Portfolio Assessment and Evaluation: Developing and Using Portfolios in the Classroom;* Cypress, California: Creative Teaching Press, 1992.

Ashley Bishop and Suzanne Bishop, *Teaching Phonics, Phonemic Awareness, and Word Recognition;* Westminster, California: Teacher Created Materials, 1996.

Beverly Casebeer, *Missiles to Learning: Beyond the Left-Right Brain;* Novato, California: Academic Therapy, 1996.

Diane Heacox, *Up from Underachievement: How Teachers, Students, and Parents Can Work Together to Promote Student Success;* Minneapolis: Free Spirit Publishing, 1991.

Allan Lifson, *Taming the Tornado in Your Classroom and at Home;* Costa Mesa, California: Educational Consultant Group, 1980.

H. Light and Pamela Morrison, *Beyond Retention: A Survival Guide for Regular Classroom Teachers;* Novato, California, Academic Therapy, 1990.

Stephen Nowicki and Marshall Duke, *Helping the Child Who Doesn't Fit In;* Atlanta: Peachtree Publishers, 1992.

Betty Osman, and Henriette Blinder, *No One to Play With: Social Problems of LD and ADD Children* (revised edition); Novato, California: Academic Therapy, 1995.

Dianne Schilling (editor), *Fifty Activities for Teaching Emotional Intelligence* (series of three: elementary, intermediate, and high school); Carson, California: Jalmar Press, 1996.

Jeanne Schumm and Marguerite Radencich, *School Power: Strategies for Succeeding in School* revised ed.; Minneapolis: Free Spirit Publishing, 2001.

Michele Tamaren, *I Make a Difference! A Curriculum Guide Building Self-Esteem and Sensitivity in the Inclusive Classroom;* Novato, California: Academic Therapy, 1992.

John Taylor, *Answers to A.D.D.: The School Success Tool Kit*, a VHS videotape; Salem, Oregon: A.D.D. Plus, 1992.

John Taylor, *Ayudando a los Ninos Hiperactivos con Deficiencia de Atencion (DDA)*, a VHS videotape; Salem, Oregon: A.D.D. Plus, 1994.

John Taylor, *Especially for Teachers: Motivating the ADD/ADHD Student*, an "Answers to A.D.D." audiotape; Salem, Oregon: A.D.D. Plus, 1998.

John Taylor, *Motivating the Uncooperative Student: A Guidebook for School Counselors*; Warminster, Pennsylvania: Mar-Co Products, 1990.

John Taylor, *Social Skills Solutions: Strategies for Teaching Children and Teens*, a VHS videotape; Salem, Oregon: A.D.D. Plus, 1995.

John Taylor, *The Attention Deficit/Hyperactive Student at School* (revised edition); Warminster, Pennsylvania: Mar-Co Products, 1995.

Barbara Vitale, *Unicorns Are Real: A Right-Brained Approach to Learning*; Torrance, California: Jalmar Press, 1982.

Susan Winebrenner, *Teaching Kids with Learning Difficulties in the Regular Classroom*; Minneapolis: Free Spirit Publishing, 1996.

Chapter 15

Rosemarie Clark, Donna Hawkins, and Beth Vachon, *The School Savvy Parent: 365 Insider Tips to Help You Help Your Child*; Minneapolis: Free Spirit, 1999.

Jo Fitzpatrick, *Reading Strategies That Work: Helping Young Readers Develop Independent Reading Skills*; Cypress, California: Creative Teaching Press, 1998.

Scott Flansburg, *Math Magic for Your Kids: Hundreds of Games and Exercises from the Human Calculator to Make Math Fun and Easy*; New York: Harper, 1998.

Meredith Gall and Joyce Gall, *Making the Grade* (revised edition); Roseville, California: Prima, 1993.

Barbara Johnson, *Helping Your Child Achieve in School: Strategies for Caring Parents*; Novato, California: Academic Therapy, 1985.

H. Light and Pamela Morrison, *Beyond Retention: A Survival Guide for Regular Classroom Teachers*; Novato, California: Academic Therapy, 1990.

Dawna Markova and Anne Powell, *Learning Unlimited: Using Homework to Engage Your Child's Natural Style of Intelligence*; Berkeley: Conari Press, 1998.

Gail Mengel, *The Homework Organizer: Assignment Notebook and Guide* (revised edition); South Hadley, Massachusetts: Get Organized, 1998.

Marguerite Radencich and Jeanne Schumm, *How to Help Your Child with Homework* (revised edition); Minneapolis: Free Spirit Publishing, 1997.

Dorothy Raymond, *What You Can Do with a Word: 300 Classroom Reading Activities*; Novato, California: Academic Therapy, 1981.

Jeanne Schumm and Marguerite Radencich, *School Power: Strategies for Succeeding in School* revised ed.; Minneapolis: Free Spirit Publishing, 2001.

Robyn Spizman and Marianne Garber, *Helping Kids Get Organized: Activities That Teach Time Management, Clutter Clearing, Project Planning, and More!* Torrance, California: Good Apple, 1995.

Murray Suid, *Demonic Mnemonics: 800 Spelling Tricks for 800 Tricky Words*; Torrance, California: Fearon, 1981.

John Taylor, *Ayudando a los Ninos Hiperactivos con Deficiencia de Atencion (DDA)*, a VHS videotape; Salem, Oregon: A.D.D. Plus, 1994.

John Taylor, *Answers to A.D.D.: The School Success Tool Kit*, a VHS videotape; Salem, Oregon: A.D.D. Plus, 1992.

John Taylor, *Especially for Teachers: Motivating the ADD/ADHD Student*, an "Answers to A.D.D." audiotape; Salem, Oregon: A.D.D. Plus, 1998.

John Taylor, *Especially for Teachers: Understanding the ADD/ADHD Student*, an "Answers to A.D.D." audiotape; Salem, Oregon: A.D.D. Plus, 1998.

John Taylor, *Especially for Teens: Shortcuts to School Success*, an "Answers to A.D.D." audiotape; Salem, Oregon: A.D.D. Plus, 1998.

John Taylor, *The Attention Deficit/Hyperactive Student at School* (revised edition); Warminster, Pennsylvania: Mar-Co Products, 1995.

Kathy Troxel, a series of cassette tapes with activity books: *Grammar Songs, Geography Songs, States and Capitals Songs, History Songs, Multiplication Songs, Addition Songs, Subtraction Songs;* Newport Beach, California: Audio Memory Publishing.

Susan Winebrenner, *Teaching Kids with Learning Difficulties in the Regular Classroom;* Minneapolis: Free Spirit Publishing, 1996.

Homework Helpmate (homework supplies organizer); Sensible Solutions, P.O. Box 3761, Gaithersburg, MD 20885.

Chapter 16

Robert MacKenzie, *Setting Limits: How to Raise Responsible, Independent Children by Providing Clear Boundaries* (revised edition); Roseville, California: Prima, 1998.

John Taylor, *Anger Control Training for Children and Teens: The Adult's Guidebook for Teaching Healthy Handling of Anger* (revised edition); Warminster, Pennsylvania: Mar-Co Products, 1995.

John Taylor, *Correcting Without Criticizing: The Encouraging Way to Talk to Children About Their Misbehavior* (revised edition); Warminster, Pennsylvania: Mar-Co Products, 1995.

John Taylor, *Creative Answers to Misbehavior: Getting Out of the Ignore-Nag-Yell-Punish Cycle;* Warminster, Pennsylvania: Mar-Co Products, 1992.

John Taylor, *Diagnostic Interviewing of the Misbehaving Child;* Warminster, Pennsylvania: Mar-Co Products, 1989.

John Taylor, *Helping Hands and Smiling Faces: Getting Cooperation on Household Chores* (revised edition); Warminster, Pennsylvania: Mar-Co Products, 1995.

John Taylor, *Limits with Love: Effective Discipline Strategies*, an "Answers to A.D.D." audiotape; Salem, Oregon: A.D.D. Plus, 1998.

John Taylor, *No More Tantrums: Anger Control Training*, an "Answers to A.D.D." audiotape; Salem, Oregon: A.D.D. Plus, 1998.

John Taylor, *Understanding Misbehavior: Using Misbehavior as a Guide to Children's and Adolescents' Needs;* Warminster, Pennsylvania: Mar-Co Products, 1993.

John Taylor and Carrie Ivey-Cone, *Quiet Time: Very Pleasant Relaxation Training for Children*, an audiotape; Salem, Oregon: Sun Media, 1994.

Winnifred Taylor, *Anger Answers: High Impact Interventions for Anger Management and Violence Prevention*, an audiotape set; Salem, Oregon: A.D.D. Plus, 1996.

Winnifred Taylor, *Anger Answers: Strategies for Anger Management and Violence Prevention;* Salem Oregon: A.D.D. Plus, 1995.

Chapter 17

Daniel McKeever, *Guide to Summer Camps and Summer Schools;* Boston: Porter Sargent Publishers, 1995.

Jolene Roehlkepartain and Nancy Leffert, *What Young Children Need to Succeed: Working Together to Build Assets from Birth to Age 11;* Minneapolis: Free Spirit, 2000.

Organizations

American Camping Association, 5000 State Road 67 North, Martinsville, IN 46151 (317-342-8456, 800-428-CAMP); www.acacamps.org

The National Camp Association, 610 5th Avenue, New York, NY 10185; (800-966-CAMP); www.summercamp.org; contact for a free advisory service that works with parents to identify the best location, price, and facilities as well as special dietary needs.

Chapter 18

Organizations

AD/HD, 280 West Shuman Boulevard, Suite 110, Naperville, IL 60563 (800-429-4272).

Autism Network for Dietary Intervention, P.O. Box 17711, Rochester, NY 14617 (www.AutismNDL.com).

Ch.A.D.D., 8181 Professional Place #201, Landover, MD 20785 (www .chadd.org).

Developmental Delay Registry, 6701 Fairfax Road, Chevy Chase, MD 20815.

Feingold Association of the United States, P.O. Box 6550, Alexandria, VA 22306 (800-768-3287, www.feingold.org).

Learning Disabilities Association, 4156 Library Road, Pittsburgh, PA 15234.

National Down Syndrome Society, 70 West 40th Street, New York, NY 10018.

National Self-Help Clearinghouse, 33 West 42nd Street, New York, NY 10036.

Parents Against Ritalin, 225 South Brady, Claremore, OK 74017 (800-469-5929, www.p-a-r.org).

Tourette Syndrome Association, 42–40 Bell Boulevard, Bayside, NY 11361.

Appendix B: Study and Discussion Questions

This book is designed to be exquisitely usable in support groups, discussion groups, and classes. Although geared to a group of parents, these questions can easily be adapted for use with college students, interns in the helping professions, and other groups. For each chapter, add the following two questions: "What are the three most meaningful sentences for you in this chapter?" and, "What surprised you most in this chapter?" Pretend an additional instruction, "Explain and elaborate on your answer," appears at the end of every question.

Chapter 1
1. List at least four reasons why ADHD is so controversial.
2. Give an example from your personal experience of inconsistency among helping professionals with regard to diagnosis or treatment of your child.
3. Of the mental difficulties listed, which two are the most significant for your child?
4. Of the physical difficulties listed, which two are the most significant for your child?
5. Of the emotional difficulties listed, which two are the most significant for your child?
6. Of the fetal, birth, early infancy, toddlerhood, and preschool indicators mentioned, which apply for your child?
7. What are your child's score and level of hyperactivity on the Taylor Hyperactivity Screening Checklist?

Chapter 2
1. Why do you think I included this chapter in a book on ADHD?
2. A psychiatrist tells you: "Autism is psychological and has nothing to do with diet. The only way to treat it is with pharmaceuticals." Provide three refutations.
3. If you were to select two other chapters from this book to show to the parent of an autistic child, which two would you select? Why?
4. Attempt to show this chapter to a mental health professional. Report results to the group.
5. Why is this chapter likely to be highly controversial?

Chapter 3
1. Rate your child's physician on a 10-point scale of helpfulness and effectiveness.
2. If your physician would agree to read and follow the principles and instructions in any one paragraph from this chapter, which paragraph would you select?

3. Rate your child's and your family's mental health professional on a 10-point scale of helpfulness and effectiveness.
4. Give examples from your experience of trying to be a facilitator of professional help for your child: (a) when you were too insistent, (b) when you were not insistent enough, and (c) when you were insistent without being pushy.

Chapter 4

1. Of the A through H effects, which have occurred most prominently for your child?
2. Rate your child's current medication on the Taylor Medication Effectiveness Report and compare it with ratings of other participants in the group.
3. If you have ever observed an overdose condition or sensitivities/allergies in response to medication, report what you observed.
4. Using the guidelines given, track down the probable sources of a "bad day" your child has had and report results.
5. Discuss which methods for troubleshooting side effects have been successful for your child.
6. What are some of the advantages of using prescribed medication for individuals with ADHD?
7. Suppose you are asked to discredit the medication treatment method. To make your case, cite at least five passages to exaggerate and to quote out of context.

Chapter 5

1. Of the objections by outsiders about medication treatment, which have been expressed to you?
2. Why is establishing a powerful pre-post contrast for the child emphasized?
3. Of the objections by children with ADHD about medication treatment, which has your child expressed?
4. Discuss which aspects of the encouragement cycle apply for your child.
5. Take turns in your group role-playing being advised against continuing medication treatment by a critical outsider who expresses some of the objections given in this chapter. Give an assertive response to the criticism.
6. Of the child's responsibilities, list a few that your child is upholding well and cite instances that provide proof.
7. Suppose you are asked to discredit the medication treatment method. To make your case, which of the objections from outsiders do you think would be the most persuasive to include in a letter to the editor of your local newspaper? Why?

Chapter 6

1. Make a poster or large drawing of the standard food pyramid, then another drawing reversing the sequence of recommended food types. Show both to the group and discuss the implications for children with ADHD.
2. A parent of a child with ADHD tells you, "I tried that Feingold program, I eliminated all the food additives, but my child was still hyperactive." What could you suggest as the logical next step?
3. Conduct a simple survey the next time you shop at a supermarket. Select 10 breakfast cereals at random and examine them for content of wheat, corn, milk products, and additives. Report results to the group.

4. What are the six organ systems to be concerned about if you are truly going to conquer ADHD? Name at least one thing that "goes wrong" in each organ system for many children with ADHD.
5. Clean out your kitchen cupboard and replace unacceptable foodstuffs with desirable foodstuffs. Bring the discarded items to the group for a show-and-tell.
6. Attempt to show this chapter to a mental health professional. Report results to the group.
7. If you were to select two paragraphs from this chapter to show to the parent of a child with autism, which two would you select? Why?
8. Why is this chapter likely to be highly controversial?
9. Why did I include this chapter?

Chapter 7
1. Describe any sensitivities or allergies you know or suspect your child has.
2. Describe your observations after a clear exposure of your child to any of the aggravating chemicals listed in appendix D, "Sources of Chemical Exposure."
3. What is the most probable reason why the food industry has spent millions of dollars to persuade people *not* to use a method that "doesn't work"?
4. What does the claim that toxinsulation works by suddenly giving the child "power and attention" show about the claimant's familiarity with children who have ADHD?
5. Pretend you work for the Nutrition Foundation or the American Council on Science and Health (food industry proponents) and offer five statements to refute or dismiss the studies cited in this chapter.
6. Ask a dietitian, mental health professional, or physician about the validity of the Feingold program of toxinsulation and try to get that person's opinion about why it works for *some* children. Share the results with the other participants in the group.
7. Why do most criticizers of the Feingold program have little or no direct experience with it?
8. Of the potential difficulties with the toxinsulation method of treatment, which are most challenging for you to overcome?
9. What are the advantages of this method?

Chapter 8
1. Why did I include this chapter?
2. A psychologist tells you, "Sensory integration therapy isn't scientific and doesn't help children with ADHD." Provide refutations.
3. A teacher tells you, "I tried combing his arms to calm him down, but all it did is make him more hyper." Suggest logical next steps.
4. Attempt to show this chapter to a counselor or mental health professional. Report results to the group.
5. Attempt to show this chapter to an occupational therapist or massage therapist. Report results to the group.

Chapter 9
1. Of the low self-esteem traits, which apply most severely to your child?
2. Report to the group your success at improving your child's self-esteem.

3. Of the anger control methods given, which are most helpful for your child?
4. Describe your child's regular exercise program or athletic participation and describe its benefits and drawbacks.
5. Of the responses to mistakes, which would be most helpful for your child to become convinced of?
6. Contrast the approaches you have noticed other adults use with those given in this chapter for teaching your child to use mistakes wisely.
7. Directly apply at least three specific suggestions and techniques from this chapter for at least one week and report results.

Chapter 10
1. Explain why the statement, "You should be more consistent," is unfair and misleading.
2. Why does this chapter emphasize the family roles for siblings of a child with ADHD?
3. Which methods for reducing sibling rivalry have been most effective for your family?
4. Of the five most common social skills difficulties for children with ADHD, which is the most difficult for your child?
5. Using the "scored" method (page 178), select one of your child's social skills that needs improvement and report results.
6. Give an example of how your child's reputation has led to unfortunate misunderstandings or problems.
7. Explain the eight A's of apology to your child and report results after *you* have had an opportunity to use them as a model for your child to follow.
8. Which friendship skills have been most helpful for your child?
9. Which refusal skills have been most helpful for your child?
10. Apply at least three specific techniques from this chapter for at least one week and report results.

Chapter 11
1. Of the five negative parental feelings, which was the most painful prior to finding a correct diagnosis for your child?
2. Share with the other participants several criticisms or other negative reactions you have received about: (a) your child's behavior, (b) your parenting skills and actions, (c) the ADHD diagnosis, and (d) the treatment methods you have attempted.
3. Cite three extremely accurate sentences that describe exactly what you have experienced.
4. Have a group member role-play a well-meaning criticizer of the diagnosis of your child as ADHD; role-play a sensitive, kind, but firm response. Repeat this exercise with several participants.
5. In which areas mentioned in this chapter have you personally felt most guilty or inadequate?
6. What have been some of your major fears and worries regarding your family?
7. Directly apply at least three specific suggestions and techniques from this chapter for at least one week and report results.

Chapter 12

1. Of the 12 destructive marital patterns, which two come closest to your situation?
2. In what ways do highly competitive persons make poor winners? Poor losers?
3. Of the suggested methods of improving your marital relationship, which three have been most helpful for you?
4. Describe a specific instance in which the co-parenting method described in this chapter would have been helpful.
5. Of the suggestions given for rebuilding harmony, which two are most likely to succeed (or have succeeded best) in your family?
6. List at least three circumstances in which: (a) you enjoy being with your child, (b) your child enjoys being with you, (c) your child enjoys doing something with the family, and (d) the family enjoys doing something that includes the child with ADHD.
7. List at least three old habits you must break in order to respond supportively to decreases in your child's symptoms as physiological treatment becomes effective.
8. Cite at least one instance from your family experience that illustrates that children misbehave in part because they fear there is not enough love to go around in the family.
9. Directly apply at least three specific suggestions and techniques from this chapter for at least one week and report results.
10. Of the advantages given for cooperative play, which seem to be the most important for helping your child?

Chapter 13

1. Of the 17 major areas of difficulty for children with ADHD at school, which three seem to be most difficult for your child?
2. Share with other group members some approaches you have found successful in gaining the teacher's cooperation in jointly assisting your child academically.
3. Give an example from your personal experience of a truly helpful attitude or approach by a school administrator, counselor, or teacher.

Chapter 14

1. Of the six major goals for effective teaching of the child with ADHD, in which area has your child experienced the least help from teachers?
2. Of the six major goals, which do you think would be the most challenging for your child's next teacher to accomplish?
3. Use the Taylor Classroom Daily Report for at least a week and report results.
4. Ask a cooperative teacher to read this chapter. Then try to get an uncooperative teacher to do the same. Report results.

Chapter 15

1. Why is note taking difficult for most children with ADHD?
2. Of the many suggestions given for supervising and assisting your child with homework, which have been (or will be) easiest to incorporate? Which have been (or will be) hardest? Why?
3. Where is your child most likely to break down in accomplishing the steps in the homework chain?
4. Of the methods given for compensating for distractibility, which have been (or will be) easiest to incorporate? Which have been (or will be) hardest? Why?

5. Why do you think this book devotes more chapters to the school adjustment of children with ADHD than to any other topic?

Chapter 16

1. Do you agree with the last sentence that good discipline maintains an atmosphere of mutual respect?
2. Although following the four S's involves considerable effort, why is it preferable to after-the-fact discipline?
3. Devise one of the three charts described, use it for a week, show it to the group, and share results.
4. Develop a fun idea list for your child, use it for a week, show it to the group, and share results.
5. List at least five advantages of the concerns notebook.
6. Conduct two PPI meetings with your child and share results.
7. Use the I CARE method for one week and report results.
8. List five advantages of logical consequences over harsh punishments.
9. Apply the recommended response to a child's lying and report results.

Chapter 17

1. Which of the recommendations for vigorous outdoor play will your child enjoy the most?
2. Change the rules of a competitive game to make it more cooperative and report results.
3. How can play be considered an important activity for a child?
4. Directly apply at least three specific suggestions and techniques from this chapter for at least one week and report results.
5. List and share with other parents the toys you have found appropriate for your child during: (a) quiet individual play, (b) vigorous individual play, and (c) vigorous group play.
6. Based on this chapter, what will you change (or expect to do) about your teen's free time activities?

Chapter 18

1. Do a survey of support groups in your area, regardless of their relevance to ADHD, and report results.
2. Briefly interview someone in any support group regarding how many of the goals and services listed in this chapter that support group actually engages in. Share results.
3. .Suggest possible topics you would like to have discussed if you had a local support group that met monthly.

Appendix C: Emerging Patterns of Behavior

Use this guide to assess for abnormally rapid development (precociousness) or abnormally slow development (developmental delay). Both are correlated with ADHD.

Neonatal Period (First 4 Weeks)

Prone: Lies in flexed attitude; turns head from side to side; head sags on ventral suspension

Supine: Generally flexed and a little stiff

Visual: May fixate face or light in line of vision: "doll's-eye" movement of eyes on turning of the body

Reflex: Moro response active; stepping and placing reflexes; grasp reflex active

At 4 Weeks

Prone: Legs more extended; holds chin up; turns head; head lifted momentarily to plane of body on ventral suspension

Supine: Tonic neck posture predominates; supple and relaxed; head lags on pull to sitting position

Visual: Watches person; follows moving object a few degrees

At 8 Weeks

Prone: Raises head slightly farther; watches moving object; head sustained in plane of body on ventral suspension

Supine: Tonic neck posture predominates; head lags on pull to sitting position

Visual: Follows moving object 180 degrees

Social: Smiles on social contact; listens to voice and coos

At 12 Weeks

Prone: Lifts head and chest, arms extended; head above plane of body on ventral suspension

Supine: Tonic neck posture predominates; reaches toward and misses objects; waves at toy

Sitting: Head lag partially compensated on pull to sitting position; early head control with bobbing motion; back rounded

Reflex: Typical Moro response has not persisted; makes defense movements or selective withdrawal reactions

Social: Sustained social contact; listens to music; says "aah, ngah"

At 16 Weeks

Prone: Lifts head and chest, head in approximately vertical axis; legs extended

Supine: Symmetrical posture predominates, hands in midline; reaches and grasps objects and brings them to mouth

Sitting: No head lag on pull to sitting position; head steady, held forward; enjoys sitting with full truncal support

Standing: When held erect, pushes with feet

Adaptive: Sees pellet, but makes no move to it

Social: Laughs out loud; may show displeasure if social contact is broken; excited at sight of food

At 28 Weeks

Prone: Rolls over; may pivot

Supine: Lifts head; rolls over; squirming movements

Sitting: Sits briefly, with support of pelvis; leans forward on hands; back rounded

Standing: May support most of weight; bounces actively

Adaptive: Reaches out for and grasps large object; transfers objects from hand to hand; grasp uses radial palm; rakes at pellet

Language: Polysyllabic vowel sounds formed

Social: Prefers mother; babbles; enjoys mirror; responds to changes in emotional content of social contact

At 40 Weeks

Sitting: Sits up alone and indefinitely without support, back straight

Standing: Pulls to standing position

Motor: Creeps or crawls

Adaptive: Grasps objects with thumb and forefinger; pokes at things with forefinger; picks up pellet with assisted pincer movement; uncovers hidden toy; attempts to retrieve dropped object; releases object grasped by other person

Language: Repetitive consonant sounds (mama, dada)

Social: Responds to sound of name; plays peek-a-boo or pat-a-cake; waves bye-bye

At 52 Weeks (1 year)

Motor: Walks with one hand held; "cruises" or walks holding on to furniture

Adaptive: Picks up pellet with unassisted pincer movement of forefinger and thumb; releases object to other person on request or gesture

Language: 2 "words" besides mama, dada

Social: Plays simple ball game; makes postural adjustment to dressing

At 15 Months

Motor: Walks alone; crawls up stairs

Adaptive: Makes tower of 2 cubes; makes a line with crayon; inserts pellet in bottle

Language: Jargon; follows simple commands; may name a familiar object (ball)

Social: Indicates some desires or needs by pointing

At 18 Months

Motor: Runs stiffly; sits on small chair; walks up stairs with one hand held; explores drawers and wastebaskets

Adaptive: Piles 3 cubes; imitates scribbling; imitates vertical stroke; dumps pellet from bottle

Language: 10 words (average); names pictures

Social: Feeds self; seeks help when in trouble; may complain when wet or soiled

At 24 Months (2 Years)

Motor: Runs well; walks up and down stairs, one step at a time; opens doors; climbs on furniture

Adaptive: Tower of 6 cubes; circular scribbling; imitates horizontal stroke; folds paper once imitatively

Language: Puts 3 words together (pronoun, verb, object)

Social: Handles spoon well; often tells immediate experiences; helps to undress; listens to stories with pictures

At 30 Months

Motor: Jumps

Adaptive: Tower of 8 cubes; makes vertical and horizontal strokes, but generally will not join them to make a cross; imitates circular stroke, forming closed figure

Language: Refers to self by pronoun "I"; knows full name

Social: Helps put things away

At 36 Months (3 Years)

Motor: Goes up stairs alternating feet; rides tricycle; stands momentarily on one foot

Adaptive: Tower of 9 cubes; imitates construction of "bridge" of 3 cubes; copies a circle; imitates a cross

Language: Knows age and sex; counts 3 objects correctly; repeats 3 numbers or a sentence of 6 syllables

Social: Plays simple games (in "parallel" with other children); helps in dressing (unbuttons clothing and puts on shoes); washes hands

At 48 Months (4 Years)

Motor: Hops on one foot; throws ball overhand; uses scissors to cut out pictures; climbs well

Adaptive: Copies bridge from model; imitates construction of "gate" of 5 cubes; copies cross and square; draws a man with 2 to 4 parts besides his head; names longer of 2 lines

Language: Counts 4 pennies accurately; tells a story

Social: Plays with several children with beginning of social interaction and role-playing; goes to toilet alone

At 60 Months (5 Years)

Motor: Skips

Adaptive: Draws triangle from copy; names heavier of 2 weights

Language: Names 4 colors; repeats sentence of 10 syllables; counts 10 pennies correctly

Social: Dresses and undresses; asks questions about meaning of words; domestic role-playing

For children older than 5 years of age, the Stanford-Binet, Wechsler, and other scales offer the most precise estimates of developmental level. They should be administered only by an experienced and qualified person.

Appendix D: Sources of Chemical Exposure

Exposure to these substances can sometimes worsen ADHD symptoms or trigger a symptom-reactive state.

Bathroom. Deodorant, perfume and cologne, hair spray, rubbing alcohol, hand lotion, colored and perfumed soap, facial powder, eye shadow, fingernail polish and polish remover, artificially dyed or flavored toothpaste, lip balm, preshave and aftershave lotions, bubble bath, dental cleaning agent, fluoride treatment, adhesive bandages, artificially dyed or flavored medicine.

Heating. Gas appliances and furnaces; kerosene; oil heat or spills; odorous space heaters; burning of chemically treated wood; smoke from fireplace, wood stove, or coal; propane appliances.

Home. Mothballs, fresh newsprint, typing correction fluid, holiday decorations of fresh evergreen branches, evergreen trees, formaldehyde from new carpeting, scented candles, menthol cigarette smoke, air freshener, dog and cat repellent, odors from a new mobile home (first seven years after construction), damp basements.

Home workshop. Paint, shellac, varnish, and similar substances; particleboard, especially if being sawed; wood coatings; airborne particles from sanding wood; fresh paneling; plaster and drywall substitutes and fillers; formaldehyde from foam insulation; all-purpose glues; glue used in flooring, wallpaper, and paneling; petroleum products, engine cleaners and chemicals.

Kitchen. Scouring powder, soap, wax, polish, aerosols, chlorine, disinfectants containing methyl salicylate, pine scent, oven cleaner, rug shampoo, colored dishwasher detergent.

Laundry. Soap and detergent, especially nonwhite and heavily scented; scented fabric softeners; fabric softener dryer sheets; freshly dry-cleaned clothing; TRIS flame retardant in clothing.

Playroom. Scented stickers or toys; ballpoint or invisible ink on skin; felt-tip marker on skin; colored chalk or chalk dust; fingerpaint; scratch and sniff stickers; puttylike and claylike modeling compounds; caps and fireworks; white powder inside new balloons; Easter egg dyes; photographic chemicals; odorous marking devices; glue and paste; paint and other art materials.

School. Freshly applied waxes and plastic coatings on gymnasium and hall floors, mimeograph paper, duplicating machines, freshly painted walls, formaldehyde from newly laid carpet, chemically treated paper, school bus exhaust fumes, strong chemical odors from science labs, pets or pet food, moldy odors in lavatories and locker rooms, previously flooded basements or other damp areas of the school, aroma of food to which the child is allergic (such as popcorn), dust, mold, mites.

Yard/Neighborhood. Tar and pitch, smoke from large outdoor fires, exhaust fumes, freshly poured blacktop, roof resurfacing chemicals, pesticides, swimming pool chemicals, lawn chemicals.

Appendix E: Salicylates

Salicylates are a group of naturally occurring phenol-containing molecules that have been reported by parents to worsen symptoms of attention deficit hyperactivity disorder in their children who have a sensitivity to them. While certainly not the whole story with regard to dietary maneuvers that can be helpful, their removal can sometimes become a significant part of total intervention.

High sugar intake seems to increase salicylate sensitivity reactions. Usually an individual is sensitive to just a few—not all—of the high salicylate-containing foods. Removing offending salicylate foods from your child's "food vocabulary" can usually be easily managed.

The customary procedure is to *temporarily eliminate all* high-salicylate foods as well as any other substances that may be triggering a symptom-reactive (S-R) state. At a time when your child seems to be free of ADHD symptoms give *one* of the high-salicylate foods in its pure form and watch for distinct behavior deterioration within three hours. Repeat the test at a later time to confirm the result. (Use the Taylor/Latta Diet Diary on page 142 to track symptoms in response to the reintroduction of foods.) When foods are identified as causing symptoms, completely eliminate them from your child's diet. Don't allow your child to consume them in any form. Find substitute foods and assist in changing food habits accordingly. Allow consumption of the remaining, non-offending high-salicylate foods.

The salicylate content of any one food varies with the season, growing conditions, and the type of cooking or processing the food has been exposed to. High-salicylate foods include the following:

almond	cucumber (& pickle)	plum
apple	currant	prune
apricot	grape (& raisin)	tamarind
berry	mint	tangerine
cherry	nectarine	tea
chili powder	olive	tomato
cinnamon	orange	wine
cloves	passion fruit	wintergreen oil
coffee	peach	
cranberry	pepper (bell, chili)	

Substitute these fruits that have very low salicylate content during the period in which your child is eliminating salicylates:

avocado	fig	papaya
banana	grapefruit	pear
bread fruit	guava	pineapple
cantaloupe	honeydew melon	pomegranate
casaba melon	kiwi	watermelon
coconut	lemon	
date	lime	

Virtually all vegetables other than cucumbers, peppers, and tomatoes are devoid of salicylates and can be eaten without fear of triggering a salicylate-caused S-R state. Profoundly sensitive individuals might notice a reaction to banana, pineapple, or white potato.

Appendix F: Boredom-Prevention Ideas

These suggestions were provided by many parents of children with ADHD who are successfully using a "fun idea list" to prevent boredom and misbehavior. These activities are effective in helping children channel their energy into constructive pursuits and can become the starting point for your own fun idea list. You will want to modify it and add to it to fit your family's specific needs.

FUN IDEA LIST

Outdoor Play with Others
- Have a popcorn and fruit-drink stand.
- Camp in the backyard in sleeping bags or tents.
- Do water play with hose and plastic slide cloth.
- Have a water fight with squirt guns and cups, using buckets of water as the source of "ammunition."

Indoor Play with Others
- Make a tent with a sheet and a card table
- Gather shoes from around the house and play shoe store.
- Using a comb, brush, cup with water, and towel, play barber or hairdresser.
- Put things in a mystery sack and give clues about what it is, allowing the child to reach into the sack and feel the object as the last clue.
- Make up a pretend radio or television interview and talk into a tape recorder.

Outdoor Solitary Play
- Watch the stars through a telescope.
- Look through binoculars.
- Work on gardening.
- Line up pop cans and throw pebbles at them.
- Draw pictures of your yard to show the seasons of the year.
- Make a collection of leaves from the yard
- Volunteer to sweep a neighbor's sidewalk without pay.
- Train and groom pets.
- Build something for backyard (birdhouse, bird feeder).
- Earn money by washing cars or mowing lawns.
- Write or draw on the sidewalk with chalk.
- Collect interesting rocks.

Indoor Solitary Play

- Listen to music.
- Punch a punching bag.
- Make muffins.
- Make an item for a model railroad or toy car set out of popsicle sticks, toy logs, or building toys.
- Plan a day trip for the family.
- Write letters to relatives or friends.
- Make a crossword puzzle for family members to solve.
- Organize a home slide show.
- Make a collage out of pictures from old magazines.
- Practice a musical instrument.
- Start or work on a collection (stamps, butterflies, bottle caps, coins, trading cards).
- Make a "food bingo" card by cutting and pasting pictures of food from a magazine. Play bingo on the next trip to the supermarket.
- Make shadow pictures on the wall.
- Paste a picture on cardboard, then cut into pieces for a homemade jigsaw puzzle.
- Stand dominoes on end in a pattern or a long winding line, then knock them down.
- Write down some good charades titles and topics for the family to use later.
- Juggle with balloons.
- Use a tape recorder to record sounds around the home.
- Sort family photos and put them in an album.
- Make personalized stationery using stencils.
- Make holiday decorations such as ornaments.
- Measure things with a measuring tape then make up a quiz for family members about the measurement results.

Whole-Family Activities

- Have a backward dinner—dessert first.
- Tell a story-in-the-round in which each member adds the next passage to the story.
- Tell fill-in-the-blank stories in which each member adds a word when invited to do so by the storyteller.
- Watch home movies.
- Read aloud from a favorite book and act it out.
- Do a benevolent project anonymously for a needy person or family.
- Play musical instruments and sing.

FUN IDEA DRAWER

- **Arts and crafts.** Crayons, safe paints, pieces of sponge, paint brushes, art and drawing paper, colored construction paper, felt markers, colored pencils, watercolors, play modeling dough, stencils, glitter, white glue, cotton balls, rulers, sequins, buttons, yarn, hole punch, craft sticks, clothespins, oatmeal boxes, cardboard bathroom tissue rolls, stamp pad and stamps (make your own from foot pads), scissors, old magazines with pictures, used greeting cards, poster board.
- **Games.** Table game boards, markers, dice, and spinners; children's playing cards; carrom board (over 100 games and relatively indestructible).
- **Writing equipment.** Typing paper, notebooks and notebook paper, ballpoint pens, pencils, erasers, stationery for writing to friends.

Notes

Chapter 1
1. R. Brown, et al., "Gender Differences in a Clinic-Referred Sample of Attention Disorder Children," *Child Psychiatry and Human Development*, 1991, 22, pp 111–127.
2. G. DuPaul and R. Barkley, "Situational Variability of Attention Problems: Psychometric Properties of the Revised Home and School Situation Questionnaires," *Journal of Clinical Child Psychology*, 1992, 21, pp 178–188.
3. L. Goldschmidt, N. Day, and G. Richardson, "Effects of Prenatal Marijuana Exposure on Child Behavior Problems at Age 10," *Neurotoxicology and Teratology*, May-June 2000, 22 (3), pp 325–336.
4. N. Day, et al., "Effects of Prenatal Marijuana Exposure on the Cognitive Development of Offspring at Age Three," *Neurotoxicology and Teratology*, March-April 1994, 16 (2), pp 169–175.
5. Barbara Ingersoll, "Psychiatric Disorders Among Adopted Children: A Review and Commentary," *Adoption Quarterly*, 1997, 1, pp 57–73.

Chapter 2
1. T. Felicetti, "Parents of Autistic Children: Some Notes on a Chemical Connection," *Milieu Therapy*, 1981, 1, pp 13–16.
2. B. A. O'Reilly and R. H. Waring, "Enzyme and Sulphur Oxidation Deficiencies in Autistic Children with Known Food/ Chemical Intolerances," *Journal of Orthomolecular Medicine*, 1993, 8, pp 198–200.
3. K. Dorfman, "Improving Detoxification Pathways," *New Developments*, 1997, 2, p 4
4. R. H. Waring, "The Biochemistry of the Autistic Syndrome," in *Autism on the Agenda*, P. Shattock and G. Linfoot, editors, London: NAS, 1996, pp 125–127.
5. K. Reichelt, et al., "Biologically Active Peptide-Containing Fractions in Schizophrenia and Childhood Autism," *Advances in Biochemistry and Psychopharmacology*, 1981, 28, pp 627–643.
6. K. Reichelt, J. Edram, H. Scott, "Gluten, Milk Protein, and Autism: Dietary Intervention Effects on Behavior and Peptide Secretion," *Journal of Applied Nutrition*, 1990, 42, pp 1–11.
7. V. Hakeem, et al., "Salivary IgA Anti-Gliadin Antibody as a Marker for Celiac Disease," *Archives of Diseases of Childhood*, 1992, 67, pp 724–727.

8. H. Al-Bayaty, et al., "Salivary and Serum Antibodies to Gliadin in the Diagnosis of Celiac Disease," *Journal of Oral Pathology and Medicine*, 1989, 18, pp 578–581.

9. P. Shattock et al, "Role of Neuropeptides in Autism and Their Relationships with Classical Neurotransmitters," *Brain Dysfunction*, 1990, 3, pp 328–345.

10. P. Shattock et al, "Proteins, Peptides and Autism, Part 2: Implications for the Education and Care of People with Autism," *Brain Dysfunction*, 1991, 4, pp 323–334.

11. P. D'Eufemia et al, "Abnormal Intestinal Permeability in Children with Autism," *Acta Paediatrica*, 1996, 85, pp 1076–1079.

12. C. Gillberg, "The Role of Endogenous Opioids in Autism and Possible Relationships to Clinical Features," in *Aspects of Autism: Biological Research*, L. Wing, editor, London: Gaskell, 1988, pp 31–37.

13. A. M. Kniusberg et al, "Dietary Interventions in Autistic Syndromes, *Brain Dysfunction*, 1990, 3, pp 315–327.

14. A. M. Kniusberg et al, "Probable Etiology and Possible Treatment of Childhood Autism," *Brain Dysfunction*, 1991, 4, pp 308–319.

15. K. L. Reichelt et al, "Gluten, Milk Proteins and Autism: Dietary Intervention Effects on Behavior and Peptide Secretion," *Journal of Applied Nutrition*, 1990, 42 (1), pp 1–11.

16. V. Singh, et al., "Changes of Soluble Interleukin-2, Interleukin-2 Receptor, T8 Antigen, and Interleukin-1 in the Serum of Autistic Children," *Clinical Immunology and Immunopathology*, 1991, 61, pp 448–455.

17. R. Warren, et al., "Brief Report: Immunoglobulin A Deficiency in a Subset of Autistic Subjects," *Journal of Autism and Developmental Disorders*, 1997, 27 (2), pp 187–192.

18. V. Singh, et al., "Antibodies to Myelin Basic Protein in Children with Autistic Behavior," *Brain, Behavior, and Immunity*, 1993, 7 (1), pp 97-103.

19. A. Weizman, et al., "Abnormal Immune Response to Brain Tissue Antigen in the Syndrome of Autism," *American Journal of Psychiatry*, 1982, 139 (11), pp 1462–1465.

20. R. Schulman, "Optometry's Role in the Treatment of Autism," *Journal of Visual Development*, 1994, 25, pp 259–268.

21. M. Rose and N. Torgeson, "A Behavioral Approach to Vision and Autism," *Journal of Visual Development*, 1994, 25, pp 269–275.

Chapter 3

1. John Taylor, *ADD/ADHD in Childhood: An Overview* (audiotape); Salem, Oregon: A.D.D. Plus, 1998.

Chapter 4

1. John Taylor, *Using Medication Treatment Effectively* (audiotape); Salem, Oregon: A.D.D. Plus, 1997.

Chapter 6

1. S. Carlson, et al., "Alterations of Monoamines in Specific Central Autonomic Nuclei Following Immunization in Mice," *Brain, Behavior, and Immunity*, 1987, 1, pp 52–64.

2. R. Blank and H. Remschmidt, "Hyperkinetic Syndrome: The Role of Allergy Among Psychological and Neurological Factors," *European Child and Adolescent Psychiatry*, 1994, 3 (4), pp 220–228.

3. N. Ward, et al., "The Influence of the Chemical Additive Tartrazine on the Zinc Status of Hyperactive Children: A Double-Blind Placebo-Controlled Study," *Journal of Nutritional Medicine*, 1990, 1, pp 51–57.

4. R. Hagerman and A. Falkenstein, "An Association Between Recurrent Otitis Media in Infancy and Later Hyperactivity," *Clinical Pediatrics*, 1987, 26, pp 253–256.

5. G. Scadding and J. Brostoff, "Immunological Responses to Food" in J. Hunter and D. Jones (Eds.), *Food and the Gut*; Philadelphia: Saunders, 1985, pp 94–112.

6. T. Graxen, et al., "Intestinal Permeability in Patients with Eczema and Food Allergy," *The Lancet*, 1981, 1, pp 1285–1286.

7. Challacombe, *Food Allergy and Intolerance*; London: Bailliere Tindall, 1987, pp 209–222.

8. T. M. Nsouli et al, "Role of Food Allergy in Serious *Otitis Media*," *Annuals of Allergy*,1994, 73 (3), pp 215–219.

9. J. Egger, et al., "Controlled Trial of Oligoantigenic Treatment in the Hyperkinetic Syndrome," *The Lancet*, 1985, 1, pp 540–545.

10. M. Carter, et al., "Effects of a Few Foods Diet in Attention Deficit Disorder," *Archives of Disease in Childhood*, 1993, 69, pp 564–568

11. M. Bekarolu, et al., "Relationships Between Serum Fatty Acids and Zinc and ADHD: A Research Note," *Journal of Child Psychology and Psychiatry*, 1996, 37 (2), pp 225–227.

12. John Burgess, et al., "Long-Chain Polyunsaturated Fatty Acids in Children with Attention Deficit Hyperactivity Disorder," *American Journal of Clinical Nutrition*, 2000, 71 (1), pp 327–330.

13. A. Richardson and B. Puri, "The Potential Role of Fatty Acids in Attention Deficit Hyperactivity Disorder," *Prostaglandins, Leukotrienes, and Essential Fatty Acids*, 2000, 63 (1–2), pp 79–87.

14. Laura Stevens, et al., "Essential Fatty Acid Metabolism in Boys with ADHD," *American Journal of Clinical Nutrition*, 1995, 62, pp 761–768.

15. Neil Ward, "Assessment of Chemical Factors in Relation to Child Hyperactivity," *Journal of Nutritional and Environmental Medicine*, 1997, 7, pp 333–342.

Chapter 7

1. Tuula Tuormaa, "The Adverse Effects of Food Additives on Health: A Review of the Literature with Special Emphasis on Childhood Hyperactivity," *Journal of Orthomolecular Medicine*, 1994, 9, pp 225–243.

2. Michael Jacobson and David Schardt, *Diet, ADHD, and Behavior: A Quarter-Century Review*; Washington, D.C.: Center for Science in the Public Interest, 1999.

3. I. C. Menzies, "Disturbed Children: The Role of Food and Chemical Sensitivities," *Nutrition and Health*, 1984, 3, pp 39–54.

4. R. S. Pore, "Detoxification of Chlordecone Poisoned Rats with Chlorella and Chlorella-Derived Sporopollenin," *Drug and Chemical Toxicology*, 1984; 7 (1), pp 57–71.

5. B. Vadiraja, N. Gaikwad, and K. Madyastha. "Hepatoprotective Effect of C-Phycocyanin: Protection for Carbon Tetrachloride and R-(+)-Pulegone-Mediated Hepatotoxicity in Rats, *Biochemical and Biophysical Research Communications*, 1998, 249 (2), pp 428–431.

6. Jeffrey Bruno, *Super Microalgae: A Research Monograph*; Pacifica, California: Health Advisory Group, 2000.

Chapter 8

1. T. Field, F. Scafidi, and S. Schanberg, "Massage of Preterm Newborns to Improve Growth and Development," *Pediatric Nursing*, 1987, 13, pp 385–387.
2. T. Field, et al., "Massage Therapy for Infants of Depressed Mothers," *Infant Behavior and Development*, 1996, 19, pp 109–114.
3. A. Wheeden, et al., "Massage Effects on Cocaine-Exposed Preterm Neonates," *Journal of Developmental and Behavioral Pediatrics*, 1993, 14, pp 318–322.
4. T. Field, et al., "Autistic Children's Attentiveness and Responsibility Improved After Touch Therapy," *Journal of Autism and Developmental Disorders*, 1997, 27, pp 329–334.
5. T. Field, et al., "Children with Asthma Have Improved Pulmonary Function After Massage Therapy," *Journal of Pediatrics*, 1998, 132, pp 854–858.
6. S. Porges, "The Integrative Neurobiology of Affiliation," *Annals of the New York Academy of Sciences*, 1997, 807, pp 62–77.
7. T. Field, O. Quintino, and M. Hernandez-Reif, "Adolescents with Attention Deficit Hyperactivity Disorder Benefit from Massage Therapy," *Adolescence*, 1998, 33, pp 103–108.
8. J. Lubar and M. Shouse, "Use of Biofeedback in the Treatment of Seizure Disorders and Hyperactivity," *Advances in Clinical Child Psychology*, 1976, 1, pp 203–265.
9. J. Lubar and M. Shouse, "EEG and Behavioral Changes in a Hyperkinetic Child Concurrent with Training of the Sensorimotor Rhythm (SMR): A Preliminary Report," *Biofeedback and Self-Regulation*, 1976, 3, pp 293–306.
10. J. Lubar, et al., "Spectral Analysis of EEG Differences Between Children With and Without Learning Disabilities," *Journal of Learning Disabilities*, 1985, 18, pp 403–408.
11. C. Mann, et al., "Quantitative Analysis of EEG in Boys with Attention-Deficit/Hyperactivity Disorder (ADHD)," *Pediatric Neurology*, February 1992, 8, pp 30–36.
12. E. Grunewald-Zuberbier, F. Grunewald, and A. Raske, "Hyperactive Behavior and EEG Arousal Reactions in Childhood," *EEG and Clinical Neurophysiology*, 1975, 38, pp 149–159.
13. E. Callaway, R. Halliday, and H. Naylor, "Hyperactive Children's Event-Related Potentials Fail to Support Underarousal and Maturational-Lag Theories," *Archives of General Psychiatry*, 1983, 40, pp 1243–1248.

Chapter 13

1. George Hynd, Richard Marshall, and Jose Gonzalez, "Learning Disabilities and Presumed Central Nervous System Dysfunction," *Learning Disability Quarterly*, 1991, 14, pp 283–296.
2. S. Epps, J. Ysseldyke, and B. Algozzine, "Impact of Different Definitions of Learning Disabilities on the Number of Students Identified," *Journal of Psychoeducational Assessment*, 1983, 1, pp 341–352.
3. S. Smith, et al., "Familial Dyslexia: Use of Genetic Linkage Data to Define Subtypes," *Journal of the American Academy of Child and Adolescent Psychiatry*, 1990, 29, pp 204–213.
4. S. Witelson and D. Kigar, "Asymmetry in Brain Function Follows Asymmetry in Anatomical Form: Gross, Microscopic, Postmortem, and Imaging Studies" in F. Boller and J. Grafman (editors), *Handbook of Neuropsychology*; New York: Elsevier Science Publishers, 1982, pp 111–142.
5. G. Hynd and M. Semrud-Clikeman, "Dyslexia and Brain Morphology," *Psychological Bulletin*, 1989, 106, pp 447–482.

6. C. Weller, et al., "Adaptive Behavior of Adults and Young Adults with Learning Disabilities," *Learning Disability Quarterly*, 1994, 17 (4), pp 282–295.

7. W. Bender and J. Smith, "Classroom Behavior of Children and Adolescents with Learning Disabilities: A Meta-Analysis," *Journal of Learning Disabilities*, 1990, 23, pp 298–305.

8. D. Huntington and W. Bender, "Adolescents with Learning Disabilities at Risk? Emotional Well-Being, Depression, Suicide," *Journal of Learning Disabilities*, 1993, 26, pp 159–166.

9. Richard Carlton, et al., "Rational Dosages of Nutrients Have a Prolonged Effect on Learning Disabilities," *Alternative Therapies*, 2000, 6 (3), pp 85–91.

10. William Bender and Maureen Wall, "Social-Emotional Development of Students with Learning Disabilities," *Learning Disability Quarterly*, 1994, 17, pp 323–341.

11. D. Huntington and W. Bender, "Adolescents with Learning Disabilities at Risk? Emotional Well-Being, Depression, Suicide," *Journal of Learning Disabilities*, 1993, 26, pp 159–166.

12. "Learning Disabilities and the American Public: A Look at American Awareness and Knowledge," Emily Hall Tremaine Foundation/Roper Starch Worldwide national poll, March 1995.

13. W. Bursick and M. Epstein, "Current Research Topics in Learning Disabilities," *Learning Disability Quarterly*, 1987, 10, pp 2–7.

14. W. Bender, "Teachability and Behavior of Learning Disabled Children," *Psychological Reports*, 1986, 59, pp 471–476.

15. S. Kupietz, "Sustained Attention in Normal and Reading Disabled Youngsters with and without ADDH," *Journal of Abnormal Child Psychology*, 1990, 18, pp 357–372.

16. R. Paul, "Language and Speech Disorders," in S. Hooper, G. Hynd, and R. Mattison (editors), *Developmental Disorders: Diagnostic Criteria and Clinical Assessment*; Hillsdale New Jersey: Lawrence Erlbaum Associates, 1992, pp 209–238).

17. J. Snow, "Mental Flexibility and Planning Skills in Children and Adolescents with Learning Disabilities," *Journal of Learning Disabilities*, 1992, 25, pp 265–270.

18. Carol Weller, et al., "Adaptive Behavior of Adults and Young Adults with Learning Disabilities," *Learning Disability Quarterly*, 1994, 17, pp 282–295.

19. Jeffrey Glanz, "Effects of Stress Reduction Strategies on Reducing Test-Anxiety Among Learning-Disabled Students," *Journal of Instructional Psychology*, 1994, 21 (4), pp 313–317.

20. Carol Weller, et al., "Adaptive Behavior of Adults and Young Adults with Learning Disabilities," *Learning Disability Quarterly*, 1994, 17, pp 282–295.

21. Arthur Seiderman and Steven Marcus, *20/20 Is Not Enough: The New World of Vision*; New York: Fawcett Crest, 1989.

22. Richard Kavner, *Your Child's Vision: A Parent's Guide to Seeing, Growing, and Developing*; New York: Simon & Schuster, 1985.

23. J. Stein, P. Riddell, and S. Fowler, "The Dunlop Test and Reading in Primary School Children," *British Journal of Ophthalmology*, 1986, 70, pp 317–320.

24. J. Stein, P. Riddell, and S. Fowler, "Disordered Vergence Control in Dyslexic Children," *British Journal of Ophthalmology*, 1988, 72, pp 162–166.

25. Hoffman, "Incidence of Vision Difficulties in Children with Learning Disabilities," *Journal of the American Optometric Association*, 1980, 51, pp 447–451.

26. J. Grisham, *Computerized Visual Therapy— Year 1 Report*; Palo Alto: American Institutes for Research, 1986.

27. K. Kavale, "Meta-Analysis of the Relationship Between Visual Perceptual Skills and Reading Achievement," *Journal of Learning Disabilities*, 1982, 15, pp 42–51.

28. A. Sherman, "Relating Vision Disorders to Learning Disability," *Journal of the American Optometric Association*, 1973, 44 (2), pp 140–141.

29. L Hoffman, "The Effect of Accommodative Deficiencies on the Development Level of Perceptual Skills," *American Journal of Optometry and Physiological Optometry*, 1982, 59, pp 254–262.

30. H. Haynes and L. McWilliams, "Effects of Training on Near-Far Response Time as Measured by the Distance Rock Test," *Journal of the American Optometric Association*, 1979, 50, pp 715–718.

31. R. Dowis, "The Importance of Vision in the Prevention of Learning Disabilities and Juvenile Delinquency," *Journal of Optometric Vision Development*, 1984, 15, pp 20–22.

32. R. Snow, "The Relationship Between Vision and Juvenile Delinquency," *Journal of the American Optometric Association*, 1983, 54, pp 509–511.

33. Mary Biaggio and Erika Bittner, "Psychology and Optometry: Interaction and Collaboration," *American Psychologist*, 1990, 45 (12), pp 1313–1315.

34. S. Lieberman, "The Prevalence of Visual Disorders in a School for Emotionally Disturbed Children," *Journal of the American Optometric Association*, 1985, 56, pp 800–805.

35. M. Williams, J. Brannan, and E. Latrigue, "Visual Search in Good and Poor Readers," *Clinical Vision Sciences*, 1987, 1, pp 367–371.

36. R. Solman, H. Cho, and S. Dain, "Colour Mediated Grouping Effects in Good and Disabled Readers," *Ophthalmological and Physiological Optics*, 1992, 11 (4), pp 320–327.

37. R. Solman, S. Dain, and S. Keech, "Color-Mediated Contrast Sensitivity in Disabled Readers," *Optometry and Vision Science*, 1991, 68 (5), pp 331–337.

38. M. Livingstone, et al., "Physiological and Anatomical Evidence for a Magnocellular Defect in Developmental Dyslexia," *Proceedings of the National Academy of Science U.S.A.*, 1991, 88, pp 7943–7947.

39. S. Lehmkuhle, et al., "A Defective Visual Pathway in Children with Reading Disability," *New England Journal of Medicine*, 1993, 328, pp 989–996.

40. G. Robinson, "Coloured Lenses and Reading: A Review of Research into Reading Achievement, Reading Strategies, and Causal Mechanisms," *Australasian Journal of Special Education*, 1994, 18 (1), pp 3–14.

41. Helen Irlen, *Reading by the Colors*; New York: Penguin-Putnam, 1991.

42. Irlen Institute, 5380 Village Road, Long Beach, CA 90808 (562-496-2550; www.Irlen.com).

Chapter 16

1. John Taylor, *Correcting Without Criticizing*; Warminster, Pennsylvania: Mar-Co, 1995.

2. J. Egger, et al., "Effect of Diet Treatment on Enuresis in Children with Migraine or Hyperkinetic Behavior," *Journal of Clinical Pediatrics*, 1992, 31 (5), pp 302–307.

Chapter 17

1. National Coalition on Television Violence, "Nintendo Tainted by Extreme Violence," *NCTV News*, 1990, 11 (1–2), pp 1, 3–4.

2. C. S. Clark, "TV Violence," *CQ Researcher*, 1993, 3 (12), pp 167–187.

Glossary

absorption Taking a substance (e.g., medicine or food) across tissues, such as through the intestines. Unabsorbed medication is ineffective.

achievement test A measure of a person's knowledge level in a particular topic, such as reading or mathematics. Usually expressed as percentile scores or grade equivalents.

ADHD Attention deficit hyperactivity disorder.

ADHD imitator disorders Medical and psychiatric conditions whose symptoms overlap some of the components of the ADHD syndrome.

alexia Inability to read written or printed language; sometimes evident in children with ADHD.

allergy An abnormal body response to a substance during which the immune system is mobilized, usually involving histamine release with associated reddening and swelling of tissues.

amphetamines A group of stimulant medications noted for their enhancement of certain functions of the cortex of the brain. A popular category of medications prescribed for children with ADHD; Dexedrine is an example.

anoxia Reduced supply of oxygen during the birth process; can cause damage to brain tissue, resulting in ADHD symptoms.

anticonvulsant Medication that reduces seizures; also known as antiepileptic medication.

antidepressant Medication that reduces depression and uplifts mood and energy; some antidepressants help control ADHD symptoms though not contributing an uplift of mood.

anxiety State of being nervous, worried, tense, and stressed, not to be confused with eagerness, which is generally a positive condition. Severe anxiety is an ADHD imitator condition.

aphasia Impaired ability to understand or express thoughts through ordinary language; also called dysphasia.

aptitude test An estimate of ability or capacity for learning.

Asperger's syndrome   A developmental disorder involving extreme compulsivity, stereotyped language processes, and disturbed interpersonal relatedness; often regarded as related to autism.

assertiveness training   Methods for stating personal needs and wants, setting limits on others' undesirable actions, negotiating, and using refusal skills.

A through H effects   A summary of the desired effects of physiological treatment on children with ADHD: activity control, brain in gear, conscience, diligence, emotional control, focusing, gentleness, and helpfulness.

attention deficit   Impaired ability to maintain alertness, to avoid distractibility, and to select purposeful stimuli to focus on; a key symptom in the ADHD syndrome.

auditory discrimination   Ability to note differences between similar sounds, such as "bat" and "bet," which is important for learning to read.

auditory perception   Ability to interpret information coming through the sense of hearing, including discriminating sounds.

auditory sequential memory   Ability to remember an oral sequence, such as a list of items in alphabetical order or a telephone number.

autism   A developmental disorder characterized by severe impairment of interpersonal relatedness and numerous other symptoms, many of which overlap ADHD. The majority of children with autism have food allergies and/or toxic processes occurring in the brain.

behavior modification   A system of intervention to change a person's behavior by reinforcements of desired behavior (rewards) and extinguishers of undesired behavior (ignoring, punishing).

biofeedback   A method of treating pain and other symptoms by making the individual more aware of internal body processes normally thought to be outside of conscious control. *See* neurofeedback.

blue-green algae   Nutrient-dense algae occurring naturally in freshwater or saltwater; one of the best foods for children with ADHD.

caffeine   A xanthene derivative known to speed the metabolism of various substances and drugs, including some prescribed medications; sometimes it can reduce ADHD symptoms.

carcinogenic   Capable of causing cancer.

cardiovascular   Pertaining to the blood vessels and heart. A side effect of some of the medications used in treating ADHD is increased cardiovascular rates, reflected in elevated blood pressure and heart rate.

career education   Educational programs fostering awareness, exploration of alternatives, and vocational and social skills relevant to the world of work.

central nervous system (CNS)   The brain and spinal cord, which comprise the parts of the nervous system that receive sensory messages and send out muscle-movement messages.

certified U.S. food colors   Dyes based on coal tar and petroleum added for cosmetic purposes to foods and beverages and certified to be the exact substances that are registered with the FDA. Certification does not mean safe or unlikely to cause adverse reactions in individuals sensitive to them.

child abuse   Excessively harsh treatment of children, commonly divided into emotional (rejection), verbal (yelling, name calling, swearing), physical (excessive spanking, slapping, hair pulling, or assaulting), sexual (force or enticement to witness or participate in sexual activity) and ritual (satanic cult mistreatment of the child).

chronological age (CA)   Real age in years and months, as used in psychological testing. A child who is eight years, nine months old would be CA 8-9.

clinical effect   The desired effect of prescribed medication, as contrasted with side effect. *See* side effect.

clonidine hydrochloride   A blood pressure medication useful in reducing the tics of Tourette's syndrome; a trade name is Catapres.

cognitive behavioral training (CBT)   A method of improving performance and self-control with self-reminding statements said silently or out loud throughout the sequence of actions being learned.

cold-pressed   Processed without applying heat, in order to preserve nutrients.

colic   Acute abdominal pains; a term more generally describing digestive upset, crying, and difficult feeding in a young infant; correlated with ADHD.

communication disorder   An impairment in the ability to communicate because of a speech problem or the inability to use language effectively; includes difficulty in articulation, voice characteristics (pitch), or fluency (stuttering).

comorbid   Occurring simultaneously, such as learning disabilities and ADHD.

compulsivity   An irresistible impulse to perform an irrational act; more generally, a tendency to be overly concerned with orderliness to the point of double-checking everything and writing everything down.

concerns notebook   A method of anger control, disciplinary supervision, and communication between children and their parents. A special notebook in which the child enters concerns, to be discussed regularly at the PPI (*see* personal private interview).

contraindication   A factor impeding the effectiveness of a medication or causing it to create harmful side effects.

correlated   Occurring together or associated with each other. Many of the predictors and symptoms of ADHD are correlated with each other and with the occurrence of ADHD in any one individual.

counseling   A type of psychotherapy involving emotional support and reassurance, advice, and education. Intervention includes discussing alternative plans of action, discipline techniques, study skills, and similar topics. *See* psychotherapy.

decoding   Converting symbols into understandable concepts, such as reading words or interpreting facial expressions.

depression   A syndrome marked by sadness, pessimism, low energy for coping with ordinary tasks, lack of zeal or enthusiasm, frequent crying, loosened emotional control, weakened mental alertness, low productivity, and social withdrawal.

developmental delay   Temporary lag or delay in a child's development of a trait or skill, such as the ability to talk or walk (also known as maturational delay). *See* developmental milestones; precociousness.

developmental milestones Stages in normal progression of accomplishing increased skills, such as walking or talking. Passing of milestones abnormally late is a developmental delay; abnormally early is precociousness.

Dexedrine The generic name is dextroamphetamine sulfate. *See* amphetamines.

dextroamphetamine sulfate Generic name for an amphetamine stimulant. *See* Dexedrine.

diagnostic prescriptive teaching An educational approach that assesses a student's strengths and weaknesses, then designs and implements special instructional procedures to compensate for weaknesses.

diagnostic test An in-depth measure of a person's skills, including strengths and weaknesses and style of approach to tasks.

diet diary A form for use with the Feingold program, or any special diet, to record chemical exposure or behavioral effects.

disinhibition Difficulty controlling an impulse to act in a certain way or do a certain thing; roughly equivalent to hyperactivity.

distractibility An impaired ability to block out irrelevant stimuli, such as noises while working on a task, and to remain on-task after perceiving the irrelevant stimuli. One of the key traits in the ADHD syndrome.

dopa A neurotransmitter derived from tyrosine; transforms into dopamine near the end of the nerve cell (presynaptic cell) prior to the cell's sending dopamine on to the next cell.

dopamine A neurotransmitter derived from dopa near the end of the nerve cell (presynaptic cell); migrates to the next nerve (postsynaptic cell), where it transforms into norepinephrine as part of the process of transmitting a nerve impulse.

dosage The amount of medication administered at one time; usually expressed in milligrams (mg.).

double-blind A research design in which neither the person giving the treatment nor the person receiving it knows whether the treatment or medication being used is genuine or merely an imitation (placebo). Double-blind experiments eliminate the effects of bias on the research results and are regarded as among the most scientific and reliable forms of research.

drug Any nonfood substance that affects living tissue and is present in abnormal concentration in the blood. All medications are drugs, as are most food additives.

drug addiction Persistent drug use and overwhelming involvement with the drug, securing its supply, and returning to its use after attempts to discontinue using it, despite adverse social and medical consequences.

drug holiday A temporary discontinuance of prescribed medication for the purpose of ascertaining whether symptoms reappear and whether continued use of the medication is indicated (also known as a medication holiday or drug-free period).

due process A system of legal procedures guaranteeing that persons are treated fairly and can raise issues or objections about the services they are receiving. *See* IDEA.

dysarthria Impaired ability to pronounce words because of difficulty controlling muscle movements in the mouth, resulting in slurred or distorted speech.

dyscalculia   Impaired ability to perform mathematical computations, either because of perceptual problems (such as difficulty aligning decimals) or conceptual problems (such as not understanding a ratio).

dysgraphia   Impaired ability to produce legible handwriting because of difficulty controlling muscle movements.

dyslexia   Impaired ability to read.

eclampsia   Convulsions in an expectant mother.

educational disability   *See* learning impairment.

egocentrism   A reaction to every situation from a self-centered or selfish point of view.

eight A's of apology   A method of teaching children how to apologize: admit, account, acknowledge, apologize, ask forgiveness, affirm, amends, and adjust.

emotional lability   Rapidly changing types and severity of emotional display.

encephalitis   An inflammation of brain tissue, causing a variety of severe symptoms; an ADHD imitator disorder.

encoding   Transforming ideas into symbols, such as in speaking and writing.

encopresis   Involuntary defecation while fully clothed, usually without awareness.

enuresis   Involuntary urination while fully clothed or asleep, usually without awareness.

epilepsy   Recurring episodes of changing states of consciousness caused by temporary alteration in brain biochemistry, with or without accompanying sensory or muscle involvements.

exceptional child   A global term for a child whose needs differ from agemates' and who requires specially designed educational programs.

expressive language dysfunction   Impaired ability to encode or express thoughts with well-selected words; evidenced by searching for the correct words and stammering (also known as expressive language disability or disorder).

failure-to-thrive syndrome   A combination of colic and slow weight gain in an infant.

family therapy   A form of psychotherapy in which family members are seen as a group by the therapist; focuses on issues such as sibling rivalry, emotional communication, conflict solving, and power structure within the family.

FDA (Food and Drug Administration)   A regulatory agency of the U.S. government responsible for assuring that food is safe and wholesome; that drugs, biological products, therapeutic devices, and diagnostic products are safe and effective; that cosmetics are safe; and that all of these products are honestly advertised and labeled.

Feingold Association of the United States   A nonprofit organization of and for parents of children with ADHD or autism. Provides information and resources to assist in using the "toxinsulation against phenols" treatment method for ADHD and autism.

Feingold, Benjamin, M.D.   Pediatrician and allergist, instructor of pediatrics at Northwestern University, discoverer of the sensitivity reactions underlying some ADHD, and originator of the Feingold program.

Feingold diet   Former name of the Feingold program.

Feingold program A method of treating ADHD and autism symptoms by limiting exposure to chemicals to which the children are sensitive. Equivalent to toxinsulation against phenols.

fetal alcohol syndrome A syndrome noted at birth that includes low birth weight, small head size, birth defects, withdrawal symptoms, ADHD, and mental retardation; caused by an expectant mother's excessive consumption of ethyl alcohol.

figure-ground perception Ability to differentiate between a prominent item or design and the less prominent background. Auditory figure-ground perception involves hearing the difference between the speaker's voice and other voices or background noise.

fine-motor coordination Small-muscle movement ability, such as in handwriting or tying laces.

formal test A test that has explicit instructions for administration and scoring, such as an IQ test.

free agency An individual's responsibility for and control of his or her own behavior.

fun idea list A list of suggested activities prominently displayed and referred to whenever boredom or misbehavior starts to occur.

gastrointestinal Referring to the intestines and stomach.

generic medication Medicine manufactured after the developer's 17-year period of protected marketing, often by firms who merely copy the formula.

generic name The chemical, official, or nonproprietary name for a medication, as contrasted with the trade name.

grade equivalent The difficulty level of academic tasks expressed in terms of the average difficulty of similar tasks in U.S. schools (sometimes called grade-level equivalent). A child who scores 5.5 in reading would be able to read as well as the average fifth-grader in the fifth month of instruction (January).

gross-motor coordination Large-muscle movement ability, such as in running, balancing, or throwing a ball.

group counseling Several participants in a therapeutic group discussion with one or two leaders.

growth rebound The sudden increase in height, weight, and muscle development that results from cessation of medication treatment for a period of weeks or months; caused by the temporary termination of drug interaction effects with growth hormones.

heavy metals A subset of minerals whose molecules have high molecular weight, such as lead, aluminum, cadmium, and mercury. They disrupt iron metabolism when lodged in the brain, worsening ADHD and autism symptoms.

homework chain Thirteen steps between a teacher's giving a homework assignment and a student's turning the finished work in.

home schooling An alternative to public education in which the child receives instruction at home, usually with the parent as teacher.

homovanillic acid One of the main discharge products, along with MHPG, from the neurotransmitter molecules at the junctions of nerve cells. Children with ADHD have reduced homovanillic acid, which provides evidence for neurotransmitter shortage as the cause of ADHD. Use of stimulants increases homovanillic acid, which provides evidence that medications used to treat ADHD increase neurotransmitter supply.

hyperactivity   In its narrowest sense, excessive movement, excitability, fidgetiness, and restlessness. It represents a key symptom in the ADHD syndrome and often is used as a synonym for that syndrome. Formerly known as hyperkinesis. *See* disinhibition; ADHD.

hyperthyroidism   A condition involving high blood pressure and accelerated heart rate that arises from an overly active thyroid; an ADHD imitator disorder.

hypoglycemia   Abnormally low blood sugar; results in poor emotional control and mental problems. An ADHD imitator disorder and sometimes a comorbid disorder with ADHD. *See emotional lability.*

I CARE   An acronym for a five-step procedure of disciplinary intervention for use with children: intervene, cool off, affirm, redirect, and educate.

IDEA   Acronym for the Individuals with Disabilities Education Act, also known in earlier versions as Public Law 94-142 and the Education for All Handicapped Children Act of 1975. The major U.S. federal law providing for free, appropriate public education of handicapped children, including those with ADHD.

imipramine   Generic name of tricyclic antidepressant imipramine hydrochloride. A trade name is Tofranil; widely used to treat ADHD symptoms.

impulsiveness/impulsivity   A tendency to respond too quickly without careful consideration of alternatives and without preplanning; a key symptom in the ADHD syndrome.

incidence   The number of new cases of a disease or disorder over a certain period of time; often expressed as the number of cases per 1,000 live births. *See* prevalence.

inclusive   A classroom in which students with special educational needs are mixed with regular students; IDEA requires a maximizing of inclusive classroom services for handicapped students. Also called mainstreamed.

individualized education program (IEP)   A written plan for a special education student; includes the student's strengths and weaknesses, goals and objectives, educational services and their starting dates, and procedures for evaluating progress. It is devised by a team of school personnel along with the parents and is required as part of IDEA.

individualized instruction   Academic instruction specifically adapted to a given student's learning style and readiness. *See* learning style; readiness.

inflexibility   *See* perseveration.

insomnia   Disturbed quantity and quality of sleep. Often included as part of the ADHD syndrome and as a side effect of medication used to treat it, though more appropriately called presleep agitation side effect. *See* presleep agitation.

intelligence quotient (IQ)   A percentage figure expressing the apparent intelligence of a person. Determined by mental age (as reported on a standardized test) divided by chronological age and multiplied by 100. For example, an 8-year-old with the thinking and learning abilities of a 6-year-old would have a mental age approximately three-fourths the chronological age. The IQ would be 75.

interaction In medicine, the modification of the effects of a medication by giving a different medication at the same time, with either desirable (positive interaction) or undesirable (negative interaction) results.

Irlen syndrome A collection of visual skill deficits that contributes to dyslexia, at least partially redeemable by the use of colored filters and lenses.

kinesthesis The sense of movement of body parts, such as arms and hands while writing or throwing; one of the major emphases in sensory integration therapy.

learning disability Severe impairment of the ability to learn through ordinary classroom instruction, based largely on difficulties with processing sensory information, memory, understanding and using spoken or written language, listening, thinking, talking, reading, writing, spelling, performing mathematical calculations, refining muscle coordination skills, and developing adequate social skills.

learning impairment Mental, physical, or emotional factors impeding the ability to learn and necessitating specially designed instruction. Also called educational disability.

learning style The behaviors that characterize a person's approach to learning; includes ability to focus attention, plan ahead, and remain on-task. *See* psychoeducational evaluation.

least restrictive environment A standard established by IDEA for placement of students in special education programs. Requires a setting that meets their educational requirements and closely matches the regular education program offered to their schoolmates.

lipid metabolism The chemical processing of fats in a living organism.

logical consequences A disciplinary response logically related to a misbehavior, such as paying the offended person back in service for the inconvenience caused by the misbehavior.

mainstreaming Placement of an educationally disabled student in a regular classroom; also known as inclusion.

mental age In intelligence testing, a score indicating overall ability to learn, think, and absorb knowledge; expressed as equivalent to the average performance of other children of a given chronological age. *See* intelligence quotient.

metabolism The chemical processes needed to sustain life functions in a living organism.

methylphenidate A stimulant medication structurally similar to naturally occurring dopamine; seems to work by releasing stores of dopamine and norepinephrine in the brain. It is the most popular medication for treating ADHD. A trade name is Ritalin.

MHPG One of the main discharge products, along with homovanillic acid, from neurotransmitter molecules at the junctions of brain cells.

migration The process of a chemical's movement from one cell to a nearby cell, such as the movement of the neurotransmitter dopamine from one brain cell to the next as part of the process of sending an impulse along a nerve pathway.

mineral An inorganic substance naturally occurring in the earth, expressable with a chemical formula and having a distinct set of physical properties. Minerals perform crucial functions in metabolism. All metals are minerals.

minor tranquilizers A group of psychotropic medications for reducing anxiety and increasing calmness; includes diazepam (Valium), chlordiazepoxide (Librium), and hydroxyzine pamoate (Vistaril). Sometimes inappropriately prescribed in an attempt to slow down children who have ADHD.

motor performance Ability to perform coordinated movement of large- or small-muscle groups.

multimodal approach An instructional technique incorporating several senses simultaneously, as in teaching reading by having the student say the letter, write it in the air with a finger, and read it at the same time.

natural consequences A disciplinary approach naturally related to a behavior if no special intervention is provided; whatever will happen anyway. An example would be allowing a carelessly placed bicycle to rust and requiring the child to earn money for a replacement.

neurofeedback An ADHD sensorimotor treatment method employing EEG measurements while the child performs simple tasks; the child learns through a biofeedback procedure how to control brain electrical activity. *See* biofeedback.

neurologist A physician specializing in diagnosis and treatment of disorders of the brain, spinal cord, and other parts of the nervous system.

neurotransmitter A chemical manufactured in the nerve cells for use in sending impulses along nerve pathways. Deficits in the production of the neurotransmitters tyrosine, dopa, dopamine, and norepinephrine appear to be involved in ADHD.

norepinephrine One of the four key neurotransmitters often undersupplied in the brains of children with ADHD.

norm The average score obtained by a group on a test, to which any one person's score can be compared.

nortriptyline A tricyclic antidepressant sometimes used to treat ADHD. A trade name is Aventyl.

occupational therapist A specialist in treatment to integrate mental and muscle-movement processes more purposefully and efficiently, especially severe problems of locomotion or coordination.

off-medication trial *See* drug holiday.

off-task A descriptive term for someone who is not paying attention to or participating in the correct activity in a classroom setting.

on-task A descriptive term for someone who is paying attention to or participating in the correct activity in a classroom setting.

otitis Abnormal collecting of fluid in the ears. Often occurs as an allergic reaction in infants and toddlers with ADHD. *See* allergy.

overdosage An inappropriately high amount of medication taken at one time.

parent education programs Training in child-rearing methods and philosophy, usually small groups with a leader and resource materials.

pathway The series of chemical reactions by which a given chemical affects organs, systems, or other chemicals in the body. Prescribed medication creates pathways or series of chemical reactions to produce its clinical effects and side effects.

peer monitoring   Using a classmate or other agemate to supervise the work and behavior of a certain student at school.

percentile   A child's test score on a scale of 100; indicates what percent of similar children scored higher and lower. For example, a child in the 90th percentile scored higher than 89 percent and lower than 10 percent of comparable children.

perception   The ability to recognize, process, organize, and interpret stimuli received through the senses.

perceptual-motor task   An activity requiring coordination of perception (usually vision) and muscle movement (usually hand or foot), such as in batting a baseball, kicking a football, or handwriting.

perseveration   Continuing to repeat a movement or act when doing so is no longer appropriate; finding it difficult to switch smoothly from one activity to another.

personal private interview (PPI)   A technique for monitoring a child's adjustment and maintaining constant parent-child communication; consists of regular brief interviews of the child. *See* concerns notebook.

phenol compounds   Substances whose molecular structure is characterized by a benzene or phenol group at the core; many phenol compounds interfere with neurotransmitter formation and thereby contribute to ADHD symptoms.

phenylketonuria (PKU)   An inherited disorder in brain biochemistry in which tyrosine is greatly underproduced; results in the severe loss of neurotransmitter functions, producing mental retardation and ADHD symptoms.

phonics   Connecting sounds with the letters and letter combinations that make them.

physical therapist   A specialist in treatment to improve muscle-movement skills and increase strength and endurance, especially of body parts weakened by injury or disease.

physiological treatment   Treatment of ADHD or a related condition by attempting to normalize the abnormal brain chemistry causing the disorder with prescribed medications, dietary changes, or toxinsulation against phenols.

PKU   *See* phenylketonuria.

placebo   An inactive medication, inert substance, or therapeutic procedure with no value or potency; false medication often used in double-blind research studies to make the recipient believe treatment is occurring when there is no physical effect.

placebo effect   An explanation for some improvements that occur with apparent treatment when in fact the treatment had no curative power. The observed changes are assumed to occur because the recipient believed that treatment was occurring (also known as the power of suggestion).

postmaturity   Being born after 10 or more months' gestation.

postsynaptic nerve cell   A nerve cell that receives dopamine from an adjacent presynaptic cell as part of the process of relaying a nerve impulse from the adjacent cell. *See* presynaptic nerve cell.

precociousness   Acceleration in a child's passing of developmental milestones such as the ability to talk or walk. *See* developmental delay; developmental milestones.

precursor　An intermediary substance along a chemical pathway from which other substances derive.

prematurity　Low birth weight, generally regarded as less than five pounds; it is correlated with ADHD.

pre-post contrast　The observed differences in behavior, thoughts, and feelings between the period prior to receiving treatment and the period after the treatment is well established.

presleep agitation　A rebound effect caused by wear-off of medication for ADHD near bedtime; often inappropriately called insomnia. The child is agitated and can't get to sleep, despite intentions of doing so, for at least an 80-minute period.

presynaptic nerve cell　A nerve cell from which the nerve impulse is to be relayed to the next cell. *See* postsynaptic nerve cell.

prevalence　The total number of cases of a disease or disorder in a specific geographic area over a certain time period; often expressed as a percentage. For example, the prevalence of ADHD is generally estimated at 5 to 10 percent of all U.S. children. *See* incidence.

proprioception　Awareness of the position of various body parts; one of the major senses focused on by sensory integration therapy.

proteins　Complex compounds consisting of combinations or chains of amino acids comprising most of the mass in living cells. Neurotransmitters are protein derivatives, and the main cause of ADHD probably involves abnormalities in protein and lipid metabolism.

psychiatrist　A physician who specializes in the diagnosis and treatment of mental and behavioral disturbances and is qualified to prescribe medication for them.

psychoeducational evaluation　Comprehensive assessment of a child's learning style, academic knowledge, intelligence level, learning disabilities, and related factors; includes formal tests as well as observation.

psychologist　Holder of an advanced degree, usually a doctorate, in psychology. A clinical or counseling psychologist has specialized training in diagnosis and treatment of mental and behavioral disturbances, normal life-adjustment processes, psychological testing procedures and psychometrics, and research strategies.

psychometrics　Psychological tests and measurements, such as IQ tests and measures of eye-hand coordination.

psychotherapy　A general term for intervention into a person's life to improve adjustment; in its narrowest sense, an intense experience involving deep, basic issues such as self-esteem. *See* counseling.

readiness　The level of skills needed for learning a specific academic subject or task.

rebound　Temporary magnification of symptoms that occurs when medication wears off. *See* growth rebound.

receptive language dysfunction　Impaired ability to understand spoken language (also known as receptive language disability or disorder).

receptive vocabulary　Understanding of what words mean; expressed as an approximate total number of words understood.

refusal skills   Methods of resisting invitations and peer pressure to misbehave; one aspect of assertiveness training. *See* assertiveness training.

remediation   The processes used to correct or counteract areas of academic weakness; for example, drill, practice, special instructional techniques, and tutoring.

resource room   A room in which students with academic problems receive remedial instruction from a specially trained teacher.

Ritalin   *See* methylphenidate.

Ritalin SR (sustained release)   Long-acting Ritalin.

salicylates   Phenol-based compounds found in various fruits; usually associated with a tangy, bittersweet taste. Many children with ADHD are sensitive to them.

school survival skills   Minimal levels of performance required to function in an ordinary classroom with a regular curriculum; includes attendance, class preparedness, remaining on-task, and getting help when needed.

seizure threshold   The minimal state of disturbance in brain chemistry necessary to create an epileptic seizure; as the threshold lowers, seizures occur more frequently.

self-contained classroom   Academic placement of special-needs students of a particular diagnosis or learning-style impairment together in one room, often for full-time or nearly full-time instruction. It is an alternative to mainstreaming and is to be minimized under the provisions of IDEA.

sensation   Excitation and activation of nerves designed to help the person be aware of stimuli, such as in the eye, ear, nose, mouth, or skin. Precedes perception during the process of experiencing the environment.

sensitivity   Abnormal use or processing of a chemical by the body not involving the immune system but creating symptoms of biochemical imbalance or distress.

sensorimotor   Involving muscles, skin, and sense organs.

sensory integration   A sensorimotor treatment method for ADHD and other conditions involving normalizing of tactile, vestibular, kinesthetic and proprioceptive senses, usually performed by occupational therapists.

sequencing deficit   Impaired ability to perceive stimuli such as letters or numbers in a particular order or stepwise progression.

side effect   An effect of a drug or medication that occurs in addition to the intended or desired effects; also known as untoward reaction or toxic effect. *See* clinical effect.

social skills   Ability to choose appropriate actions in social settings, such as being tactful, making friends, and settling conflicts peaceably.

sociopathy   Lack of normal conscience; results in abusive, manipulative, exploitative, or criminal behavior toward others. Also known as character disorders.

sound blending   Segmenting or combining components of a word to recognize or pronounce it. *See* phonics.

special education   Educational approaches designed to meet the unique needs of a handicapped child; includes comprehensive evaluation, intensive instruction matched to needs and readiness, specialized materials and equipment, specially trained teachers, and ongoing progress monitoring.

stimulant A type of medication that increases mental and motor performance and uplifts mood in depressed persons. Generally regarded as the medication treatment of choice for children with ADHD.

support group A group of interested individuals who meet regularly and provide programs and services to assist each other.

symptom-controlled (S-C) state A temporary symptom-free condition, as when medications are taken at correct dosage level.

symptom-reactive (S-R) state A temporary symptomatic condition, as when medication has worn off.

syndrome A set or collection of symptoms or traits occurring together and characterizing a particular disorder; several such traits occurring from one person to the next who have the same disorder.

Taylor-Latta Diet Diary *See* diet diary.

TCDR Taylor Classroom Daily Report; a method of maintaining daily contact between the teacher and parents of a child whose classroom behavior or academic productivity needs daily monitoring.

THSC Taylor Hyperactivity Screening Checklist; a simple form for quick, accurate assessment of the severity of hyperactivity in anyone from age 2 through adulthood.

tic Spasm-like movement of a muscle, especially twitching of facial muscles.

titration Establishing the correct dosage of a medication by observing the effects created by progressively higher dosages.

TMER Taylor Medication Effectiveness Report; a method of monitoring the clinical and side effects of medication prescribed for the individual who has ADHD. Submitted by the parent to the physician. *See* TSMER.

Tofranil *See* imipramine.

tolerance Decreased response to an identical dosage of a medication after its repeated use. Tolerance toward the clinical effects of a medication is undesirable and usually indicates the need to switch to a different medication. *See* clinical effect.

Tourette's syndrome A disorder featuring extreme compulsivity, uncontrollable body movements, and up to 50 other symptoms. It is comorbid with ADHD.

toxemia Blood poisoning.

toxic Causing disturbance in chemistry or function of body tissues or organs.

toxinsulation Limiting or preventing exposure to potentially harmful or toxic substances; one of the three chief physiological methods of treating ADHD and autism.

trade name The proprietary or brand name, protected by a patent and trademark laws, under which a medication is sold.

transition plan A program for helping a student cope with a change in school environment, as when changing from an elementary school to a junior high school.

trauma Extreme stress or shock; results in symptoms such as anxiety or depression. *See* depression; anxiety.

treatment of choice Preferred method of treating a disease or disorder.

tryptophane   An amino acid precursor of neurotransmitters that has a favorable effect on ADHD symptoms and helps children with ADHD get to sleep at bedtime. *See* precursor.

TSMER   Taylor School Medication Effectiveness Report; a method of monitoring the clinical and side effects of medication prescribed for a child with ADHD. Submitted by the teacher to the physician. *See* TMER.

tyrosine   A neurotransmitter chemical that transforms into dopa near the end of the presynaptic nerve cell prior to the cell's sending a nerve impulse on to the postsynaptic cell.

validity   The extent to which a checklist or test measures what it is intended to measure. The Taylor Hyperactivity Screening Checklist, for example, is valid to the extent that it correctly categorizes children in terms of their level of hyperactivity.

vestibular   Having to do with the sense of balance; one of the major focuses of sensory integration therapy.

visual memory   Ability to retain information obtained through the sense of sight, such as remembering the image of a word when trying to spell it.

visual-motor integration   A category of perceptual-motor tasks; involves perceiving something visually and reproducing it with the hands, such as copying designs with paper and pencil.

visual perception   Ability to interpret information coming in through the sense of sight, including discriminating designs or symbols (such as words and letters).

visual tracking   Following visual stimuli through space, such as reading a line of words from left to right. Difficulty with visual tracking is correlated with ADHD.

visual training   One of the sensorimotor methods useful in treating ADHD and learning disabilities. It involves improving the coordination of eye muscle movements.

wake effect   The impact of a negative reputation on an individual's social relationships; analogous to the wake that occurs when a boat moves through water.

wear-off period   The time during which medication rapidly decreases in its effectiveness and symptoms increase as the medication's molecules are depleted.

withdrawal symptoms   Physical or behavioral symptoms occurring after stopping use of a medication or drug, especially after sudden stoppage of medication that was taken for a long time at a high dosage level.

word finding   Associating an idea with the correct word to express it (also known as verbal encoding). *See* encoding.

Index

About the Author

John F. Taylor, Ph.D., is a consulting clinical family psychologist specializing in children, adolescents, and adults with ADHD and related conditions (such as oppositional defiant disorder, depression, Asperger's syndrome, autism, and learning disabilities). An authority on the diagnosis of children, he is the author of *Diagnostic Interviewing of the Misbehaving Child* and some of the test items on Wechsler and other intelligence scales.

A prolific producer of innovative techniques, he is the author of over 250 creative works, including 11 books and numerous articles in professional journals. His series of parent education resources includes *Helping Hands and Smiling Faces: How to Get Cooperation on Household Chores, No More Sibling Rivalry, Encouraging the Discouraged Child, Correcting Without Criticizing, Creative Answers to Misbehavior,* and *Answers to ADD.*

He is a contributing editor to *The ADHD Challenge*, a popular national newsletter. He has also written the popular counselor's guidebooks *The ADHD Student at School, Motivating the Uncooperative Student, Understanding Misbehavior, Anger Control Training for Children and Teens,* and *Positive Prescriptions for Negative Parenting.*
Dr. Taylor is one of the pioneering authorities in the field of attention deficit disorder. He is coauthor of *Why Can't I Eat That: How to Keep Your Child on Any Prescribed Diet.* His book *The Hyperactive Child and the Family: The Complete What-to-Do Handbook,* published in the early 1980s, was the first to provide a major in-depth discussion of family relationship and self-esteem issues for children with ADHD. Featuring over 125 techniques, his *School Success Tool Kit* is the most comprehensive video ever produced on classroom and home-based techniques for assisting students with ADHD.

His "Answers to A.D.D." audiotape library is the most comprehensive available, with over a dozen titles, many of which are also available in Spanish. His videos *Social Skills Solutions* and *Nutrition and Neurochemistry: The ADD Link* are at the cutting edge of psychological and dietary techniques for assisting ADHD and autistic children.

His Medication Effectiveness Report Form and Hyperactivity Screening Checklist are used throughout North America by pediatricians and psychiatrists.

An entertaining and popular lecturer and frequent guest on broadcast interviews, Dr. Taylor is president of A.D.D. Plus, a resource provider to parents and professionals for help with ADHD and related conditions. He frequently gives training workshops to professionals throughout North America. He resides in Salem, Oregon, and is the father of eight children, five of whom have ADHD.

He is willing to come to your conference, convention, public program, or in-service training event.

For information on Dr. Taylor's publications or for making arrangements for training workshops or other programs, write: A.D.D. Plus, P.O. Box 4326, Salem, OR 97302, or visit www.ADD-Plus.com.